A PRESSING PROBLEM

Verity Worth was faced with a dilemma. Her charge, Miss Cecily Pettiforth was furious that Lord Rathbone neglected to court her properly while he improperly pursued Verity. At the same time, Lord Rathbone refused to take Verity's no for an answer as he probed for a chink in her armor.

But now she faced an even more pressing problem as she found herself scandalously secluded with the relentless Rathbone. Doing her best to conceal her desperate haste, she tried to leave.

"Do not run away," he said softly, and shifted so that she would have to press against him to go through the doorway. She lifted her eyes to meet his gaze. His eyes were glinting with laughter and a disturbing warmth.

"Pray let me pass, my lord," she said as icily as she could.

But even as she spoke, she felt her flushed color rise. The problem she faced now was not Cecily's fury or Rathbone's wicked charm, but her own wildly beating heart. . . .

SIGNET REGENCY ROMANCE
COMING IN JANUARY 1995

Dawn Lindsey
The American Cousin

Emily Hendrickson
The Contrary Corinthian

Anne Douglas
The Fourth Season

AT YOUR LOCAL BOOKSTORE
OR ORDER DIRECTLY
FROM THE PUBLISHER
WITH VISA OR MASTERCARD
1-800-253-6476

Lord Rathbone's Flirt

Gayle Buck

A SIGNET BOOK

SIGNET
Published by the Penguin Group
Penguin Books USA Inc., 375 Hudson Street,
New York, New York 10014, U.S.A.
Penguin Books Ltd, 27 Wrights Lane, London W8 5TZ, England
Penguin Books Australia Ltd, Ringwood, Victoria, Australia
Penguin Books Canada Ltd, 10 Alcorn Avenue,
Toronto, Ontario, Canada M4V 3B2
Penguin Books (N.Z.) Ltd, 182–190 Wairau Road,
Auckland 10, New Zealand

Penguin Books Ltd, Registered Offices:
Harmondsworth, Middlesex, England

First published by Signet, an imprint of Dutton Signet,
a division of Penguin Books USA Inc.

First Printing, December, 1994
10 9 8 7 6 5 4 3 2 1

Copyright © Gayle Buck, 1994
All rights reserved

 REGISTERED TRADEMARK—MARCA REGISTRADA

Printed in the United States of America

Without limiting the rights under copyright reserved above, no part of this publication may be reproduced, stored in or introduced into a retrieval system, or transmitted, in any form, or by any means (electronic, mechanical, photocopying, recording, or otherwise), without the prior written permission of both the copyright owner and the above publisher of this book.

BOOKS ARE AVAILABLE AT QUANTITY DISCOUNTS WHEN USED TO PROMOTE PRODUCTS OR SERVICES. FOR INFORMATION PLEASE WRITE TO PREMIUM MARKETING DIVISION, PENGUIN BOOKS USA INC., 375 HUDSON STREET, NEW YORK, NEW YORK 10014.

If you purchased this book without a cover you should be aware that this book is stolen property. It was reported as "unsold and destroyed" to the publisher and neither the author nor the publisher has received any payment for this "stripped book."

One

The young lady had been traveling since early that morning. An hour past, she had obeyed the instructions written to her and left the mail coach at the small posting house. She had stepped down from the crowded coach, stiff and weary and wondering what was yet to come. A frosty November wind had begun blowing out of the north, and she stood in the inn yard, pulling close her pelisse.

While her portmanteau and her bandboxes were being retrieved by the coachman, she had been approached by a manservant, who had addressed her by name and indicated that she was to travel the remaining miles in the master's own carriage.

Miss Verity Worth had gratefully climbed up into this well-sprung vehicle, her luggage had been stowed, and the servant had taken his seat on the box. A crack of the whip over the team, and the carriage had been well off. Miss Worth had thus been afforded but the most fleeting impression of the posting house yard and of the village through which the carriage passed, before tall hedgerows had obscured her vision.

The carriage jolted over the potholes of the lane, but Miss Worth paid little heed to what she considered to be a minor discomfort. She was grateful for this respite. Despite the lack of a brick to warm her feet or a lap rug, the carriage still offered a much more comfortable ride than had the mail coach, which she had endured in the company of several other passengers. She had never before experienced the crowding and the noise of travel by mail and she hoped that she would not soon again.

Miss Worth concernedly scanned the leaden sky that was swiftly darkening to dusk. She knew that she would arrive at her destination at an inconvenient hour, but it could not be helped. The mail had been put off schedule when one of its leaders had tossed a shoe. She only hoped that her cousins, who were now to be her employers also, would not be thrown into a state of censorious disapproval by her later arrival.

Certainly nothing could have been more unfortunate, since she did not know her cousins except in a vague way. She had been anxious to make a favorable impression, for this was to be her first post.

Miss Worth's anxiety stemmed from the fact that she did not recall much about her cousins, the Pettiforths. She had met them once, perhaps twice, during the course of her girlhood. The families had not been close, either in relationship or geographically, and so there had not been the concourse that one might have otherwise expected.

However, Miss Worth's father had been a man of considerable correspondence. Sir Montague Worth, Baronet, had been active in the House of Commons. He had also held the post of justice of the peace and he had taken an interest in all that took place in his particular county. He had firmly believed that one should cultivate as many people as possible for, he had once said, one never knew when a connection would prove to be useful. And so he had pursued a comfortable correspondence with a distant cousin that through the years had become immensely satisfying to both gentlemen.

It was a connection that was now standing Sir Montague's eldest daughter in good stead. Miss Worth had few illusions about what her options would have been had her father not supported such a wide-flung acquaintance. She sighed with regret as her thoughts turned on the past several months.

Sir Montague's premature death had been a shock to all who had known that robust gentleman. His widow, especially, had been devastated. It was not to be wondered at, agreed her acquaintances, when there were two sons still in school and a daughter at an expensive select seminary in Barchester to be provided for.

Lady Worth's widow portion amounted to one third of the income from her dead husband's estate. Her ladyship was shocked at how meager was the amount. There was scarcely enough left over from the upkeep of the huge house to see to all the other necessary expenses incurred by a large estate. Those expenditures that must be made on behalf of the Worth offspring had been in addition to all the rest.

Of course, there would not have been a problem at all if it had not been for the unfortunate timing of Sir Montague's passing. By all rights, the baronet should have enjoyed several more years before giving up the reins, at a time when it could be expected that the restless heir would have become willing to quit a military career.

The estate was entailed to the eldest son, Charles, who unfortunately was serving with the British army somewhere in America. Word about Sir Montague Worth's untimely death had at once been sent out on one of the sailing ships, but naturally Charles could not be expected to return to England for several months. Nothing could be done about releasing the rest of the income from the estate until that day, since only the heir could do so.

The months had crept by without a single communication from the heir. Word was again launched, this time with the object of learning why the new baronet had not already returned. In the meantime, the matter of finances had become rather pressing, and so the remainder of the family had been faced with the prospect of the strictest economizing to remain afloat.

"We shall simply have to bring the boys and poor Elizabeth home," Lady Worth sighed. Even as she put into words the ugly necessity, her rounded chin trembled.

"No, I will not have it," Verity declared. "It is unthinkable to interrupt the younger boys' education. As for Elizabeth, it is equally unthinkable that my sister should be denied the same advantage that I enjoyed. You know how very well Elizabeth has settled in, Mama."

"What choice is there, Verity? You know as well as I do

that nothing can be done about the sudden shortfall in finances until Charles returns," said August Worth, his kind face lined by worry. He did not voice it, but the thought that something might have befallen his brother was never far from his thoughts.

August was next in age after his elder brother but no two young men could have been more dissimilar. Where Charles was reckless and somewhat hard, August had always been contemplative and deliberate. He was by no means a weak man, for his gentle nature was also one of resilience and conviction.

He did not wish for the baronetcy to fall on his shoulders, but if it should, he meant to bear its responsibilities with stoicism and give up his calling with the least amount of repining of which he was capable.

August Worth was in orders and he was genuinely sincere in the work that had been given to him. His living was not a rich one, but nevertheless he had offered to put at his mother's disposal whatever meager sum he could manage.

Lady Worth had been greatly touched by her son's sacrifice, but she had declined, declaring that nothing could persuade her to take the food out of her grandsons' mouths. Her daughter-in-law, Sally, had gently protested that it was no such thing. But Lady Worth had been adamant and, indeed, had become so agitated, that the subject was allowed to drop.

"Crofthouse must be closed and most of the servants released to find other employment," said Verity with mingled regret and decisiveness. "Then only a portion of the salaries need be paid until Charles returns and reopens the house."

At Lady Worth's despairing moan, Verity smiled with understanding. She laid her hand over her mother's. "I am sorry, Mama, but we must. You have said it yourself—we are very nearly run off our feet. If we knew for certain when Charles was going to return—"

"Yes, and I shall not disguise from you all that I am most disturbed that your brother has not yet come home, nor sent us a single reassurance as to his safety," said Lady Worth. "Sometimes I cannot but wonder whether—but I shall not say it. I dare not!"

The others looked at one another in dismay, their eyes acknowledging the shadow of fear that beset them all. There was a war going on in America, after all, and Charles had always been a neck-or-nothing sort of fellow.

With determined cheerfulness, Verity said, "You shall not stay here amongst the holland covers, Mama. You must write to Great-aunt Mary and accept her kind invitation to reside with her for a time at Brighton. You know how she urged you to come after Papa died."

"Yes. Of course it is necessary. I should have realized it sooner. It is just that I shall hate it so!" said Lady Worth, looking about the familiar sitting room with tears in her eyes.' "I have lived here since that first day when your dear papa brought me in as a new bride. It will be so very difficult to leave."

"Charles will come home as soon as he can," offered Sally. She put her arms around the afflicted widow, who was searching wildly for a handkerchief.

Verity handed her own handkerchief to her mother. She said encouragingly, "It is only for a very little while, Mama. You know that Charles will want you to come back."

"Yes, I do know it, dearest. And I mean to be brave," said Lady Worth, dabbing at her eyes. She sat up straighter, though there was still a forlorn cast to her expression. "There, do I not appear brave?"

"Yes, indeed, Mama. You will do," said Verity, smiling.

"This is all very well, Verity. Certainly, closing Crofthouse and sending away the servants is practical. But it is not enough, as you well know," said August, clasping his hands behind his back and regarding his sister from his angular height.

Brother and sister were much alike in appearance, both tall and sharing the same gleaming chestnut locks and gray eyes. They were generally acknowledged to be handsome. But whereas August's even features could sometimes assume an austere aspect, Verity was held to be more lively in countenance. It was but a trick of expression with its origin in the eyes, but it had won for her much notice with the gentlemen in the past.

Verity's expression was now uncharacteristically subdued. "Yes, I know. There is still the tuition to be thought of and

Elizabeth also," said Verity, sighing. "I have racked my brains and I still cannot quite see how it is all to be brought about."

"Oh, why doesn't Charles come? I vow that I am being driven quite distracted with the whole wretched business. My mind is in a constant whirl, wondering what is to be done," said Lady Worth. "If Crofthouse is to be closed I am sure I do not know what is to become of Elizabeth or the boys, for certainly they cannot come home."

"But *I* have just had a thought to the purpose," said August. A singularly charming smile touched the corner of his mouth as he inclined his head respectfully to his parent. "Our mother will not accept pecuniary help from me; however, I fancy that she will not deny me the right to lend a hand in another direction. The boys must come to me at Highcroft and I will become their tutor."

"August, it is the very thing! How very clever of you to think of it,' exclaimed Sally. She beamed at her husband with such adoring approval that he flushed a gratified crimson.

"I own, it does seem a very good notion," said Verity. She turned to Lady Worth. "What do you think, Mama? Will that suit you?"

Lady Worth nodded. There was a measure of relief in her eyes and her voice trembled. "It is so very good of you, August. You are a true comfort in this time of affliction. I need not wonder how my boys are going on when you have them in hand."

August cleared his throat, somewhat embarrassed by such expressions of gratitude. "Then it is settled. Timothy and Bart will board with us until such time as they may return to school."

"But what of Elizabeth? Oh, surely there must be a way to provide for her, as well?" asked Sally hopefully.

She had expressed all their thoughts. With the satisfactory solution for the continuance of the boys' education, there had also to be found a way to continue to provide for their remaining charge.

"I have already thought of it," said Verity. She looked down at her hands. "I had not wanted to say anything when the boys' future was still at stake, for I did not believe that what I had in mind would support all three. But now that Timothy and Bart are comfortably settled, I shall tell you all at one time."

She raised her eyes and took a steadying breath, for she well knew what reaction to expect from her pronouncement. "I mean to take a post."

Her family stared at her, held momentarily speechless by the shock, but then almost instantly there was a strenuous outcry. Lady Worth's firm voice was distinguishable above the others. "My dear! No, I will not countenance it. I shall not see you so degraded. You will go with me to Brighton."

Verity appealed to her mother's practical nature. "Mama, it will not do. Great-aunt Mary's town house could not possibly contain the three of us. And Elizabeth's needs are of far greater moment than my pride, which even you must admit."

"But what will people say? How will I explain it to our friends? I know that everyone will suspect that your father left us penniless or some such thing. They will talk about him so. Oh, Verity, it is just too horrible to contemplate!" exclaimed Lady Worth.

"Our true friends will think no such thing. They know that Charles is away and how things stand with us. I do not believe that they will hold it against Papa, and only a little against me, that I accept a temporary post under the circumstances," said Verity.

"You have friends in London. Surely there is someone that you might call upon," said August.

Verity shook her head even as her gray eyes twinkled up at her brother. "Really, August, how can I descend upon any one of my friends for an unspecified time and be totally dependent upon their hospitality? I think that would go more against your pride than the notion of my seeking honorable employment. I know that it does mine. Besides, if I were to do so, it would not make it possible for Elizabeth to remain in Barchester, which I am determined that she will be able to do. So that is why I have decided to become a governess or a companion."

At her mother's moan, Verity allowed the flicker of a smile to cross her lips. "It is only for a time, I promise you. I am counting upon Charles to rescue me, you see. He shall enjoy that, don't you agree? But all levity aside, Mama, can you not see that it is for the best?"

Lady Worth could only shake her head, not agreeing but unable to deny the truth of what her daughter had said.

"Well, I do not see it, Verity. No, Verity! You will do no such thing," said August roughly. "You will come to live with us."

"Yes, that is by far the best possible solution. And Elizabeth shall go to Brighton. Oh, Verity, we do want you with us," said Sally.

Verity smiled rather mistily at her brother and sister-in-law. "Oh, August, dearest Sally, I would like that, indeed I would. But I could not possibly. You will already have Timothy and Bart and the babies."

August's lips parted. Verity threw up her hand to forestall her brother's counter to her statement. "Pray do not let us argue, August. I have quite made up my mind, you see. By taking a post, I shall be able to provide something for my sister and also I will not be a charge upon you or on Mama."

"Verity, you could never be a charge upon any of us," exclaimed Sally, distressed.

"Indeed, indeed, dearest child, I would far rather live in a garret than watch you make such a sacrifice for me," assured Lady Worth.

"There is one other alternative open to me," said Verity.

"Anything else would be infinitely preferable!" exclaimed August.

"I could marry Mr. Plimpton," said Verity quietly.

Two

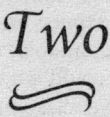

An instant consternation came over Verity's companions. Lady Worth passed a hand over her eyes. Her brother and sister-in-law exchanged an eloquent glance. "I apprehend that the possibility does not meet with unqualified approval," said Verity dryly.

August took an agitated turn about the room. He flung over his shoulder, "It is an unhappy thought, Verity!"

Sally looked at her sister-in-law and faltered, "Oh, my dear sister! Mr. Plimpton?!"

They were all very well-acquainted with Mr. Plimpton. He had been a good friend of Sir Montague Worth's. The gentleman had been hanging out after Verity for more than a year. It had been a very good joke to begin with to all the family, not the least to Sir Montague himself; but it had palled some time past. The gentleman's attentions had become even more marked since Sir Montague Worth's death.

"I am on the shelf, Sally. One cannot be too particular at my advanced age," said Verity, trying to lighten the moment with a bit of gallow's humor.

August growled under his breath, but he did not object to his sister's statement as might have been expected of a fond brother. He was a realist and he understood the society in which they lived and were bound by birth and tradition. Each year young misses emerged from the schoolroom to be introduced to society for the express purpose of snaring the most superior offer of marriage possible.

Verity was twenty and could not now be expected to wed to advantage. Though she was a stylish young woman and had acquired the ease necessary to a well-bred lady who moved in society, she was still two years older than most of the rest of the unmarried females. As far as society was concerned, Miss Verity Worth was passé.

It had not always been so. Upon her come out, Verity had had several suitors. Only just out of the schoolroom, her heart had been engaged and an offer for her hand had been accepted. But her fiancé had been almost immediately killed in an action on the Peninsular.

Though Verity had not been completely without suitors in the intervening two years, she had never formed another deep attachment. She had enjoyed her visits to town; she had liked keeping in touch with old friends, both male and female; and she had accepted the gallantries of admiring gentlemen. But she had not shown a clear preference for anyone.

"Oh, how I wish that you had cared for that nice Mr. Crawford who appeared so smitten with you several months ago," said Sally, deeply distressed. "Even though he has since emigrated to America, and we would have sorely missed you, I am certain that he would have seen to your comfort."

"Yes, hindsight is certainly more sure," agreed Verity. She laughed, shaking her head at her sister-in-law. "You goose, Sally. I did not accept Mr. Crawford's offer because it would not have been fair to the gentleman. I knew that we would not suit."

"Nevertheless you would have been credibly settled. I cannot disguise from you that I have often bewailed the fact that you could not find it in your heart to accept one of the several offers that have been made for you," said Lady Worth with an unexpected note of reproach.

"I know, Mama. But I am such a peculiar female. I don't wish to simply be 'settled,' " Verity said.

"Perhaps you have been too nice in your notions, Verity," commented August, still frowning as he thought about his sister's suddenly bleak future. He did not like what he saw. Verity was too precious to waste herself on either a marriage of necessity or in service. Perhaps better than did his sister, he realized that once she had stepped over the line marking the difference between a young lady of family and a young female who found it necessary to accept employment, it would be very difficult thereafter to set aside the inevitable stigma and resume her former life.

Verity would be tainted by the brush of snobbery. Those who had once found nothing to find fault with in Miss Verity Worth of Crofthouse would look askance at her and smile in their worldly superiority. It was not to be thought of, but for the life of him, he could not discover another alternative. How much he wished that Verity had already married!

"I never thought my requirements were too high. I still do not, though now that it has come down to it, it seems very hard that those opportunities offered to me should have come to naught," said Verity with characteristic frankness.

She herself had not been unduly concerned about her unwed state, for she had had a vague notion that somewhere, somehow, she would cross the path of just the sort of gentleman who would once more stir that slumbering part of her heart to life again. She had only to wait for him to appear; and so she had been content to remain in her favored place as her father's daughter.

But now her father was dead and there was suddenly no time left to Verity. If she was to succeed in her determination to help her family, her present options appeared limited. She could cold-bloodedly enter into a loveless marriage with Mr. Plimpton, the only suitor at that moment on her horizon, or she could take a genteel post.

Though Verity liked and respected Mr. Plimpton, it was another thing altogether to actually contemplate being wed to a gentleman who had been a contemporary of her father. Mr. Plimpton would no doubt do all in his power to help any members of her family who were in need, but Verity shuddered to think of an obligation such as that used as the basis for marriage. No, it was far better to go into service as a governess or a companion and keep intact her dream of finding love again just a little longer.

She did not air that very private hope to her family, but said, "I have as little desire to sacrifice my person or my consequence as any of you wish to see me do so. However, if Elizabeth is not to be made to suffer, I feel that I have small choice in the matter."

"I do not hesitate to tell you, sister, that you have an uncanny ability to cut to the bone of a matter," said August heavily.

"Does that mean that you do not prefer Mr. Plimpton, after all?" asked Verity, with a little laugh.

Her brother reluctantly grinned at her. "Charles shall undoubtedly break a cane about my shoulders, but I do not see that I have any other choice except to allow you to go your own way."

Verity rose from her chair and went over to embrace him. "Dear August. You could not prevent me in any case, for I am very much my own mistress."

Lady Worth was bravely wiping away her tears. "It is not what I wish for you, my dear. But I quite see how you might prefer not to wed poor Mr. Plimpton. He is undoubtedly a most worthy man, but I have never approved of young women marrying gentlemen so much older. Especially when the young lady in question can quite look over the top of the gentleman's head."

Verity allowed herself a small smile. "I know that it is very bad of me, but I have the most lowering suspicion that Mr. Plimpton has always found his view of me most satisfactory."

Since the gentleman's glance fell little higher than the vicinity of Verity's bosom there was some justice for her sister-in-law's choke of outraged laughter. "Verity! You will say such things!"

"Most unbecoming indeed, my dear," said Lady Worth, her lips trembling for the first time in several weeks from something other than grief or worry.

Verity's brother lowered his brows in a surprisingly fierce frown. "Do you mean to say that the gentleman has offered you insult, Verity? For if he has made any lecherous advances, I shall—"

"No, no, nothing of that sort. The poor man can scarcely be blamed for allowing his glance to fall where it naturally must.

I must own, however, I shall not miss the gentleman's frequent visits. I do not care to be ogled, even by such a dear as Mr. Plimpton," said Verity.

"No, I should say not!" exclaimed August, revolted. "If I had had any notion that—Or Charles, either!"

"Well, you did not so there is not the least cause for this show of outrage now, August. Besides, I am very well able to take care of myself. Mr. Plimpton has been harmless enough, believe me," said Verity.

Since at that moment the butler entered to announce the arrival of the gentleman in question, August had to swallow whatever hasty words he was on the point of saying. But his stern countenance and his chilly manners upon being greeted by Mr. Plimpton were such that the gentleman anxiously wondered whether he had at some time inadvertently insulted the young reverend.

"Dear ladies, I need not ask how you go on. You are all radiant as ever," said Mr. Plimpton, greeting Lady Worth and Mrs. Sally Worth, but reserving his largest smile for the daughter of the house. He looked at Miss Worth with patent admiration. In truth, she was a veritable Venus. He hoped that she would rise from her seat to greet him. It always did his heart good to view her in her full magnificence.

Disappointingly, Verity did not rise from her chair to give her hands to him. She had learned that Mr. Plimpton was too much the gentleman to allow his eyes to stray from her face if he was on a level with her. It was quite another thing, however, if she was standing before him. She smiled. "Good morning, sir. I hope that we see you well."

"Oh, indeed, indeed! I am never ill, you know. I am as feisty as a colt on a chill autumn morning," said Mr. Plimpton heartily and laughed at his own witticism. He seated himself beside Lady Worth and he addressed his hostess as was proper, but even as he phrased the question, his glance flickered in Miss Worth's direction.

"We do very well, thank you, Mr. Plimpton. Indeed, it has been hard upon us all. But we shall manage," said Lady Worth.

"I know that to be true, my lady. You, and Miss Worth, are true heroines to have borne up under the recent sorrows. My only wish is that you would allow me to stand with you in whatever capacity that is within my power," said Mr. Plimpton, bowing from the waist. He was a solidly built gentleman and had recently taken to corsetting. The resulting creak which distinguished his movement was disconcerting to Mrs. Worth, who had not previously been privileged to hear it. Her expression was such that Verity had difficulty choking back a gurgle of laughter. Verity shot a brimming glance at her brother, urging him to share in her amusement.

But the humor quite escaped August Worth. He cleared his throat and the gaze with which he favored Mr. Plimpton was uncharacteristically hard. "My father would have been grateful for your kind offices toward his ladies, Mr. Plimpton, as I am myself. I shall indeed call upon you on my mother's behalf if there is the least necessity to do so. We need not stand on ceremony with you, I know, since you are such an old, *old* friend."

"No, indeed," faltered Mr. Plimpton, sensing something not quite friendly in August's words. Really, the boy need not make him out to be a graybeard, he thought, pardonably peeved when he caught the faint hint of amusement in the glance that Miss Worth threw at her brother.

Shaking off his annoyance, he turned his attention to making genteel conversation, but for some reason he could not understand, he was not coming off at his best. His companions seemed somewhat preoccupied and all his efforts to entertain seemed to fall short of expectation. At last, concerned that he was boring on, Mr. Plimpton allowed himself only a short visit with the ladies before taking himself off.

As soon as Mr. Plimpton had left, the others reverted to the topic still uppermost in all their minds. The alternative of welcoming Mr. Plimpton into the family had been universally rejected without a word spoken between them and Verity's other avenue had become in a fair way to being accepted, though not without a good deal of residual resistance.

"How shall you go about it, Verity?" asked Sally.

"I shall place an advertisement in the *London Gazette* and hope for the best. There must be any number of positions available, so that I feel assured of finding one suitable to my qualifications," said Verity quietly.

She spoke with more confidence than she felt. Her inner

being actually quailed at the thought of being interviewed for a post. She did not know whether she would be able to carry it off with the proper humility, for she was, after all, the daughter of a proud baronet. However, that would be but the first hurdle. The true test of her pride would be to submit on a daily basis to the role that she would be taking upon herself.

"I cannot like it," said August, his countenance again weighted with a heavy frown.

Verity smiled across at him. "I know, none of you do. I own, I do not much care for it myself." She recognized the swift altering of her brother's expression and she shook her head. "But I shall not change my mind, so it is of no use to hammer away at it."

"You will not go away until I am settled, I hope?" asked Lady Worth, almost pathetically. "I do not know how I shall go on otherwise."

Verity shook her head. "No, Mama. I shall be here to help you with all the details."

Over the next few days, August and Sally, individually and together tried to sway Verity from her purpose but she stood firm. They were at last forced to acknowledge failure, August remarking, "At least Charles cannot say that I did not try. He knows what an obstinate streak you can exercise when you take something into your head, however, so I hope that he will forgive me."

"Charles will say nothing to you, dear August. It is I who shall bear the brunt of his displeasure, for I have done nothing to turn my own dear child from this determined course of madness," said Lady Worth sadly.

"You are both being quite nonsensical. If Charles has anything to say, he shall say it to me. Indeed, I hope that he may do just that, and with the greatest anger imaginable, for then I shall be handed a valid excuse for giving up my post," said Verity with a laugh.

"I know that Charles will come home soon," said Sally, repeating the hopeful words that she had taken to saying ever since notice had first been sent out of Sir Montague Worth's death.

Lady Worth's chin trembled. "I do hope so."

"Of course he shall," said August staunchly, as much to reassure himself as to calm his mother's fears.

Three

A few days later August and Sally took reluctant leave of Lady Worth and Verity. It was time to collect the boys from school and thence return home to Highcroft. Lady Worth exchanged kisses with her twin grandsons, making many promises to visit them in a few weeks.

Lady Worth and Verity stood on the steps of the manor, their shawls wrapped tightly about them against the chill, and waved until the carriage had bowled round the bend in the drive and was lost to sight. They turned, shivering, and went back into the house.

Lady Worth squared her shoulders. She wore a wavering smile as she tipped her head to look up into her daughter's face. "Well, my dear? Shall we begin this dreadful business this evening?"

"Why do we not spend our usual quiet evening tonight, ma'am? I own that August and Sally's leavetaking has left me feeling low and I do not think that I have the heart just yet for the other," said Verity. She was rewarded by the swift relief in her mother's expression.

Lady Worth caught Verity's hand and gave it a quick squeeze. "Thank you, my dear. Yes, that would be very pleasant."

The ladies dined and took coffee in the drawing room. Each busied herself with an embroidery hoop while they conversed quietly. At ten o'clock, they went upstairs and when they separated to go to their rooms, Lady Worth bade Verity her usual fond goodnight. Then she said, "I shall rise early, never fear. I do not mean to leave everything to you to handle, dearest."

Verity felt tears sting her eyes. "We shall manage together, Mama."

"Yes, dear."

The following morning Lady Worth, whose habit was generally to take a leisurely breakfast in bed, was as good as her word and presented herself downstairs at an unusually early hour. Verity was already at the table. "Good morning, Verity dear," Lady Worth said brightly.

"I am happy to see you feeling so lively, Mama," said Verity, surprised.

"Oh, I am full of high spirits. Now, how shall we begin?" Lady Worth sat down opposite with a cup of tea and some strips of toast.

Verity hesitantly began to ennumerate, but as her mother seemed encouraging, she warmed to the subject. It was not until several minutes had passed that Verity suddenly took note that Lady Worth's countenance, once so bright and sparkling, had steadily turned more woebegone. She broke off what she was saying to exclaim, "Oh, Mama! Forgive me, I am a veritable beast not to have realized!"

"No, it is completely my own fault." Lady Worth made use of a handkerchief to dab at her brimming eyes. "I am sorry, dear. I do try to keep up my spirits but it is all so very sad."

"Yes." Verity reached out and touched her mother's hand. "Never mind, Mama, you may safely leave it to me."

So it was that the responsibility for making most of the decisions fell upon Verity's shoulders. The business of closing down the huge house that had been the family home for generations was more onerous than she had ever dreamed. Lady Worth was by turns helpful and lachrymose. Often she apologized to her daughter that she was not of more use. "But it is just so affecting, you see."

"Yes, Mama, I do see." Verity sighed, pushing back a tendril of hair. It was indeed a sad time, made even more so when

Verity let go the servants who would no longer be needed. All she could do was to assure herself and others that the drastic measure would not exist for long.

It was odd to know that the house would stand forlorn and empty, except for the retainers, whose job it would be to keep it in repair. However, Verity's optimistic hope was that her brother, now Sir Charles, would set things to rights again once he returned.

There was still no word of Sir Charles, and when Verity realized how desperately she was holding to the hope that he would suddenly materialize before the door of Crofthouse was finally closed, she scolded herself. It was vexing to discover that she was not as resolute as she had supposed.

All this combined to oppress her spirits, but perhaps the most trying circumstance was the visit made to her by Mr. Plimpton.

Mr. Plimpton had heard through the gossip in the village that the servants had been let go at Crofthouse and of the intended move by the Worth ladies. He at once set out in his gig to discover the truth for himself.

When he showed himself into the sitting room, he found Verity seated on the settee and engaged in packing away some of the odd knickknacks that were her mother's personal treasures. "Miss Worth!"

She looked up in surprise. "Mr. Plimpton!"

Mr. Plimpton approached and at once caught up her hands, exclaiming, "My dear Miss Worth! I have but just heard or I would have been here sooner. I had hoped the rumors were in error, but I apprehend that it is all too horribly true. You are actually closing Crofthouse! I have never been more overset, I assure you. Only tell me what I must do to help you and dear Lady Worth, for I cannot bear to watch you driven from your home."

Verity gently reclaimed her hands from his agitated clasp. She smiled reassuringly. "I do appreciate your sentiments, Mr. Plimpton. You have always been a kind friend, both to my father and to us. But there is not the least necessity to put yourself in such a taking. My mother and I, yes, and August, too, discussed the matter in detail and it was decided that it would be for the best if Crofthouse was closed, at least until Charles should return."

"But what will you do? Where will you go?" he asked, very upset.

"My mother has accepted an invitation to stay with my great-aunt in Brighton," said Verity, completely sidestepping any mention of her own plans. It was best to let the gentleman assume that Brighton was also her own destination.

"With Mrs. Moffett? But that dear lady's accommodations are scarcely of a nature to allow for so many additions to her household. There will be yourselves and your personal servants. No, no, the squeeze is not to be thought of. It is not at all what you are used to, my dear Miss Worth," said Mr. Plimpton.

Too late, Verity realized that the gentleman was perhaps more familiar with the members of her family and their circumstances than she had appreciated. "We shall manage very well, however."

Mr. Plimpton took an agitated turn about the room. He stopped before her. "Miss Worth! This is not the most felicitous moment for what I would say to you, but I must speak. Miss Worth, I am offering for your hand. I am not a young man nor a particularly wealthy one, but I fancy that what I can give to a wife is respectable, nevertheless. I—"

Verity threw up her hand. "Mr. Plimpton, pray say no more!" She realized that she had risen to her feet as she had spoken and that Mr. Plimpton's eyes had settled of their own volition upon the deeply curved front of her gown. Verity firmly pulled her shawl close about her. "I am naturally flattered by the honor that you do me. However, I cannot in all conscience accept. Such a bargain would be a disappointment to us both."

"Not at all, my dear Miss Worth. Quite the contrary. I should feel myself a young man again," said Mr. Plimpton, his gaze never wavering.

Verity found that the gentleman stood directly between herself and the door. She was practically boxed into her little corner. It would be most noticeable if she were to step deliberately around him and go to the door. No amount of kind words would disguise that she wished to escape from his attention. She knew that such a course would wound Mr. Plimpton's sensibilities, and however unwelcome his ardency, she did not wish to hurt the gentleman.

Mr. Plimpton unsuccessfully tried to take her free hand. "Miss Worth, I cannot be silent any longer. I must speak what has been my dearest wish for many months."

Verity made a show of untangling a fringe of her shawl. "How vexing that these should knot up so easily."

Mr. Plimpton was not indifferent to her agitation. "Ah, you are shy. Yes, yes! I see it fully and honor you all the more, Miss Worth."

Verity tried to edge around the gentleman, giving a laugh to cover her stealthy movement. "Mr. Plimpton, you startle me, certainly."

Verity cast a glance over the gentleman's head at the open door. She wondered where her mother was or the butler. Surely Mr. Plimpton had not been shown in without someone being made aware that she was alone in the sitting room. A young lady did not receive gentlemen by herself, not even somewhat elderly ones such as Mr. Plimpton. She glanced down into Mr. Plimpton's face, and the thought speeded through her mind that the gentleman was regarding her in a distinctly unpaternal fashion.

Almost on the heels of the astounding thought, Lady Worth came into the sitting room. "Verity, I—"

She saw all at once that her daughter was not alone and read the desperate appeal in Verity's eyes. The frown disappeared from her brow and she stepped forward with a welcoming expression, determined to do her duty as a good parent. "Why, dear Mr. Plimpton, forgive me. I was not aware that you had called. We are in a state of some confusion, as no doubt you have noticed. Have you come to wish us good-bye?"

"Yes. That is—" Mr. Plimpton squared his plump shoulders and opened his mouth to deliver himself of a dignified declaration.

But the moment was snatched from him as Lady Worth hurried into speech. "How kind of you. You are a true friend, and I am so glad that you have appeared just now, for I have a favor to ask of you," said Lady Worth, smiling. She had taken his arm and drawn him after her toward the settee that Verity had so lately abandoned.

Mr. Plimpton bowed. "You may ask anything at all of me, my lady."

"You are so very good, Mr. Plimpton." Lady Worth sat down and indicated with a gracious gesture that Mr. Plimpton should join her. After the smallest hesitation, the gentleman did so, but not without throwing an undecided glance in Verity's direction. Lady Worth said firmly, "Verity, I have just recalled that there is a list of items on my desk that need attending. Will you see to it, my dear, while I speak with Mr. Plimpton?"

"Of course, Mama," said Verity quietly. She knew that she was being handed her chance and murmuring her apologies, she made good her escape.

Verity did not return downstairs, but waited for her mother in the upstairs parlor. When Lady Worth at length appeared, Verity smiled at her parent. "I have never been more thankful to be sent on an errand in my life, Mama! I did not know what to do. Mr. Plimpton offered for me, but he did not seem in the least put out when I refused him. Indeed, for a moment I quite thought that he was on the brink of taking liberties with me. That would certainly have been an embarrassment to us both."

"Well, you need not be anxious any longer. I explained the matter perfectly to poor Mr. Plimpton." Lady Worth shook her head. "The dear man was quite crushed to learn that you have no thought of marriage at all, but he understood when I told him that you were still wearing the willow for that unfortunate young man."

"You didn't! You know very well that I am not, it is just that—Why, Mr. Plimpton must think me to be a ninny," said Verity, regarding her mother with a fascinated gaze. She had not known that there was such a streak of ruthlessness in her dear mother.

"Not at all. He quite appreciated the loyalties that are bound up in a blighted love. You know, I had never before realized what a strong romantic streak is harbored by that little man. It was quite a surprise, I assure you," said Lady Worth. "Now, have you marked off any of those items on my list?"

Verity laughed, seeing that the affair was well and truly

closed. Mr. Plimpton had at least been forced to accept that she was not for him. It was just as well that she was going away, for she did not think that she would care to meet the gentleman after he had been dealt such a blow. "Poor Mr. Plimpton. He is forgotten in the pursuit of sheets," she remarked, showing the list to her mother.

"Yes, well, we do have an inventory to finish," said Lady Worth practically. "Charles must not find the accounting wanting when he returns."

The ladies bent their energies to finishing the task of closing the large house. At last the packing was begun. Lady Worth and Verity were taking away little more than their wardrobes and a few personal items. Soon all that was left to be done was to order out the horses and carriage. However, strange as it was, neither Lady Worth nor Verity were in any great hurry to do so.

One morning over breakfast, Lady Worth said, "Verity, I have had a very nice letter from your Great-aunt Mary. She is impatiently awaiting my arrival." Lady Worth hesitated, then said, "I shall write her that I am not certain of the date of my arrival. I do not wish to go to her until I know what your situation is to be, my dear."

"Yes, I know." Verity sighed. She set down her cup. "I have been curiously reluctant to take the irrevocable step, Mama."

"Then do not, my dearest! You will come with me to Brighton," said Lady Worth quickly.

"You know it will not do, for then we would have to take Elizabeth from the seminary and she, too, would need to stay with Great-aunt Mary. I cannot see how we might contrive that," said Verity.

"Nor I, I am afraid. Your great-aunt lives very quietly due to her straitened circumstances," said Lady Worth, sighing. She shook herself and summoned up a wavering smile. "Very well, dearest; put in your advertisement."

"I have already done so, these two weeks past. I just have not gotten up the courage to open my mail," confessed Verity.

"You awful girl. And you did not tell me. Well, you shall open those letters this very moment. Now go and bring them down," said Lady Worth.

Verity rose obediently from the breakfast table, but as she went round the corner she dropped a kiss on her mother's head. "Thank you, Mama. I would rather not be alone during this time."

Lady Worth gave a watery sniff. She reached up to catch hold of her daughter's fingers for a quick squeeze. "You are my daughter. Of course I shall stand by you to face together whatever unpleasantness may come."

Verity returned to the breakfast room quickly. In her hands were half a dozen letters. "I shall rely upon you to help me sort them out, Mama."

"Of course. I hope that I take my duty too well to allow you to accept just any position. It must naturally be a respectable household," said Lady Worth with forlorn determination.

Verity divided the letters with her mother and they went about the task of opening them. The second letter that came to Verity's hand was from Mr. Pettiforth.

Verity was both surprised and curious to receive correspondence from a distant relation that she had met very seldom and she broke the seal on it at once. As she read, she gasped with astonishment.

"What is it, dearest?" asked Lady Worth, looking up from one of the letters that she had opened.

"Why, it is the most extraordinary thing," said Verity. She proceeded to read the closely written sheets to her mother.

In his letter, Mr. Pettiforth set forth a proposal to Verity. It was felt by himself and his wife that their daughter needed the refining influence of a well-bred young lady. Miss Pettiforth was soon to be presented to society, but there was concern expressed by her present governess that the young lady was not well-enough prepared to make a success of her debut.

In short, Miss Pettiforth wanted a bit of polish and experience. Would Miss Worth, who was known to Mr. Pettiforth through the letters he had had from her father, be willing to take on the charge of his daughter? He hoped that Miss Worth's example and society would benefit his daughter.

Naturally, Mr. Pettiforth would not dream of encroaching upon Miss Worth's good nature. There would, of course, be renumeration to her both for the sacrifice of her time and as a small token against depriving her mother of her company. Mr. Pettiforth discreetly named a figure in such a way as not to give offense.

Four

Verity looked up from the letter. "What do you think, Mama?"

Lady Worth shrugged slightly. "My dear, I have disliked immensely the thought of your taking a post. But this situation with your cousins, the Pettiforths, is something different altogether. You would be a part of the family. Such a position would be far more respectable than hiring on as a governess or companion. I own, I shall not be so anxious on your behalf," she said.

Frowning, Lady Worth tapped the sheets of the letter that she had put down on the table as she had listened to Mr. Pettiforth's appeal. "Certainly it is more desirable than any such as this. Why, I immediately saw that this lady desired not a companion, but an overworked drudge. She offers room and board and her castdown wardrobe, if you please! I do not wish to sound mercenary, but I do think you could do worse than to settle for the figure that Burton Pettiforth offers."

"The salary is generous indeed. I should think that I would be more than able to save enough to provide toward Elizabeth's keep, for I do not anticipate that my needs will be onerous," said Verity.

She reflected that her clothes were good, and since they had been made up during the mourning period for her father, the dull colors were just the thing for a paid chaperone. However Mr. Pettiforth might put it otherwise, that was essentially the place that she would fill while making one of his household. It was unlikely, then, that she would need any new ball gowns or fashionable day dresses. Chaperones and paid companions did not dance or mingle with guests. She said as much to her mother. "And in the unlikely event, I am persuaded that I can make do with one of my old gowns."

Lady Worth disagreed. "A chaperone is a very different thing from an unpaid companion. You might very well be required to accompany Miss Pettiforth to various social functions. I would not wish you to appear a quiz in last year's gowns. Perhaps it would be wise to see what old silks and such are stored in those old trunks in the attic. We might wish to have one or two simple gowns made up. The village seamstress has your measurements so that you need not be present for fittings if you must leave very soon."

"Does this mean that you have no objection to my accepting the situation?" asked Verity, smiling at her mother.

"Of course I object, dear! But you are determined on this course and try as I might, I have been unable to see a way to spare you. Mr. Pettiforth's offer comes most providentially. It is a compromise of sorts," said Lady Worth.

She gathered up the other letters, opened and unopened, and with a satisfied look in her eyes, she said, "I shall burn these immediately. And you must write at once to the *Gazette* to have your advertisement taken out so that we will be spared any more of these!"

By return mail, Miss Worth respectfully indicated her willingness to accept the position of chaperone and companion to Miss Pettiforth. Mr. Pettiforth's reply was a combination of gratitude and instruction to her in how to get to her destination. And so Verity had embarked on the mail coach with the tearful good-bye and good wishes of her mother still ringing in her ears.

Verity set aside her melancholy recollections as the carriage finally swept up to the steps of a well-built manor house. It was full night and lanterns had been hung in expectation of Verity's arrival, so that when she descended from the carriage, she was able to gather an impression of the solid stability of the manor itself before she was ushered inside.

Her luggage was carried off by a footman to unknown regions while she was escorted by a solemn-faced butler into a large sitting room. The butler went away to announce her arrival.

Verity sent a curious glance about the charming room. It was well-proportioned and comfortably furnished, speaking mutely of the owners' affluence. But it was the fire in the grate that she thought to be most welcoming, and drew her immediate attention. It had been a chilly ride once she had exchanged the redolent warmth of the crowded mail coach for the solitary comfort of the Pettiforth's carriage.

Verity spread her hands to the blaze. She was just thinking of removing her gloves when the door to the sitting room was opened. Verity straightened and turned as a small-statured, deep-bosomed lady entered.

"My dear Miss Worth!" The lady bustled forward, her hands outstretched in welcome. "I am Alice Pettiforth. But I shall call you Verity, if I may, for I have been thinking you one of the family ever since Mr. Pettiforth suggested that you might come to us. May I do so?"

Verity shook hands with her cousin-in-law, aware that the shorter woman was measuring her with narrowed eyes. "Why, with my goodwill, ma'am. I assure you that it would afford me genuine pleasure to be considered one of the family."

"Very prettily said," approved Mrs. Pettiforth. "You must address me as 'Cousin,' for that is what we are, is it not?" She sat down on the tall wooden settle and gestured for Miss Worth to join her, remarking, "This settee is an old-fashioned piece and I have long wished to replace it, but Mr. Pettiforth will not hear of it. He quite likes to doze before the fire of an evening after coffee." Her voice became a shade cooler. "You have come late, so I must assume there was some sort of excitement attached to the journey."

"Oh, no excitement, ma'am. It was but a tossed horseshoe," said Verity quietly. She had no difficulty in detecting the shade of disapproval in Mrs. Pettiforth's tone, but she would offer no apologies for a happening that had been beyond her control.

"How annoying for you. We have already sat down for dinner, of course. You will not wish to set us back, I know, so we must forgo the pleasure of your company this evening, at least," said Mrs. Pettiforth. "Now, you must tell me quickly about your dear mama and then I will let you go up to your room."

"My mother conveys her compliments. I am charged with a missive to you which I have carried in my reticule. Here it is, ma'am," said Verity, handing the folded letter to her employer.

Mrs. Pettiforth took the letter in her hand, but she scarcely glanced at it before setting it aside on an occasional table. "I shall read it at my leisure after dinner. You are tired from your journey, I daresay, and would like nothing better than tea and a bowl of soup in your room before retiring. I shall ring now for a footman to show you upstairs. We will talk more in the morning when I shall be free to explain to you what is required. Mr. Pettiforth shall wish to interview you as well, of course."

Mrs. Pettiforth had gotten up to pull the bell while she was yet speaking. Miss Worth had scarcely time to murmur her thanks and acquiescence before the footman appeared. Mrs. Pettiforth walked out of the sitting room with Verity, but at once parted from her, saying, "I must return to the dining room. I know that you will excuse me, Verity." The dismissal was clear.

Verity followed the footman upstairs, her thoughts somber. She had been taken aback by Mrs. Pettiforth's manner, which had seemed to her to be a strange mixture of familiarity and civil superiority. She hoped that her interview on the morrow with Mr. Pettiforth would be more informative and enlightening. The tone of Mr. Pettiforth's letter had persuaded her to accept the proposal outlined in it. In light of what she had believed, Mrs. Pettiforth's behavior toward her was confusing. Verity was now uncertain what her actual position might be in the household, whether that of a surrogate family member or that of a mere employee.

Misgivings rose in her at thought of being relegated to the role of a menial. She had naturally resigned herself to having to bear indignities and slights when she had found a post either as a companion or a governess. That was to be expected.

However, Mr. Pettiforth's letter had set forth the position in his household with such discretion and obvious care for Verity's sensibilities that Verity had rather hoped that she need not be concerned for such things. Her spirits had risen even higher when she had been met by the Pettiforth's own carriage. However, Mrs. Pettiforth's odd conduct upon their first meeting hinted that all might not be as cozy as Verity had come to anticipate.

Verity was once more heartened when she was shown to the bedroom that was to be for her use. The bedroom was on the second floor where the family's own apartments would naturally be located. After talking with Mrs. Pettiforth, she had half-expected to be given a cold garret under the attic rafters and it was a most pleasant surprise to discover that she was accorded the courtesy of a place on the same floor as her employers.

The room was of a good though irregular size and contained a large four-poster, an old-fashioned wardrobe, a washstand with pitcher and basin, and a dressing table. There was in addition a small sitting area near the curtained windows.

A maid was building up the fire on the grate. She cast a curious glance and half-smile over her shoulder when the footman ushered in the stranger. "Good evening, miss."

Verity returned the maid's greeting. She saw that her luggage had already been unpacked and that her bedgown and overrobe had been laid across the coverlet on the bed. She took off her bonnet and pulled off her gloves as she surveyed the room. "This is a comfortable room, indeed," she said, smiling.

"Aye, miss. There will be fresh water in the basin so that you can wash, and as soon as I have the fire started good and proper, I will go fetch up a tray of supper for you," said the maid. She sat back on her heels, surveying the result of her efforts. "There now. That will soon take the chill off."

"Thank you." Verity smiled her appreciation as the servant-woman left the bedroom. She unbuttoned her pelisse and laid it with her bonnet and gloves on a chair. Then she washed her face and hands in the basin.

Lord Rathbone's Flirt

By the time that she had finished with her toilette and tried to fluff her crushed hair, the maid had returned with a tray. There was soup, tea, and buttered bread.

The maid offered to undo the buttons down the back of Miss Worth's dress before she left. "For I'm certain that you'll not easily manage all of them for yourself, miss."

Verity agreed. She thought that it would be an adjustment for her to make do without a maid. For several weeks she had shared a dresser with her mother and it had been agreed that the woman would go with Lady Worth to Brighton. Verity's own maid had some time before gone to help her sister with a new baby and when the decision to close Crofthouse had been made, the woman had been sent notice that she need not return until Miss Worth was once more in a position which would require the offices of a personal maid.

With the maid's help, Verity undressed and made ready for bed. The maid ran a warming pan between the bedsheets, recommended that Miss Worth enjoy her supper, and left once more. In gown and dressing gown, Verity sat down to the small table and disposed of her lukewarm soup and bread. She discovered that she really was hungry and the soup was very satisfying.

Afterward, she snuffed out the candle and slid under the heavy coverlet. She was asleep almost at once. It had been a long fatiguing journey and not even her natural anxiety over her future in the Pettiforth household could keep her awake.

In the morning at breakfast, Miss Worth met Mr. Pettiforth. They were the only ones in the breakfast room at the time, since Mrs. Pettiforth and Miss Pettiforth did not come out of their rooms until later, while the younger children took breakfast in the schoolroom with their governess. This much Verity learned in the matter of minutes of their introduction to one another.

Mr. Pettiforth assured her that she was to consider herself part of the family. "You are not to stand on ceremony with us, my dear. I consider you almost one of my own daughters due to the close correspondence that your father and I enjoyed for so many years."

"I know that he derived as much pleasure out of your letters, sir," said Verity.

Mr. Pettiforth was pleased to hear that it was so. He inquired after Lady Worth and Verity's brothers and sisters in detail, initially surprising Verity as to how well-informed he was; but, of course, her father must have told him much over the years. As a consequence, Verity felt rather more free in talking about her family to him than she might have otherwise.

Mr. Pettiforth shook his head, frowning in sympathy at her confessed misgivings over her brother's continued absence from England. "And not a word, you say. That is certainly cause for anxiety. But nevertheless I do not doubt that Sir Charles will return. From everything that your father wrote me of him, Sir Charles has something of a wild turn in his character. I expect that we shall discover he was delayed through being engaged in some odd enterprise or other and that the word of your father's death did not reach him at once."

"I trust that you are right, sir," said Verity. She found that she was cheered by her cousin's observation. It was perfectly true that her brother could have gone off on some start or other. Indeed, how very like dear Charles that would be!

As they continued to converse, Verity decided that she liked Mr. Pettiforth very much. His was a quiet personality, and he listened with sincere interest to all that was said. Her own questions about the household and her duties were answered thoughtfully and completely.

She was surprised to learn that there had been some discussion between the Pettiforths and that it had been decided that she would be accompanying Miss Pettiforth to most of their social obligations. She had assumed that her responsibility would be limited to the daily rounds of activity and an occasional excursion. Verity had naturally thought that Mrs. Pettiforth would herself wish to chaperone her daughter into society, but according to Mr. Pettiforth that was not the case.

With Mrs. Pettiforth's conduct vividly in mind, Verity thought that it would be wise to establish just what was expected of her by that lady. "I shall hold myself available to fulfill whatever needs are required of me by Mrs. Pettiforth, of course. Will she wish anything else of me, sir?" she asked.

"Thank you, my dear. You will discover that your role is

just as I have said and that you will soon feel quite comfortable with us," said Mr. Pettiforth.

Mrs. Pettiforth entered the breakfast room just as Mr. Pettiforth was rising. She inclined her cheek for her husband's salute. "Dear Mr. Pettiforth, good morning. And Verity, too!. You have had an opportunity to talk, then?"

"Yes, indeed. I believe our cousin shall be an asset to us, Mrs. Pettiforth," said Mr. Pettiforth.

Mrs. Pettiforth nodded. She allowed her husband to seat her at the table. "Just as I thought. We shall deal famously, I do not doubt."

Mr. Pettiforth excused himself once more to the ladies and exited.

Five

Mrs. Pettiforth poured herself a cup of tea, but she did not serve herself anything from the sideboard. "I never touch a morsel before luncheon, but I see that you are a fine trencherwoman, Verity. But then you are a rather tall young woman, are you not? Not at all like myself or my dear Cecily. I do hope that you have a store of gowns, for I should not like the fitting of you."

"Pray do not be anxious on that account, ma'am. I assure you that I am decently wardrobed," said Verity quietly. She did not give any indication that she was aware that Mrs. Pettiforth had offered insult. One did not give notice to another's ill-breeding.

It was becoming obvious to her that however much Mr. Pettiforth wanted her in the house, Mrs. Pettiforth held hidden resentments over her presence. Verity smiled slightly. "However, you have raised a question. Mr. Pettiforth told me that I would be accompanying Miss Pettiforth to several social functions. May I inquire more closely into what you desire of me?"

Mrs. Pettiforth fiddled with the lace at her bosom. "Yes, well, that was talked of. Mr. Pettiforth hopes to spare me anxiety by having a companion whose sole responsibility will be to provide an example for our daughter. Of course, you are not quite out of mourning, but Mr. Pettiforth does not consider that a true objection, since you will not be dancing in any event." She looked up and bestowed a patently false smile on Verity. "I would not wish you to go against the dictates of your conscience, however."

Verity smiled also. She was very well able to discern Mrs. Pettiforth's true desires. The lady did not want an interloper chaperoning her daughter, but at the same time she did not want to run counter to her husband's expressed wishes. As for herself, Verity rather thought that she would take her cue from Mr. Pettiforth himself. It was him to whom she owed her present position and so that was where her strongest loyalties must incline. Indeed, she would far rather accept Mr. Pettiforth's description of her place in the house rather than that to which she suspected Mrs. Pettiforth would prefer to relegate her. But the matter had to be handled with as much diplomacy as possible, for she had no wish to make an enemy of Mrs. Pettiforth. If she so chose, the lady of the house could undoubtedly make Verity's position very uncomfortable indeed.

"I am out of black gloves, ma'am. I do not believe that the conventions will be outraged if I were to pursue the charge that you have laid upon me. Indeed, it would be a dereliction of my duty if I were to cry off for such a reason when I am certain that you have much planned for Miss Pettiforth's entertainment," said Verity.

Mrs. Pettiforth's stiff expression eased. "Indeed, we do have ambitious plans in train for my beloved Cecily's edification. I was never one to see the sense of throwing a sheltered young miss willy-nilly onto the London social scene without first having some experience behind her."

"I do agree, Mrs. Pettiforth. Nothing is more detrimental to a young girl's chances, especially if she is the least bit spirited," said Verity, venturing to draw a bow in the dark.

Her arrow struck the target. Mrs. Pettiforth nodded and unbent even further. She said proudly, "There is no denying that Cecily is exceedingly high-strung and sometimes her playfulness can lead her too far. Cecily is a beauty, of course, and much can be forgiven her for that reason. You understand that there are those whose envy of Cecily's superior looks leads them to catty whisperings which put my dear girl out of all patience."

Mrs. Pettiforth shrugged. "However, I wish Cecily to put forward her very best foot no matter what the circumstance. She must learn to behave with all the cool disdain that a lady should possess when faced with direct insult. That is where you come in, dear Verity. You shall be Cecily's example in how to go on in society, for Mr. Pettiforth assures me there could be no person better qualified to handle the task. In addition, I wish you to shield my girl as much as possible from those unfortunate remarks that sting her sensibilities and lead her into rash retaliation."

"I understand you, I think," said Verity slowly. "Miss Pettiforth is both high-strung and perhaps overly sensitive to possible slight. That is indeed an awkward combination when one is to make one's debut. Polite society is rarely compassionate where a *faux pas* is concerned, and especially when it is committed by a young lady unestablished in the world."

"Exactly," said Mrs. Pettiforth. She was very nearly beaming her approval of Verity's quick grasp of the situation. "I see that Mr. Pettiforth was precisely right in his estimation of your character. My anxieties may be put to rest, indeed! I shall rely upon you, dear Verity, for I hope that Cecily will go off exceedingly well. In point of fact—"

Abruptly, Mrs. Pettiforth seemed to realize that she had very nearly confided something that she should not. She had leaned over the table in a conspiratorial posture, but now she straightened. She picked up her teacup. "But I should not say anything more at present. You will understand a mother's hopes, I know, for Lady Worth must have cherished much the same for you. It is such a pity that you did not take, my dear."

Verity was rather taken aback by Mrs. Pettiforth's assumption. She did not quite know what to say, and so she made a noncommittal statement that could be taken in any way. "My hopes were also rather dashed, ma'am. However, I do not regret the opportunities that were given me."

Mrs. Pettiforth chose to accept Verity's reply as agreement with her observation. She actually smiled. "I can now understand why Mr. Pettiforth's thoughts naturally turned directly to you, my dear Verity. You have a very superior understanding.

Sir Montague's letters indicated a pride in you. Indeed, in all of his family. I was never more shocked than to hear of his death. I would have been at the funeral with Mr. Pettiforth except that I was laid down on my bed with an ailment. It was nothing serious, I do assure you, but nevertheless it barred me from any exertion. I do hope that Mr. Pettiforth properly conveyed my respects to your dear mama."

Verity recalled from that terrible time a rare visit from Mr. Pettiforth to her mother, and though she did not actually know what had passed in that interview, she thought it was safe to assume that Mr. Pettiforth had indeed discharged this duty. "Yes, he did, ma'am. My mother was much appreciative of the gesture of condolences, I know."

Mrs. Pettiforth nodded. "Very good. I know that you will be anxious to settle into your duties with us. You will undoubtedly meet Cecily at luncheon."

Verity realized that she had been dismissed again. Since she had already finished her breakfast, there was nothing else to keep her in the room. She therefore rose and gracefully took her leave.

Upon exiting the breakfast room, Verity inquired of a footman the location of the library. She went directly there, assured of finding stationery and pens available. She wrote at once to her mother, outlining for that lady the welcome that she had found. Also, she requested that her evening gowns, and the new gowns that had been ordered, be sent to her since she would require them after all. She also wrote letters to her brother and sister-in-law, with a special word each for Timothy and Bart, and to her sister, Elizabeth. Much of the morning passed quickly and pleasantly at the task. When she emerged from the library with her finished letters, she requested that the butler frank them for her, Mr. Pettiforth having put this courtesy at her command.

Verity then went upstairs to idle away the time remaining before luncheon. On the landing she chanced to meet a superior female of stern demeanor, who was herding three young females of varying ages down the hall. Correctly divining that this must be the governess and the younger ladies of the house, Verity paused to introduce herself.

The governess regarded Verity with what could only be

called a measuring look. Verity wondered at the sharpness of the woman's glance and what it could possibly mean. The woman briskly shook Verity's hand. "I am Miss Tibbs. These young ladies are Miss Sophronia, Miss Dorothy, and Miss Rebecca." Each of the girls curtsied in turn as they were introduced, silently staring with wide eyes at the new member of their household.

Verity smiled at them. "How do you do, girls. I am glad to make your acquaintance."

The girls murmured polite acknowledgments. The tallest girl said hesitantly, "Perhaps Miss Worth would like to join us, Miss Tibbs?"

Miss Tibbs glanced at the girl, permitting a small smile of approval to touch her lips. She lifted her gaze from the girl's gratified expression. "We are on our way to take a turn about the walking gallery. Would you care to join us, Miss Worth?"

"Yes, thank you. That would indeed be very pleasant." Verity turned about and accompanied the little group. It was still early and she had wondered what she was to do with herself until the luncheon bell sounded. Nothing could have suited her better than to meet more of the household and learn something about them. In addition, she was not used to being physically idle and she was grateful for the opportunity to take a little exercise.

The party traversed the halls to the walking gallery, whereupon the younger members broke away to dash to the far end. "The exercise will do them good. They will sit more quietly at their stitching later," said Miss Tibbs, as though she was replying to a query about the latitude that she allowed the girls.

"I recall that my governess disliked it very much whenever I stepped out at more than a sedate walk. She scolded me many times for my lack of ladylike restraint," said Verity, smiling. "But girls become young ladies so very quickly in any event."

"Indeed they do," said Miss Tibbs. "It is the nature of things, after all. One hopes that in the process valuable lessons are learned so that the transition is relatively painless. I am fortunate that my present charges are fine, sensitive girls."

"It is wonderful that you can say so," said Verity. "I understand it is not always the case."

Miss Tibbs chuckled. "No, that is true; it is not. Do you have family, Miss Worth?"

Verity replied and, encouraged by Miss Tibbs's casual question, had soon divulged much of her background. Miss Tibbs gave out her own history in a dry way. The conversation between Verity and Miss Tibbs was of this moderate polite nature until the governess abruptly put a question that quite turned its character. "Have you any reservations about your position here, Miss Worth?"

Verity looked at the governess in considerable surprise. She had not judged the governess to be the sort to inquire so closely into what assuredly did not concern her. "Why, how should I?"

Miss Tibbs smiled understandingly. "You are astonished. Forgive my bluntness, Miss Worth. I am not rude, as a rule. However, I have taken a liking to you. It was my thought to offer any insights that I might have if you should care to inquire."

"That is kind of you, Miss Tibbs. I shall certainly call upon you if I should ever have a question," said Verity in gentle rebuff.

Miss Tibbs nodded and turned aside to speak to one of the girls who had come running up to her. She dealt with the child's breathless question with a patience and affection easily recognized by Verity.

Verity saw that under the governess's blunt exterior hid a kind heart and that rarity of rarities, a genuine interest in others. Verity realized then that the governess had not spoken as she had out of a desire to enter into gossip or even out of simple curiosity. Miss Tibbs's offer had been sincere.

A frown formed between Verity's brows. The governess obviously had something of moment that she wished to say, but she would not do so unless invited. Verity made up her mind. Perhaps it would be well to have some insight into the kind of young woman with whom she would be dealing.

When the girl had run off again to join her sisters, Verity said, "Miss Tibbs, I would be grateful to know anything that you may be able to tell me about Miss Pettiforth's character and her likes and dislikes. I have not yet met her, you see, and I do wish to establish a friendly footing as soon as possible.

Mr. and Mrs. Pettiforth have stressed that my duty is to influence Miss Pettiforth to acquire social ease. I think that shall be a much simpler task were I to have some insight into her."

Miss Tibbs regarded her for a moment. "Of course, Miss Worth. I shall be glad to tell you what I can. I was Miss Pettiforth's governess until very recently. In fact, it was at my recommendation that Miss Pettiforth was emancipated from the schoolroom."

"Then surely you must consider Miss Pettiforth ready to enter polite society," said Verity.

Miss Tibbs smiled. "No, I do not. However, Cecily is grown into a very pretty young miss and she is of a character that will no longer submit to lessons and instruction. She has never possessed a bent for study, but in the last several months that inattention became markedly worse. Cecily gives thought to very little else but fashions and prospective entertainments and her impending come out. It was natural enough, I suppose. However, her continued presence in the schoolroom was proving most disruptive to the education of the younger girls."

"I see. I gather that Miss Pettiforth is very much like most young misses, then, as they begin to come of age," said Verity, smiling. After the slightest hesitation, Miss Tibbs agreed to it. Recognizing Miss Tibbs's reservation, Verity probed a little further. "Mrs. Pettiforth has told me that her daughter is rather high-strung."

"Perhaps that is a bit of an understatement," suggested Miss Tibbs.

Verity sent a swift glance at the governess's bland face. "Oh dear. I suppose that I am in for a rare ride, then. Headstrong and mad for fashions and grown-up society, rather like a scampering puppy that has not been quite housebroken. Well, I am nothing if not resolute. Miss Pettiforth shall be whipped into shape if I have anything to say on the matter. I shan't allow her to disgrace herself too far."

"I should perhaps tell you that Mrs. Pettiforth dotes on her eldest daughter," said Miss Tibbs.

Verity mulled over that piece of information for a moment. She thought that it fit into what she already knew of the lady's leanings. Mrs. Pettiforth's favoritism, coupled with the fact that the lady had not really wanted Verity to come into the household, all made for a very interesting situation. She would have to be on her guard, for obviously Miss Tibbs was warning her to tread lightly where Mrs. Pettiforth was concerned. Verity sighed in resignation. "And Mr. Pettiforth?"

"Mr. Pettiforth has a fondness for all of his daughters," said Miss Tibbs. "I think that you will find him to be a fair man, albeit somewhat retiring. The youngest girl takes most after her father. Rebecca dislikes intensely any sort of ruckus or confrontation."

"Better and better," Verity murmured to herself.

Nevertheless, Miss Tibbs heard her. The governess gave a dry little laugh. "Pray do not allow me to put you off, Miss Worth. Indeed, that was not my intention. I only wished you to have your eyes open from the first so that you may avoid the most obvious pitfalls," she said.

"I am grateful to you, Miss Tibbs. Certainly I can be more confident of how I am to go on, for you have given me some valuable insight," said Verity.

Miss Tibbs called to her charges. "It is near the quarter hour, girls. You shall have to hurry if you are to tidy yourselves for luncheon." The governess turned back to say, "I hope that what I have imparted serves you well, Miss Worth. I should dislike to lose you too soon."

Verity laughed. "Oh, I have no intention of crying uncle, Miss Tibbs. I am not easily intimidated, I do assure you. In any event, I expect to rub along so famously with Miss Pettiforth that we will quickly become great friends."

Miss Tibbs smiled, a twinkle in her sharp eyes. "I trust that it will chance just as you expect, Miss Worth."

The girls joined them then and by tacit consent the ladies did not speak any more about Verity's concerns. The small group turned about and retraced their steps out of the gallery and through the halls. Verity parted company with the governess and the three girls, promising to walk with them again in future.

Six

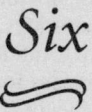

When Verity entered her room and began to tidy up in anticipation of the sounding of the luncheon bell, she had much to reflect on. She liked all whom she had met of the household with the possible exception of Mrs. Pettiforth.

Verity told herself that she should reserve judgment on the lady of the house. Perhaps Mrs. Pettiforth was feeling threatened by having someone thrust upon her. If Verity made an effort to be patient and conciliatory toward Mrs. Pettiforth, it could very well be ironed out to their mutual benefit.

Miss Tibbs had imparted little more about Miss Pettiforth than she had already guessed. Verity remained confident, despite the initial obstacle that Mrs. Pettiforth's indulgence of her daughter might prove, that she could handle a flighty, society-struck miss well enough.

Indeed, Verity felt so assured of herself that the suspicion crossed her mind that Mr. Pettiforth had extended charity to her in the thin guise of genteel employment. Surely Mrs. Pettiforth could do as well or better in the endeavor to train Miss Pettiforth in the social niceties. She was, after all, the girl's mother.

Verity concluded that she must speak to Mr. Pettiforth about his overgenerosity and persuade the gentleman that it was not necessary that he should manufacture a place for her out of the friendship he had had with her father. She could find a post with someone who truly needed her.

At sound of the bell Verity went downstairs.

When she entered the drawing room, she came unwittingly upon an appalling scene. The Pettiforths were present. The gentleman wore a pained expression, while his spouse expostulated, "Now, Cecily dear! Do calm yourself, I pray!"

Miss Tibbs stood beside the tallest of the girls, Sophronia, that Verity had met not half an hour past. Miss Tibbs's lips were tightly compressed and her hand rested upon the girl's stiff shoulder. Sophronia's face was white.

A furious beauty was facing the governess and the young girl, hurling a veritable stream of scolding at her sister's head. If she heard her mother's cajolings she paid no attention to it.

Finally, Mrs. Pettiforth exclaimed, "Sophronia! You will hand over your sister's shawl at once, if you please. I will not have Cecily's feelings so lacerated by your insensitivity. I should think that the treat of taking luncheon outside the schoolroom would have embued you with a greater sense of what is due to your elders."

Without a word, Sophronia took from her shoulders a Norwich silk shawl and held it out. The beauty snatched it away, exclaiming, "Spiteful, thieving hussy! If there is one snag, miss, you shall answer to me for it! Borrowed it, indeed! *I* know better! You meant to keep it!"

"I did not! I borrowed it because I could not find my own shawl. I did not think that you would mind so very much, since you told me yourself that you did not care for this one," Sophronia retorted hotly.

"Sophronia," murmured Miss Tibbs.

The girl cast up a glance at her governess's expression. Her cheeks had flushed. "I am sorry, Miss Tibbs! But I cannot stand silent an instant longer and let her rake me down so. She did say that she did not want it."

"Oh! So you wish to have my castdowns, do you? Well then, take it! The fringes are all knotted. I could not possibly wear it, now that you have ruined it!"

The beauty threw the shawl into her sister's face and twitched herself about, giving Verity a full view of the young woman's coutenance. Her cheeks were pink and her eyes flashed with high temper. Verity realized with a sinking heart that this catamount was her charge, Miss Cecily Pettiforth.

"Now, Cecily, dearest. Do, pray, consider your manner. A lady does not allow her emotions to overcome her, no matter how great the provocation," said Mrs. Pettiforth.

"Sophy had no right, Mama. You know that she didn't," exclaimed the beauty.

Observing Miss Pettiforth's enraged expression, Verity revised her opinion. All suspicion that Mr. Pettiforth had sent for her out of pity vanished. She thought rather ruefully that she would earn every last penny of the handsome salary that Mr. Pettiforth was to make to her.

"Enough, Cecily. Here is Miss Worth come to join us," said Mr. Pettiforth, rising. His countenance had cleared when he saw Verity, but instantly it had become shadowed by embarrassment.

Verity went forward, holding out her hand. She pretended that she had not witnessed the painful scene. With a smile, she said, "I am glad to see you again, sir."

"Thank you, Miss Worth," said Mr. Pettiforth quietly, obliquely acknowledging her tact.

Mrs. Pettiforth did not rise from her chair to make her greeting. "My dear Verity, how nice that you could join us. We gather quite informally, as you see. This is my daughter, Cecily, whom you have not previously met. Cecily, dearest, this is our cousin, Miss Verity Worth, who has come to lend her experience to you in social matters."

"How do you do, Miss Pettiforth. I hope that we shall become good friends," said Verity.

The beauty ignored her as though she had not spoken. Instead she addressed her mother. "I do not need a chaperone to tell me how to go on, Mama. I told you so before."

"Cecily, Miss Worth is waiting for your bows," said Mr. Pettiforth.

Miss Pettiforth appeared about to deliver herself of a few choice words, but catching her father's glance, she apparently thought better of it. She gave a pettish shrug. With elaborate civility and a cold smile, she said, "Miss Worth. I trust that your stay with us will be enjoyable."

Verity inclined her head, a cool expression in her eyes. "I hope so, too, Miss Pettiforth."

Mr. Pettiforth directed Verity's attention then to the others, whom Mrs. Pettiforth had so patently neglected to bring forward. "Miss Worth, this is our second eldest, Sophronia, and her governess, Miss Tibbs."

Verity gave a warm smile. "Yes, we met earlier and enjoyed a turn about the walking gallery. I look forward to joining you and the girls often for exercise on these dull days, Miss Tibbs."

"We would be delighted to include you, Miss Worth," said Miss Tibbs. Beside the governess, Sophronia gave a small smile and nodded. The girl's color appeared to have returned to normal. The shawl which had been the focus of so much distress was draped elegantly over her shoulders. Verity saw that the girl's thin fingers unconsciously stroked the smooth silk, causing her to conclude that such luxurious pieces did not often come Sophronia's way.

"You need not expect *me* to go walking in the gallery. Such boring stuff! I would not bear it," said Miss Pettiforth, tossing her head.

Verity turned her gaze on Miss Pettiforth, a glinting of anger in her eyes. Speaking quite civilly, with the hint of sympathy in her expression, she said, "In that case, I am persuaded that we shall do very well without you, Miss Pettiforth. Nothing is so tiresome as to be in the company of one who suffers from fidgets."

A quick flash of color rushed into Miss Pettiforth's face. "Fidgets? I do not *fidget!*"

Verity put up her slim brows. "Is that not what you meant? Forgive me, Miss Pettiforth. I quite misunderstood. Naturally a well-bred lady must not admit to such a failing. Why, nothing is more ruinous to one's social success than to earn a reputation for freakish starts or an uncertain temper."

The smile that she bestowed upon the beauty was guileless. Verity noticed out of the corner of her eye that Miss Tibbs was wearing the blandest of expressions, while her charge, Sophronia, started with a half-agape mouth. Verity turned at once from Miss Pettiforth to remark to Mr. Pettiforth that it was remarkably warm for November. The gentleman had hidden a smile behind his hand by giving a slight cough, but he replied suitably. The assumed gravity of his expression was belied by the twinkle in his eyes.

Mrs. Pettiforth stared at Verity with a rather hard gaze, as though turning something over in her mind. Undecided, she looked at her favorite daughter.

An astonished look had crossed Miss Pettiforth's face at Verity's setdown. She stood with uncertainty warring with the tempest in her eyes. Her small hands clenched and unclenched. The uncertainty won. She tossed her head and flounced over to the pianoforte to strike a discordant note.

Mrs. Pettiforth seemed willing to let Verity's declaration stand without challenge. She surged to her feet. "Mr. Pettiforth, pray let us repair to the dining room for luncheon."

"As you wish, my dear." Mr. Pettiforth escorted his spouse out of the drawing room, followed by his eldest daughter and Verity, Miss Tibbs and Sophronia.

Through the meal Verity listened to and watched the interaction of those seated with her at the table. It quickly became obvious that Miss Tibbs had spoken the literal truth about Miss Pettiforth. The girl could talk about nothing except her clothes, her come-out, the treats in store for her, and her future prospects. Mrs. Pettiforth entered into all of these topics with the greatest of interest and encouragement, particularly into speculations about what admirers her daughter might attach during the Season.

Mr. Pettiforth seemed to withdraw himself entirely from the intense discussion, never saying a word for or against any of the delightful notions put forward.

Miss Tibbs succeeded in capturing Mrs. Pettiforth's attention for a short time to discuss in a general way the progress and needs of the other girls. Miss Pettiforth, growing impatient of any topic that did not relate directly to herself, interrupted her mother and Miss Tibbs. She declared herself bored with all the talk of the schoolroom and her sisters' progress. "Will you not attend to me, Mama? I need a length of satin ribbon to trim that darling bonnet that I bought last week and which did not look half as well when I got it home. I am persuaded all that it requires is a knot or two of ribbon to look ever so much better."

"Very well, my love. We shall go into the village this afternoon and look for your ribbon," said Mrs. Pettiforth indulgently. She turned an inquiring expression on the others. "Have you any commissions for us, Verity? Miss Tibbs?"

"Oh no, Mama! You cannot mean to spend hours traipsing all over looking for someone else when I particularly want you," objected Miss Pettiforth.

Verity was seated next to Sophronia and so heard what the girl muttered under her breath. "Mean cat!" Verity glanced quickly sideways, but Sophronia held her head lowered so that her expression was hidden.

"I have no immediate needs, Mrs. Pettiforth," said Miss Tibbs colorlessly.

"Nor I," said Verity, having on the instant made up her mind to discover what Sophronia would most like to be brought to her from the village. "However, I would be glad to offer my help in hunting down just exactly the shade of ribbon that Miss Pettiforth desires."

Mr. Pettiforth had looked up, a sharpening in his gaze as he regarded Verity. Miss Tibbs had also glanced across the table with a suddenly thoughtful expression.

"Why, that is most kind of you, Verity," said Mrs. Pettiforth, pleased. "Is it not, Cecily?"

Miss Pettiforth did not appear to be gratified. Instead, she cast a glance of loathing at Verity. "Yes, Mama, to be sure it is. But Miss Worth need not accompany us if she does not really wish to do so. Besides, she would have to sit with her back to the horses and I am persuaded that she would dislike it."

Verity was amused by Miss Pettiforth's blatant attempt to fob her off. *It won't be so simple as that, my girl*, she thought. *I have agreed to take you on and so I shall*. She therefore said, "I shan't mind it in the least. The horses, I mean. And I am curious to discover what the shops in the village have to offer."

"You will be pleasantly surprised, no doubt. We cannot boast London quality, of course, but we do very well for ourselves nevertheless," said Mrs. Pettiforth.

Miss Pettiforth was effectively left with nothing more to say against including Verity in the outing. She did manage to express her displeasure, however, by saying sweetly, "I do hope that you do not mean to drag us all about, Miss Worth. Waiting upon another's self-interest is what I particularly dislike."

"Oh yes, I have very few doubts on that head," said Verity dryly. "Pray do not give it another thought, Miss Pettiforth." She steadily returned the beauty's glare and was satisfied when the younger woman turned away first.

As luncheon concluded, Verity rose with the others from the table. Mrs. Pettiforth and Miss Pettiforth were once more deep in discussion over various fashion matters and, as Verity made to follow them out of the dining room, Mr. Pettiforth stopped her with a word. Waiting until Miss Tibbs and Sophronia had exited, Mr. Pettiforth said, "You have rattled in in fine style, Miss Worth. I congratulate you."

"Thank you, sir. My only hope is that I can withstand the heat," said Verity with a rueful expression.

"Oh, I have every confidence in you, Miss Worth," said Mr. Pettiforth, smiling. He waited for her to proceed him through the door and took his leave.

Verity hurried up the stairs and caught up with Miss Tibbs and Sophronia on the landing. "Miss Tibbs! I wished to inquire whether there were any errands that I might discharge on your behalf while I am in the village," she said.

Miss Tibbs smiled. Her eyes held a decided twinkle. "Thank you, Miss Worth. That is most kind of you. As a matter of fact, there are a few articles for the schoolroom that I would like to acquire. I shall write out a list and have it, and the funds for you, if you would come to the schoolroom in a few minutes."

Verity agreed to this and then inquired of Sophronia what she would like from the village. The girl flushed up to her hair and stammered that she really required nothing. Verity smiled. "Never mind, I suspect that I might discover something that you and your sisters might like."

"Thank you, Miss Worth!" exclaimed Sophronia. She went quickly away, quite overcome.

"You have done a kind thing in that direction," observed Miss Tibbs.

"I dislike bullying of any sort," said Verity quietly. She met the governess's eyes and she knew that they were both thinking of the appalling scene that had taken place in the drawing room. "I must hurry off now or I shall be accused of keeping Miss Pettiforth waiting."

Miss Tibbs was surprised by her own deep chuckle. "Yes, I rather think you might."

Verity returned to her bedroom to freshen up and to put on a bonnet and a walking pelisse. When she was ready, she retrieved Miss Tibbs's list, and returned downstairs, to find that the Pettiforth ladies had just that moment stepped into the hall. The carriage was at the front door and the ladies climbed up into it, Verity seating herself with her back to the horses. The carriage rattled away, carrying the trio on the shopping expedition.

Verity quickly found that shopping in the company of Mrs. Pettiforth and her eldest daughter involved pandering to the girl's every wish. The opinions that Miss Pettiforth expressed on matters of fashion were immature and tended toward the showy. The only caveats that Mrs. Pettiforth held fast to were the proper degree of bosom that should be allowed in a gown, and that she would not countenance a damped-down or sheer muslin.

"It's of no use to wheedle me, Cecily dear. Besides the cold, I know very well what a figure you would cut, and let me tell you that in that sort of gown, it is a very different sort of lady you would appear to any peer," said Mrs. Pettiforth with unexpected firmness. "Is that not so, Verity?"

"Entirely so, ma'am. No lady of high position would be seen dressed in such a fashion," said Verity, purging her soul without compunction.

"Oh." Miss Pettiforth considered the matter for a moment. Her brow cleared. "Very well, Mama. I shall forego having the muslins made up. I do not wish to give any titled gentleman cause to think badly of me."

The afternoon was soon spent. Verity had been able to make her few purchases and held them on her lap. A welter of boxes and tied packages containing all of those things that Miss Pettiforth had seen and determined she could not do without took up every inch of space on the seats and floor, making the ride back to the manor uncomfortable for the occupants of the carriage. Somewhere lost in the profusion, and quite forgotten, was the humble parcel of satin ribbon that had been the catalyst for the orgy of buying.

Seven

"I had not thought ever to be summoned to you for such a cause as this, ma'am!" Lord Henry Alan George Sandidge, Viscount Rathbone, leaned his wide shoulder against the mantel and regarded the other occupant of the room with a sardonic expression.

"It is extraordinary, is it not?" agreed his hostess.

"Quite," said Lord Rathbone dryly. "Perhaps you will be good enough to enlighten me as to your reasoning upon this signal occasion."

Before replying, her ladyship took a few moments to regard the viscount with objective eyes. She concluded that she was well-satisfied.

There were few gentlemen that met the dictates of the day so worthily as Lord Rathbone. He was an extremely well-knit gentleman, athletic in build and inclination, the possessor of a handsome face and fortune. His tall figure was a familiar sight in London's fashionable drawing rooms and he was equally well-known amongst the sporting set known as the Corinthians.

Lord Rathbone was cultivated for his birth, his breeding, his wealth, and his reputation as a blood of the first order. He had entered into his inheritance at an early age, and from that day to the present he had embarked upon a career of gentlemanly pursuits that had become a scandal and an affront to some of his more staid relations. His progress had been attended by himself with enthusiasm, an enthusiasm which had over the intervening years turned to weary cynicism.

Now his mother, Lady Rathbone, smiled rather grimly at the viscount. She well knew the depths of her son's disillusionment and boredom. She counted upon that more than any sense of conscience to work to her advantage in forcing him into what to him could only be a repugnant course.

"You do not care to have your actions called into question," she stated.

Lord Rathbone gave a short bark of laughter. A swift grin lit his face for a bare second, then it was gone. "Frankly, my dear mother, these stories you have repeated to me this afternoon mean nothing to me. I am astonished that you give such credence to talebearers." His voice was heavily contemptuous.

"Your uncles do not have a fondness for you," said Lady Rathbone.

Lord Rathbone shifted, settling both shoulders against the high mantel. "That is a superlative understatement, ma'am, as well you know," he said softly.

Lady Rathbone nodded. Yes, she knew very well that her brothers-in-law regarded her son with loathing and considerable hatred. After all, if it had not been for his totally unexpected birth, the title and estates would have reverted to them.

She had wed a gentleman considerably older than herself. Several years of her marriage had passed without being attended by the birth of children. It would have been wonderful indeed if the eldest of her brothers-in-law had not begun to covet a title and a property that brought easily an income of a thousand pounds a year. A second property had been entailed to pass to the younger brother in the event that there was no heir from the marriage. Both brothers had thus stood to gain from Lord Rathbone's death without issue. Their ambitions had crumbled to dust with the advent of the infant heir.

Lady Rathbone drummed her fingers lightly on her chair arm, recalling the past. Her lord had been ecstatic at the birth of his son. He had disliked both of his brothers, trusting more in their obvious avarice than in their expressions of goodwill, but his advancing years had seemed to make surer and surer the likelihood of one of them inheriting his position and the other becoming overseer of his minor estate.

With the birth of his son, Lord Rathbone had taken a new lease on life. He had hoarded his energies, conserved his health, and restricted his former excesses. He had spent what was considered by outsiders to be an inordinate amount of time with the growing boy. The resulting relationship had been uncommonly close and fierce in mutual loyalty.

His lordship had lasted until his heir's fifteenth birthday. Upon Lord Rathbone's demise, his brothers had descended, swift as grinning vultures. Even though there was an heir, control of the estates would naturally fall upon the shoulders of those named as the youth's guardians until the young viscount had attained his majority. By that time, of course, there was every possibility that there would be little of substance left to inherit.

The Sandidge brothers had rubbed their hands; their eyes had gleamed. They had said everything that was proper under the somber circumstances. Lady Rathbone had received their empty condolences with a regal nod and the slightest of smiles. Her lack of emotion had been dismissed by them as stupidity.

When the will was read, Lady Rathbone stood legally acknowledged as sole legal guardian. She had swept out of the library without acknowledging even with a glance the outcries that poured from her outraged brothers-in-law. She had gone directly to her rooms and indulged in a prolonged bout of tears, for she had held back her grief until the thing should be done and over. Then she had freshened her toilette and gone downstairs to order her brothers-in-law put out of the house.

The deposition of the will had created a scandal of no mean order. The Sandidge brothers had contested it, protesting that it must have been made under duress, for no gentleman in his right mind would leave such weighty responsibility to a mere female. It was argued that his lordship's considerable years had made him vulnerable to subtle compulsion.

This claim was openly ridiculed throughout the county by gentry and rougher folk alike. Local opinion held that no gentleman in memory had ever retained both his mental faculties and his physical capabilities to such good effect and that, even hours before death, Lord Rathbone had still been considered a force to be reckoned with.

The will was proven indisputably legitimate. The document was not drafted in the waning years of his lordship's life, as had been assumed. Quite the opposite, in fact. The Sandidge brothers were infuriated to learn that the will had been drafted the very eve of the heir's birth and had not been changed by one jot for fifteen years.

Lady Rathbone's eyes drifted thoughtfully to her son's face. As always she felt great satisfaction that he did not bear the least resemblance to herself.

When the announcement was made that shortly an heir would be born to Lady Rathbone, there had been whispers bruited about of an unknown lover and that the heir was the product of an illicit union. Those rumors persisted for years, fueled by the malicious tongues of her brothers-in-law. But the slurs had gradually died as the boy had grown and matured, for there was no doubt of his lordship's stamp upon him. By the time the heir had attained his fifteenth year, the resemblance between himself and his father was uncanny. Lord Rathbone might have become a little stooped and his once coal-black hair turned snow white, but the fierce, startlingly blue eyes and the strong, wide bones of the face had not blurred.

Over the years Lady Rathbone had suffered the slurs and the slander and the malice of her husband's family with quiet dignity. If her naturally autocratic bent had become more pronounced, and she did not suffer fools easily, it was scarcely to be wondered at. She had done her duty toward her son as handily as any gentleman might have; better, perhaps, for she guarded her son and his inheritance with a ruthlessness that would not be gainsaid.

Her brothers-in-law and their families were treated with cold civility. They were never allowed to establish a foothold at Ganescourt, either by being made to feel welcome in a social way or by default in presuming to have any say in how the estate was run.

Lady Rathbone could look back with pride on all that she had accomplished. She had preserved her lord's estate from the machinations of his greedy brothers. She had raised a strong and handsome son. However, her task was not yet entirely done.

Perhaps the most profound challenge of all in the long battle to resist and to utterly vanquish her husband's family had now to be faced. Lady Rathbone knew her own strengths and weaknesses. If it was only herself who was to be involved, she had every confidence that a successful conclusion could be had. However, she was not the key actor this time. However reluctant she was to recognize it, time had inexorably and inevitably limited her power to that of a role behind the scenes.

When the new viscount had attained his eighteenth year, Lady Rathbone abruptly announced that she was relinquishing her guardianship over her son. When criticized by friends and foes alike, she had simply said that the viscount was too much his father's son to be hedged about by unnecessary restrictions. Society's astonishment was nothing compared to the boiling outrage of her brothers-in-law. Again, she had merely smiled at them. They had subsided, suspicious of her ladyship's serenity. They recalled all too vividly what had taken place once before when they had underestimated her position.

However, as the young Viscount Rathbone had embarked upon his riotous course, his uncles had taken heart. Surely such a wild young man must come to mortal grief. Surely he would break his neck riding neck-or-nothing over the roughest hunting fields, or come off the worst for a duel, or wreck one of those expensive racing curricles.

In addition, there was a war going on. With a judicious word of encouragement, a young man of such a wild bent might develop a fancy for purchasing a pair of colors, even subsequently to fall on the bloody field of battle.

It would be tragic, of course, for a gentleman of such tender years to expire in any of these violent ways; but the odds were surely against the viscount surviving the course he had set upon.

Lord Rathbone's uncles nourished their twisted malignant hopes. But the years passed and the young Lord Rathbone continued to escape unscathed the violent death that had once seemed so certain. Particularly galling to the gentlemen, Lord Rathbone had proven so contrary that he had not expressed the least desire to enter the army in order to fight for the glory of England.

Instead, Lord Rathbone had exhibited a new leaning that brought alarm to his frustrated relations. He was said to be a rake. Though his name had never been linked to that of a respectable female, it was obvious that he had considerable address with the ladies of his own order, as well, and could one day decide to wed.

The viscount was openly discussed as a very eligible *parti*. His wild reputation was overlooked in view of his birth and fortune. Several ambitious matrons had thrown their daughters at his head, but thus far he had not nibbled at any of the delectable bait offered him.

The fact that the viscount was pursued, coupled with his known predilection for a pretty female, aroused the liveliest dismay in the breasts of Lord Rathbone's paternal relations. Thus was explained the most recent stories that had been conveyed to Lady Rathbone.

"Your uncles fear daily to hear of the birth of a by-blow," said Lady Rathbone calmly.

Lord Rathbone's mouth curled, and his eyes gleamed with a curious light. "Indeed? That would put their noses out of joint, would it not? I see that I have been singularly shortsighted. It is a circumstance that I must rectify as soon as possible."

"Shall you?"

He made an impatient, abrupt gesture. "You must know that I spoke in jest only. I do not litter the streets with my get."

"I thought not, and so I assured my brothers-in-law."

The viscount uttered an oath.

Lady Rathbone smiled. The firelight cast shadows over her face so that the expression in her eyes could not be determined. "I gathered that they fear even more to read of your engagement to a respectable young miss."

Lord Rathbone glanced sharply at his mother. "What are you saying, Mother?"

Lady Rathbone leaned back in her chair, her laughter stilled. "My dear son, you need not look at me with such suspicion. You know full well that I do not plot against your interests."

"Yes, and for that reason you are the more formidable opponent," he retorted unfilially.

Lady Rathbone smoothed her skirt. "I am glad that you recognize it, my dear. It has been my overriding preoccupation since your birth to destroy your uncles' grasping pretensions, as well you should know." She paused and raised her eyes to meet his level gaze. "As it stands, Ganescourt and everything else could still pass to the Honorable Forde or Bastion Sandidge and their progeny. Your life is all that has ever stood in the way of their ambitions. For that alone, they hate you, but even more so because you are your father's image, in face and in temperament. I knew that was so. I allowed you to prove it to them."

Lord Rathbone's lips thinned. His gaze was dark as he considered the indomitable woman who sat before him. Slowly, he said, "I had not before understood why you relinquished the guardianship five years before my majority. It was a hell-born motive, ma'am!"

She shrugged. "I knew that you would run your course. I knew that the pattern would be such as to impress unmistakably and ever deeper upon your uncles how very much like your father you are."

"You are a Machiavelli, ma'am," Lord Rathbone said softly, eyeing her with mingled anger and old, formless emotions that had become so rooted that they could no longer be completely distinguished. "I have gone to the very devil and back these past years. It meant little or nothing to you, did it?"

"On the contrary. I feared often for your life. Not by word or look would I check you, however. You had to be left to run your chosen course."

"And now that my course has been run? What now, dear ma'am?" asked Lord Rathbone, an unpleasant smile upon his face.

"It is time to deal the final blow to your uncles. You must get an heir," said Lady Rathbone calmly.

Lord Rathbone gave a short harsh laugh. "Thank you, my lady! So I am to get myself legshackled for the sole purpose of cutting up my uncles' pecuniary hopes. I dislike the two gentlemen just as much as you do, ma'am, and more, for I know how they rejoiced when my father died. I shall never forgive them that. But to enter into wedlock with one of these simpering milk misses—to be tied for life to a trivial mind and running tongue! No, I think not!"

"Then get yourself a bastard," said Lady Rathbone.

Eight

There was an astonished silence. Lord Rathbone stared down at his parent, staggered. At length his expression altered, reluctant amusement entering his eyes. "You are an amazement to me, dear lady. Never did I expect to hear such a suggestion come out of *your* mouth."

Lady Rathbone sat at her ease, a peculiar smile lighting her face. "Did you not?"

"No, I did not!" Lord Rathbone's lips suddenly twisted. "I recall too well the slurs that were cast upon myself and upon your virtue. I was very small when first the lies came to my ears, and though at the time I did not completely understand what was being said, I swiftly learned. And you would have me bring forth a child who would be a bastard in truth! Your capacity for revenge runs to cruel depths that I never suspected."

"Perhaps it does. But obviously, yours does not," said Lady Rathbone unemotionally.

"No, it does not!" said Lord Rathbone explosively, coming away from the mantel.

Lord Rathbone took a hasty turn about the room. Her ladyship watched him, her face devoid of expression. Upon returning, the viscount cast a smouldering look at his mother. "My

God, what opinion you must hold of my sense of honor and decency! I could never do what you suggest. Understand me in this, Mother. I have never, nor will I ever, beget a bastard!"

"You will not wed for an heir. You will not father a bastard for an heir. You will let all that your father held for you fall into the hands of his bitterest enemies," said Lady Rathbone.

Lord Rathbone swung fully around, his fists clenched at his sides. His eyes blazed in a savage face. "You dare to accuse me of betrayal!"

Lady Rathbone did not shrink from his fury. Her voice was cold. "Well? Have I not summed up the matter most succinctly?"

He stood stock-still for a moment, his very stance a threat. Then he crossed swiftly to the window and stared down for several minutes at the busy London street. Over his shoulder, he threw, "Damn you! You have always cut too close to the bone!"

"I have had to," said Lady Rathbone, an unusual edge to her voice. "The jackals still circle and snap, waiting for their opportunity." Suddenly her voice faltered. "George, I grow so tired."

Startled, Lord Rathbone turned. He was appalled to see that his mother had shaded her eyes with her hand and that she seemed to have diminished in the chair. In two quick strides, he had dropped beside her chair. "Mother!" He grasped her thin wrist between his fingers.

Lady Rathbone straightened, though with what appeared to be some effort. Withdrawing from his hold, she pressed his hand. "I apologize, my dearest. I am ashamed of my weakness. It shall not happen again, I promise you."

Lord Rathbone clasped her hand between his. For the first time, he felt the frailty of her fingers and saw the fine webbing that mapped the skin of her face. He was shaken to realize how old she had become without his ever noticing. She had always seemed just the same, year after year, regal and indomitable.

The realization that she was no longer the same lady that had been such a strong force in his life brought with it a second realization, and a sense of inevitability. Quietly, he voiced it. "It is not you who should apologize, dear ma'am, but I. You have carried what should have been my burden for too long.

You are right, as always. It is definitely time that I wed and set up my nursery."

"You must not think that I wish to force you to it, George." Lady Rathbone's fingers closed tightly round his, surprising him by their fierce strength.

"I know better," he said slowly, wishing it were otherwise. He lifted his eyes to meet the shuttered expression in hers. Oh yes, he knew very well. He realized that it had been her sole purpose from the beginning of his visit. His mouth twisted. He was a fool to feel even the vague disappointment that was still his portion whenever he was brought face-to-face with his mother's obsession.

But Lady Rathbone was apparently satisfied with his answer, for she did not pursue it. Her fingers slipped from his clasp. "Get up, do, George. It seems so strange to see you thus."

Lord Rathbone got to his feet. He looked down at his mother, his eyes glinting. There was a cold, raw anger in him now. "For me, also, I assure you. I warn you, ma'am. My pride is monstrous. I will not be easily satisfied in my prospective bride."

Lady Rathbone nodded. "You have already voiced your opinion of those on the market and, for the most part, I agree with your sweeping assessment. You will do better to look to the schoolroom and find a miss who has not had time to be exposed to society and its corrosive influence. With care, you will be able to mold such a miss to your requirements."

Lord Rathbone once more leaned against the mantel. He regarded his mother with a mocking half-grin. "As my father did with you?"

"Just so." Lady Rathbone suddenly laughed. "It did not turn out so badly, I believe."

"No, perhaps it did not," said Lord Rathbone. He turned his eyes to the fire, a deep frown contracting his heavy black brows. The firelight reflected over the planes of his face, making his countenance appear harsh. Lady Rathbone did not interrupt the quiet. She was content to leave the viscount to his thoughts.

Then Lord Rathbone shrugged. "Very well. I shall look to the schoolroom. But how to go about it I have not the least notion. I do not number amongst my many acquaintances even one schoolroom chit."

"Whereas I am aware of the existence of several eligible young ladies of that sort. I, too, have a number of acquaintances, and many of them *will* bore on about their numerous progeny," said Lady Rathbone.

Lord Rathbone smiled. It was a peculiar smile, at once charming but underlaid with cynicism. With exaggerated politeness, he said, "I would be grateful for any suggestions that you might lay before me for consideration, ma'am."

As he had known she would, his mother seized the opening offered her. "You have a cousin," began Lady Rathbone.

He straightened like a shot. The expression in his eyes was not pleasant. "*Not* one of my uncles' daughters, ma'am! I will not stomach it, even to bring truce to the family."

"Of course not. Do you think me so unfeeling of you?" asked Lady Rathbone impatiently.

Lord Rathbone studied her face, than made an ironic bow. "Forgive me, ma'am. I was not thinking. If not one of my Sandidge cousins, then whom do you have in mind?"

"My sister's eldest girl. I forget her name now, but it will come to me. Alice married a Pettiforth, the younger son."

"Yes, I remember now," said Lord Rathbone frowning. "I have a vague memory of visiting the Pettiforths when I was a boy. There was an infant."

Lady Rathbone nodded. "Alice writes to me often. We were never affectionate sisters, so undoubtedly she does so because she cherishes hopes that I might one day sponsor her daughter. This girl figures largely in her affection. She is forever prosing on about the chit. Ah, yes, now I remember. That is the name! Cecily. In any event, Alice Pettiforth claims that her darling is a positive beauty and that she has very high hopes for the girl upon presentation to society. The girl is seventeen, old enough to emerge from the schoolroom, but possibly still young enough to be molded."

There was a short silence. Lady Rathbone studied her son's expressionless face. "What think you?"

Lord Rathbone shrugged again. "The matter is nearly one of complete indifference. I have no liking for the prospect of tying myself to a schoolroom chit. But in deference to you, I shall look over this cousin of mine. If she is as attractive and malleable as you have painted, then perhaps she will suit me well enough."

"I will arrange a meeting, then," said Lady Rathbone.

Her ladyship's autocratic manner set up the viscount's back. As little as any man, and perhaps less than most, did he take kindly to being driven. "Take care that you do not push my head through the noose, dear ma'am," said Lord Rathbone softly. "It will still be I who shall make the choice—or not—as I please."

"I am not so crude in my methods. This is a matter to be handled with subtlety. I do not expect you to post down and give the girl a cursory inspection with all the county watching the spectacle with gaping mouths," said Lady Rathbone. "No, I shall request Alice to hold a house party. She will naturally have invited me. I will send my regrets, which you will convey on my behalf. There will be some speculation, but nothing to which anyone can actually point. It is hunting country. Take out your guns in the morning and of an evening do the pretty by the ladies. Cecily will be one of those present in the drawing room. What you do with the opportunity is completely up to your discretion, of course."

"Of course," agreed Lord Rathbone, his swift grin flashing.

Lady Rathbone held up her hand to her son. He took it in his. Her ladyship cocked her head, her shrewd eyes bright. "We have always understood one another fairly well, have we not?"

Lord Rathbone pressed her ladyship's fingers. For her sake, he uttered the meaningless lie. "Yes."

Lady Rathbone retrieved her hand, her show of affection done. "I shall write to Alice Pettiforth this same day. We shall undoubtedly have an answer by return post." Her expression flickered in a glinting half-smile that bore a startling resemblance to that of her son's most sardonic expression. "My sister Pettiforth and I are alike in one way, at least. Ambition is a cruel taskmaster, my son."

"Is it ambition or revenge that is *your* taskmaster, dear ma'am?" asked Lord Rathbone softly.

Lady Rathbone's face smoothed to the habitual mask that so completely concealed her thoughts. She looked up at the viscount with cool amusement in her eyes. "You see, you do know me very well indeed."

"Perhaps better than I wish," retorted Lord Rathbone.

"You are a disrespectful dog, but you do know where your duty lies. That is all that I shall ever require of you," said Lady Rathbone.

"I have gravely misunderstood you, then. I thought all you wanted of me was a male heir," said Lord Rathbone, a glint in his eyes.

"You are worth something more to me than a mere stud, my dear," murmured Lady Rathbone. "You have been both my instrument of revenge and my justification in the eyes of the world."

"I am more moved than you can possibly know," said Lord Rathbone ironically.

"What nonsense you speak, George."

Lady Rathbone smiled at her son. She did not quite understand the strange undercurrents that she sensed in him today, and that was dangerous where he was concerned. Besides a strong will, her son possessed a streak of contrariness that was totally unpredictable. That trait could possibly work to her disadvantage if she inadvertently roused it to full life.

Lady Rathbone made the sudden decision that she had seen enough of her son for that day. She leaned back in her chair. "Now I am weary. Send my maid in to me. I must nap before I write to my sister Pettiforth."

"As you wish, my lady," said Lord Rathbone. The faintest of mocking smiles accompanied his formal bow, for he knew that he had been summarily dismissed. Lady Rathbone had achieved her end of the moment. She therefore had no further use for his company. He took his leave, pausing outside the sitting room to convey his mother's order to her butler.

Lord Rathbone left his mother's town house with the decided opinion that he would do well not to return to enjoy her hospitality until he had wed and gotten his bride with child. If he did not tie the knot of his own will, whether with this Pettiforth cousin or another, Lady Rathbone was not one to sit idly by. He knew enough of her ladyship's machinations to realize that she would work to force his hand.

The wild possibilities that crossed his mind made him utter a short bark of laughter, but he was actually little amused. He disliked very much to be manipulated. He disliked it most when it was at his mother's hands.

He climbed up into his phaeton and swung it into the traffic. He did not notice that his groom scarcely had time to scramble up behind the vehicle. He was too deep in his own unpleasant reflections.

No, it would not surprise him in the least if his mother tried to force him into wedlock, by fair means or foul. He had seen today that she felt her age at last. Knowing herself to be mortal and having perceived the end of her life, Lady Rathbone would not rest until she had made certain that everything that she had preserved would be safe forever from the clutching fingers of the lesser Sandidges.

Lord Rathbone was no less determined that his life would not be savaged in the process. Little cause as he had himself to wish that all that was his by birth would fall by default to his uncles and their get, he would damn his soul to hell before he willingly immolated himself on an altar of Lady Rathbone's fashioning.

He would indeed wed. In truth, it was past time to think of the future. But his bride would be of his own choosing.

As Lord Rathbone maneuvered through the heavy traffic, he mentally made a swift catalog of the young eligible ladies of his acquaintance and of one or two others who might possibly fit his requirements. If this cousin of his, Miss Cecily Pettiforth, proved unsuitable to his taste, he should have other possibilities already settled upon.

It was unfortunate that he had no feelings whatsoever about any of candidates whom he could bring to mind. The milk misses were all of them insufferably boring. There was a widow of his acquaintance who had more countenance and vivacity, but he swiftly discounted that lady—the widow was a little too free with her favors. He had not found that objectionable in her before, but it would not do in one who was to be made his lady.

Little as he desired a wife, he would still require the woman who bore his name to be completely faithful to him. Not even a breath of scandal must touch her.

Lord Rathbone recognized that he had a task of monstrous proportions before him. It was not a prospect that could be expected to delight a gentleman who had agreed to the necessity of wedlock with the greatest of reluctance.

Nine

Over the following week, Verity settled into her role of companion. It was not done without considerable effort on her part. The situation in which she found herself was fraught with difficulties. Mr. Pettiforth had indicated his confidence in her abilities, but he offered no direct support of Verity's authority. Mrs. Pettiforth swung between regarding Verity with resentment, or as an ally who could be relied on to help tone down her daughter's worst starts. Mrs. Pettiforth's vacilliating attitude did not work to Verity's advantage; on the contrary, it promoted much of the hostility that Verity was faced with in her charge.

Miss Pettiforth proved to be a very hard nut to crack. She very much resented the fact of Miss Worth's presence. She needed no chaperone or companion to burden her with restrictions or to show her how to go on. Encouraged by her mother for years to think of herself as perfect, Miss Pettiforth treated all whom she came into contact with either disdain or simpering coquettishness.

Verity was appalled at the complacency with which Mrs. Pettiforth regarded her daughter's indifference toward acquaintances and servants alike; but it was Miss Pettiforth's desperate flirtations that made Verity truly shudder. She was privileged to witness Miss Pettiforth's machinations at a small dinner and dance, and again at a cotillion at a neighboring estate. Miss Pettiforth had several youthful admirers whom she played off one against another with a ruthlessness that set Verity's teeth on edge.

It was particularly galling to be forced to the realization that she could do nothing to circumvent the beauty. Verity had tried to relay a few well-meaning hints to Miss Pettiforth, but her efforts had fallen flat. Miss Pettiforth's lovely eyes had flashed and she had flounced off to wreak as much damage as she possibly could. *She* could do no wrong for she was the acknowledged beauty and reigning queen of the neighborhood. Miss Pettiforth was so certain that her credit was sterling in everyone's eyes that she served with contempt any suggestion that she might engender disgust or disapproval with her high-handedness.

The vision of Miss Pettiforth playing off her tricks at her come out in London was not to be thought of. The girl would totally ruin herself in the eyes of an unforgiving society, and though Verity did not like Miss Pettiforth, she did feel responsible for her.

It was not at all difficult to understand that pure self-interest motivated the girl. Verity wished often that there was a more noble character trait to which she could appeal, but look as she might, she was finally brought to acknowledge that there was not an ounce of fellow feeling existent in Miss Pettiforth.

Miss Cecily Pettiforth was everything that her parents and Miss Tibbs had claimed. The girl was a stunning beauty. She was also impulsive and high-strung. What all of them had neglected to mention was that Miss Pettiforth was willful, spoiled, and mean. That became perfectly obvious in how Miss Pettiforth chose to treat even her sisters.

The world was apparently created to revolve around Miss Pettiforth and her wishes. Nothing and no one else mattered.

Miss Worth had understood much of this in a flash that first shopping expedition. What had happened since then had only underscored her suspicions. The only recourse she had, if she were to at all justify Mr. Pettiforth's confidence in her, was to make herself seem more of an ally to Miss Pettiforth's interests rather than the watchdog she really was.

Quickly recognizing that Miss Pettiforth's highest ambition was to capture a wealthy peer, and that Mrs. Pettiforth entered into the same ambition, Verity did not waste additional time in serving homilies designed to bring Miss Pettiforth to an awareness of wrongdoing, but instead put everything in the context of how her behavior or her dress would affect her chances of winning the type of position that she craved.

Within a fortnight of her conclusions, Verity was able to congratulate herself, albeit with mixed feelings, that she was beginning to make progress in capturing the beauty's ear. The weeks past had been enlivened by Miss Pettiforth's tantrums and demands, and Verity's ingenuity had been taxed to the utmost.

However, in a much shorter time than Verity would have believed possible, she was grudgingly accepted by Miss Pettiforth as, if not an equal, at least someone who could be depended upon to promote that young damsel's interests.

Miss Pettiforth was even beginning to show some signs of decorum in society. Verity received several quiet compliments from various ladies of the neighborhood who quite rightly laid the change in Miss Pettiforth's manners at her door.

One neighbor, Lady Redding, went so far as to comment that her own daughter, Camilla, and Cecily had been friends when very young, but that Cecily had grown so unstable that she was glad that they were no longer bosom bows. "I shall not hide from you, Miss Worth, that I admire very much what you have been able to accomplish with that impossible child," said Lady Redding.

Verity had murmured gratitude for the compliment, but she wondered what Lady Redding and the rest would have thought had they been privy to her methods. Verity chose not to enlighten these good dames of the tactics that she had used to gain this much ground with Miss Pettiforth, for she felt the means she had been put to were reprehensible in the extreme.

However, it could not be denied that her stated observation that none of the beauty's beaus were peers had penetrated Miss Pettiforth's brain to good effect. From there and by slow degrees, Verity had worked around to pointing out that a lady desirous of high position had to display a certain knowledge of how to make herself pleasant to influential hostesses so that she would be assured of invitations and of sponsorship to Almack's; that she had to know how to draw the line between light flirtation and giving food for the gossips (the latter of which would almost certainly prejudice any well-heeled gentleman against making an advantageous offer, since no peer would tolerate a bride who made of herself a byword); and that she had to make herself agreeable even to those she considered inferiors because that was a quality that was regarded with favor by any peer who bore the responsibility for several dependents.

Verity had begun to breathe a little freer and feel more confident of her ability to exert a limited measure of control over Miss Pettiforth. Then Mrs. Pettiforth announced plans for a grand house party, to which she had invited several guests, including her nephew, Lord Alan George Sandidge, Viscount Rathbone.

A peer. A wealthy peer. An eligible *parti* of the first order.

Verity felt her heart drop into her toes, but the beauty was ecstatic.

Miss Pettiforth at once began boasting of what she would do with his lordship. "I shall have him worshipping at my feet," she declared confidently.

"No doubt, dearest. But I hope that you shall show forth only your very best side," said Mrs. Pettiforth.

"Of course I shall, Mama. I am not such a peagoose as to let slip his lordship," said Miss Pettiforth scornfully.

The viscount would be the first peer to wander into Miss Pettiforth's sphere. She was determined that Lord Rathbone would not wander out again without her mark upon him. She meant at the least to make him fall in love with her. If his lordship should make her an offer, why, there would be nothing to cavil in that. It would be a feather in her cap, indeed, if she could attach such a gentleman before her eighteenth year. She might even accept his lordship's offer if she found him to her taste.

Verity easily read the beauty's flitting expressions of satisfaction and calculation. What she knew of Miss Pettiforth's character gave her a very lively dread of the upcoming house party.

* * *

Lord Rathbone stepped down from his curricle and gave over the responsibility of his team and the vehicle to a groom who had hurried to the horses' heads. His lordship's valet also got down and set about giving orders about the luggage to the footman who had descended the steps upon the curricle's arrival.

Lord Rathbone paid no heed to the flurry of activity, but stood frowning as he pulled off his driving gloves. He looked up at the front of the attractive manor house and sighed. Of all things he detested, it was to make one of a house party in the country. But he meant to make the best of things. He had given his word. However, if this Pettiforth cousin of his proved to be less than what she had been painted, he would have no compunction in shaking the dust of the place from his feet.

He trod up the steps of the manor.

The butler greeted Lord Rathbone, taking his lordship's hat, gloves, and whip, and showed him into the formal drawing room. Lord Rathbone detested kicking his heels, as he termed it, and being left to his own devices did nothing to reconcile him to this visit. His frown grew more pronounced. However, he was not given many minutes to indulge his ill-tempered reflections before his hostess, the lady who also happened to be his aunt, entered.

Mrs. Pettiforth surged toward Lord Rathbone, her hands outstretched. "My lord! Or I suppose that I must address you as nephew, mustn't I? I doubt that you recall when last we met, for you were quite small. I am Alice Pettiforth. How do you do?"

"I do very well, and as a matter of fact, I do recall the occasion of my last visit, ma'am," said Lord Rathbone, his dark expression giving way to a determinedly pleasant smile. "There was a christening, was there not?"

"To be sure, I had forgotten! That would have been my dearest Cecily, of course. How the years do fly! And now she is so very lovely that it brings silly sentimental tears to my eyes. But come, I am certain that you would like to take tea. Horwich will see to it."

"Thank you, Mrs. Pettiforth," said Lord Rathbone.

She shook her finger coquettishly at him. "Now none of that, I pray you! I am your aunt, though we do not know one another at all well. However, I imagine that must change before the end of your visit."

Other guests were announced and Mrs. Pettiforth excused herself in order to greet the small group. The drawing room began to fill. Lord Rathbone looked about him curiously, nodding and speaking to certain acquaintances whom he had met at one time or another in London. None of the guests were particular friends of his, but that was certainly to be expected. The Pettiforths did not run in the same exalted circles as himself.

However, there happened to be one face that he knew quite well, and he was astonished to see this particular lady in the predominantly provincial company. He knew of her reputation for being a dashing hostess and had himself often enjoyed making one of the company at her table.

The lady saw him at the same time. "Lord Rathbone! This is quite a surprise, indeed." She gave her hand to him.

"Yes, it is," he agreed with a smile. He glanced about. "I do not see Arnold with you. Did he not come with you?"

Mrs. Arnold nodded, and laughed. "To be sure, he did. Herbert would not miss the pheasants for any amount, whilst I would prefer London at nearly any time of the year. But I do not repine. In winter, I allow Herbert to shoot to his heart's content wherever in the country that he wishes to go and he allows me to dissipate myself senseless during the Season. It is a very neat arrangement."

Lord Rathbone was amused. "Then you are very friendly with the Pettiforths?"

"Oh no, not at all. It is Herbert's connection, not mine. It seems that Mr. Pettiforth is an avid sportsman in his own right and somehow or other our host, Mr. Pettiforth, and my Herbert chanced to meet. An invitation was issued and here we are," said Mrs. Arnold.

"So this, then, is your first visit to the Pettiforths," said Lord Rathbone, his gaze roaming the assembled company, not with any degree of pleasure, but rather with resignation.

"Ah, but not the last, depending upon the quality and quantity of the pheasants," said Mrs. Arnold with another laugh. She looked up curiously at Lord Rathbone's sardonic face.

"You must tell me how you come here, my lord. I do not think that I have ever heard that you were particularly addicted to the sport of shooting."

"On the contrary, I like to take my guns out as well as the next man. However, this visit combines something of a family obligation with pleasure. My mother is sister to Mrs. Pettiforth and sent me in her place to tender her regrets at being unable to make one of the party. The ladies had not seen one another in a great number of years and it was thought Mrs. Pettiforth might feel herself to be unbearably slighted. My presence is to be a peace offering of sorts for my mother's refusal," said Lord Rathbone glibly.

Mrs. Arnold shook her head. "I do not envy you, my lord. It is never comfortable discharging such obligations, especially when one would rather be elsewhere."

"Just so," said Lord Rathbone, once more glancing over the company.

Mrs. Arnold cast a singularly penetrating glance up at his lordship. A small smile touched her face. She thought she understood Lord Rathbone's probable feelings upon finding himself in such a gathering as this and sympathized with his lordship. She, too, was something of an odd duck in this company. They were as out of place as rare birds that had been thrust among a gaggle of geese.

His lordship's attention was claimed at that moment by Mrs. Pettiforth. Her smile was tight and the glance she cast over Mrs. Arnold was frigid. "There you are, my lord! I see that you and Mrs. Arnold have been chatting. How marvelous it is that you have struck up an acquaintance so quickly."

Mrs. Pettiforth's tone instantly set up the viscount's bristles. How dared the woman presume to censor his conduct or whom he chose to engage in conversation. "Mrs. Arnold and her husband are old friends. We see much of one another in London," said Lord Rathbone repressively, exaggerating slightly for the sake of justice.

"Oh, I see. But, of course, you must run in much the same circles, do you not?" said Mrs. Pettiforth, her smile not losing one iota of its steely appearance.

Lord Rathbone was quick to note the appreciative glint in

Mrs. Arnold's eyes as that lady murmured a graceful excuse and moved off.

Mrs. Pettiforth put her hand through his lordship's and determinedly urged him across the floor. "How nice that you are acquainted with the Arnolds. You shall meet everyone presently, I daresay. But now I wish to make known to you Mr. Pettiforth and my eldest daughter. Cecily shall not remember you, of course, since she was still in the cradle. But you will not regard that, I know, for we are all family."

Lord Rathbone was spared the obligation of an answer when Mrs. Pettiforth hailed a portly gentleman. "Mr. Pettiforth! Here is Lord Rathbone. I am certain that you must remember his lordship, my nephew."

Mr. Pettiforth and Lord Rathbone exchanged civil greetings. Mrs. Pettiforth waited with patent impatience for the gentlemen to be done, and then she brought forward a young damsel. "And this, Lord Rathbone, is my dear daughter, Cecily. She has been so looking forward to meeting you at last, for I have told her all about her magnificent cousin."

Lord Rathbone listened to Mrs. Pettiforth's expansive words with a cynical smile, but despite his awareness of his aunt's fawning, he could scarcely take his eyes from the girl. His bored sophistication suffered a severe check.

The reports had not exaggerated. Miss Cecily Pettiforth was undeniably a beauty. Her figure had none of the immature lines usual for one of her youth. There was not a flaw to be found from her golden curls to the glimpse of a tiny slippered foot that peeped from beneath the hem of her gown. Her eyes were the color of sapphires, her skin the shade of alabaster and cream. Her pretty bow-mouth was a soft petal pink, just now curved in a delectable smile. When she spoke, even her voice lent itself to perfection, as she said in dulcet accents. "I am happy to make your acquaintance, my lord."

"As I am to make yours, Miss Pettiforth," said Lord Rathbone, bowing over the slender hand given to him. When he straightened, he thought he caught a look of satisfaction in the limpid sapphire eyes, but it vanished so quickly that he could not be certain of its existence.

Mr. Pettiforth spoke up. "And this lady is Miss Verity Worth, who is staying with us for a time."

Lord Rathbone with difficulty turned his head away from the beauty. He met the cool gaze of a tall young woman. There was something in Miss Worth's expression that instinctively sharpened his wayward attention.

He had the oddest notion that Miss Worth disapproved of him.

Ten

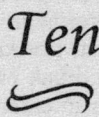

"My lord." Miss Worth's quietly modulated voice was well-bred. Her features were regular, her hair a magnificent auburn, and her well-endowed figure tastefully gowned. All this Lord Rathbone received in a fleeting impression, but it was the expression in her clear gray eyes that most struck him. She had met his regard with a candid measuring gaze that was positively disconcerting to one used to patent feminine admiration.

Lord Rathbone took her hand. Holding it, he looked at Miss Worth with narrowed eyes. "You appear somehow familiar to me, Miss Worth. Have we by chance met before?"

Mrs. Pettiforth was at once startled and jealous of the mild expression of interest that the viscount had made. She shot a fulminating glance in Miss Worth's direction. "Nonsense! How could you, indeed? Why, Miss Worth has lived quite secluded in the country," said Mrs. Pettiforth emphatically.

She was not attended to by either Lord Rathbone or Miss Worth, who continued to gaze at one another with wary curiosity.

"We have met, actually. It was in London at Almack's during my first Season, I believe," said Miss Worth, withdrawing her hand from the viscount's grasp.

"Almack's!" Lord Rathbone's swift grin flashed forth. "I

must have been in my cups, then, for I never willingly set foot in the place. It is the most tedious place imaginable."

"I daresay," said Miss Worth, very dryly.

He was pulled up short, not knowing whether she was agreeing that he had been drunk on that occasion or that Almack's was sadly lacking in entertainment. His dark brows pulled together as he studied the lady. How strange to think that she might have deliberately and yet so gently insulted him. It was an occurrence altogether outside his previous experience.

Her eyes brushed past his face, and widened slightly. Lord Rathbone almost turned to see what had so captured her attention, but forestalled himself. He was annoyed that he had almost betrayed interest. It was an old trick, certainly, and he waited to see how Miss Worth meant to build upon it. A slight smile touched his face as he awaited her explanation. But she surprised him.

Miss Worth said quickly, "Pray excuse me, my lord. I believe that I have seen an old friend." She slipped away with an ease that bespoke a wide social experience.

Lord Rathbone briefly followed Miss Worth's graceful figure with his eyes. He mentally shrugged, already banishing the lady from this thoughts as he returned his attention to the Pettiforths.

The daughter stood with a somewhat closed expression on her pretty face, a petulant pout to her lips that bespoke her displeasure at being ignored. Ah, here was something that he very well understood and he was not adverse to pandering to the little beauty. Lord Rathbone was on the point of asking some teasing question of Miss Pettiforth, but he was not to be granted the opportunity to pursue his flirtation with her so soon.

Mrs. Pettiforth was holding forth on what had just chanced, for she was one who could not let go of a thing that she did not understand. "How odd that you and Miss Worth are known to one another. I was quite astonished. Indeed, I did not think that Miss Worth was at all connected with anyone in society," she said, frowning.

"My dear lady, you must remember that Miss Worth has not always lived secluded in the country, as we have," said Mr.

Pettiforth quietly. "I believe that she has a number of friends in London and certainly she is at home in society."

Mrs. Pettiforth was not pleased to think that her own consequence was not of the same hue. "Yes, it is why we have her with us, is it not? You must know, my lord, that Miss Worth stands as a sort of companion to my dear Cecily, who is still rather shy in company."

"Oh yes, but I mean to be a credit to everyone," said Miss Pettiforth in a breathless voice. She cast a wide-eyed glance up at Lord Rathbone's face.

Her long lashes dropped to demurely hide her eyes, but not before Lord Rathbone had caught the calculation in her expression. *Oh ho, is that how it is?* he thought, and mentally shrugged his disappointment. He should have guessed that the chit would have been primed for his visit. No doubt his mother had hinted to her sister of the object of his visit and Mrs. Pettiforth in turn had encouraged Miss Pettiforth to make the most of her opportunity.

Mrs. Pettiforth patted her daughter's arm. "Of course you will be, my pet. Why, you already are, for I doubt that even a gentleman as worldly at Lord Rathbone has ever set his eyes on such a lovely face."

Lord Rathbone's cynicism was once more at full force. It was odiously obvious to him that Mrs. Pettiforth was determined that he should make an offer for her daughter. "I am flattered, ma'am. However, I can point to a dozen gentlemen far more worldly than myself."

In a deliberate move to depress the woman further, he addressed a casual question to Mr. Pettiforth concerning the sport to be had in the country, thus effectively turning the subject. Mrs. Pettiforth stood irresolute for a few minutes, as though hopeful of seeing his eyes stray once again to Miss Pettiforth. But as Lord Rathbone showed no inclination to fall in with her desires, she then took herself and her daughter off to more interesting ground.

After a few minutes, Lord Rathbone excused himself to Mr. Pettiforth and withdrew to speak to another acquaintance. As he listened to this gentleman, his bored gaze roamed the company.

His attention was caught and held by the sight of the hired

companion, Miss Worth, and Mrs. Arnold holding what appeared to be a busy conversation. The two seemed to be on very good terms. Idly, he wondered if what Mr. Pettiforth had said was true and that Miss Worth did indeed sport a London acquaintance. If so, her family must have fallen on harsh times to countenance a daughter taking the menial post of playing companion to a spoiled schoolroom chit.

He smiled faintly as he recalled how quick Mrs. Pettiforth had been to broadcast Miss Worth's position in the household. His aunt without doubt possessed a certain meanness of character. She had made such short shrift of Miss Worth, and had also detached him so swiftly from Mrs. Arnold, that it was patently obvious the lady was jealous of his passing time with any lady other than Miss Pettiforth.

Lord Rathbone decided that it would be vaguely amusing to tease Mrs. Pettiforth a little. The pretentious woman deserved to have a blow dealt to the confidence she had already expressed through her atrocious maneuverings. She would learn quickly that he did not mean to fall so tamely into line.

He glanced around to discover that Mrs. Pettiforth was engaged in the role of hostess at her spouse's side. Acting upon his ignoble impulse, Lord Rathbone strolled over to join Mrs. Arnold and Miss Worth.

Lord Rathbone was amused to catch Mrs. Pettiforth's startled eyes. Deliberately he smiled down at the ladies, saying, "I did not realize that you and Miss Worth were on terms of intimacy, ma'am."

Mrs. Arnold was too well-versed in social niceties to mistake the message in the viscount's manner. It amused her to foster it, for she well knew that her old friend was not one to put herself forward. She had long thought it a pity that Verity Worth had not seen fit to marry. The thought crossed her mind that her friend could do worse than to attract the notice of the viscount. "Miss Worth and I have a long history, my lord. We attended the same seminary and made our bows in the same season. Verity grants me the occasional visit whenever she chances to come to London."

"How is it, then, that I do not recall the pleasure of your acquaintance, Miss Worth?" he asked. "I daresay I should if you have often graced Mrs. Arnold's table. I beg your forgiveness for the oversight."

"When I go to London, I stay quietly with friends and enjoy a select circle. No doubt that is why we have not come into one another's way," said Miss Worth quietly.

"No doubt," he agreed, reflecting that most of her friends were probably not members of the *ton*. Perhaps the only influential connection that Miss Worth could claim was that moment seated beside her.

He stayed a few moments more exchanging pleasantries before taking leave of the two ladies. Aware that Mrs. Pettiforth's impotent regard was boring into his back, he half turned as though he had bethought himself of something. Then he retraced a few steps back in Mrs. Arnold's and Miss Worth's direction, enjoying the new look of dismay that passed over his hostess's face. It was certainly worth the price of exchanging a few additional banalities.

He was obliged to pause in his progress as two gentlemen deep in heated argument over the rival merits of their respective hunting countries passed in front of him. Nevertheless he had already drawn near enough to the ladies to overhear part of their conversation and realize that he was the topic under discussion.

"Oh, had you met Lord Rathbone in London? I would not have thought he would have come in your way that first Season," said Mrs. Arnold.

"I suppose that I must be considered fortunate," replied Miss Worth with a laugh that indicated quite well that her words reflected just the opposite of her thoughts. "I fear that it was not an auspicious meeting. His lordship was at Almack's in swift pursuit of a beauteous widow. He solicited my hand for a dance for the sole purpose of keeping the lady within his sights as she was led around the floor by another admirer. Lord Rathbone trod on the hem of my gown and tore it and, without a word of apology, escorted me back to my chaperone."

Mrs. Arnold laughed. With a curious look, she said, "But surely you did not hold that against him for long? After all, the viscount is accounted to be very attractive and he is extremely wealthy."

"Oh, but it was a true indication of his lordship's careless character, you see. Since then I have heard any number of tales concerning his rakish progress," said Miss Worth. "And though we never actually met again, I saw enough of his lordship in my visits to London to form what I feel to be a pretty fair estimate of his character. A handsome face and person and a deep purse cannot replace the inner man. Unfortunately, Lord Rathbone has proven his indifference to the feelings of others, being altogether arrogant and completely self-serving."

Lord Rathbone turned on his heel, in full retreat. He was seething, cut to the quick that a nonentity such as this hired companion could dish out her bad opinion of him so blithely to individuals who were acquainted with him. It did not better his temper to be followed by Mrs. Arnold's sparkling laughter at the ruthless assessment forwarded by Miss Worth.

He was intercepted by Miss Pettiforth, who had observed with very strong feelings the apparent interest that the viscount had taken in Mrs. Arnold. Though Mrs. Arnold was a matron, Miss Pettiforth recognized in her a competitor for Lord Rathbone's attentions. She dismissed Miss Worth as negligible. It was Mrs. Arnold who shared a common acquaintanceship with the viscount and who moved in the same London circles. The thought of the orgy of entertainments over which the pair could undoubtedly share reminiscences made her quite sick with envy. Miss Pettiforth decided to do something about detaching his lordship from his very annoying connection.

She laid her fingers gently on his sleeve, causing him to pause, and looked up at him with a melting glance. "My lord, I had hoped to be able to speak more with you. I am so very glad to have met someone who might enlighten me about London manners, for I shall be coming out before many more months and I am so anxious to be a credit to my dear mama. Would you be so kind as to take me under your wing?"

Lord Rathbone replied almost automatically with some driveling gallantry. Whatever he had said made Miss Pettiforth cast down her eyes in a show of pleased confusion. He continued to converse with Miss Pettiforth in a civil manner that gave no hint of his true thoughts.

Lord Rathbone was inured to disapproval from the starchiest of personages. Disapprobation had been his portion ever since he had emerged from out of his mother's guardianship. Yet he was someone of importance in his own world and so he was excused a few peccadillos. Society as a whole treated him with the deference due his consequence and wealth and overlooked any faults.

However, that a hired companion could so cavalierly pass judgment upon one who was undeniably her social better was insupportable. Lord Rathbone knew that it was beneath him to give place to Miss Worth's condemnation, but strangely enough he found it impossible to set aside.

He had been on the point of bestowing a flattering attention upon her. She had therefore dealt a blow to his pride.

He should ignore the lady and treat her only with the barest civility demanded of him, forgetting what he had overheard. But he could not do the obvious thing. Instead, he wanted to punish Miss Worth for her temerity. He wanted to teach her a salutory lesson in passing verdict upon one who was due only respect from one of her position. He wanted to make her regret that she had, even so unwittingly, spurned his condescension to recognize her.

Once tea was done, and it seemed assured that most if not all of the expected guests had arrived, Mrs. Pettiforth set about her duties. To her mind, her splendid nephew, Lord Rathbone, was the most important, and she surged toward his lordship with the object of making quite certain that he would have nothing to complain of in the treatment that he received while under her roof.

Mrs. Pettiforth laid her hand on his lordship's sleeve and smilingly appropriated Lord Rathbone from his companions.

"I wish to assure myself that you are well looked after, my lord. I shall have Horwich show you to your room." Mrs. Pettiforth ushered Lord Rathbone out of the drawing room and pointed him toward the stairs. "As you have seen, we have quite a little party gathered. I am happy that there are a few personages who are familiar to you. It is always more comfortable thus, is it not?" She told his lordship what time dinner was served and gave him over into the offices of the butler.

Eleven

Dinner was set for the unfashionable hour of six of the clock.

Verity finished setting her earrings, small glistening diamonds that had been a gift from her father upon the eve of her engagement, and regarded herself critically in the cheval glass. The gown she wore was one of her favorites. The pale rose satin suited her.

Verity picked up her shawl to drape it elegantly from her elbows and then left her bedroom. She crossed to Miss Pettiforth's door and knocked to inquire whether her charge was ready. With a wooden face, Miss Pettiforth's maid conveyed the intelligence that the miss intended to make an entrance. Verity shrugged silently and nodded. "Very well. Pray tell Miss Pettiforth that I shall await her downstairs."

Verity was not at all dismayed that Miss Pettiforth had chosen to forgo her company. If the truth was to be known, she scarcely cared. She had had ample time in which to reflect upon the situation. She had already seen that the beauty meant to run her unbridled course. Verity hoped that she had the wit not to be anxious about what could not be changed. She could only trust that those things she had managed to put across to Miss Pettiforth had taken deep enough root that the girl would not completely sink herself beyond reproach.

However, Verity did not think that Miss Pettiforth was altogether a little fool. No, the beauty might do very much as she pleased now. But she did want to attach Lord Rathbone, and he was not a gentleman to be played fast and loose. Verity believed once Miss Pettiforth learned that the viscount was of a different cut than her other admirers, she would adapt herself accordingly.

Verity trod down the stairs, a slight smile of anticipation lighting her eyes. It had been a wonderful surprise to find that one of her own friends had been included in the Pettiforth's house party. She looked forward to exchanging further quiet confidences with her friend, Betsy Arnold. Such pleasant memories had been recalled already.

Verity regretted that she had not remained in closer touch through the intervening years with one who had once been her best of friends. Oh, it was true that she had seen Betsy Arnold from time to time, whenever she visited London, but that casual contact was nothing to compare with the close relationship that they had once enjoyed. However, their relationship had inexorably altered with Betsy's marriage and debut as a prominent London hostess, while Verity's life had again revolved around the quiet doings of Crofthouse.

Lost in her thoughts, Verity was startled when she was addressed from behind. "Good evening, Miss Worth." She turned, her hand resting lightly on the banister. Her eyes widened a little to discover that it was the viscount who had thus hailed her. "Lord Rathbone!"

He stopped on the step beside her, a brow raised. His deep blue eyes glinted as he smiled at her. "Forgive me, I have startled you."

Despite his lordship's sociable tone, there was something in his expression that Verity instinctively mistrusted. "Not at all, my lord. I was merely surprised, that is all."

"You were deep in thought. No doubt you are as eager as I to sample this evening's fare."

"Perhaps, my lord," said Verity, smiling, as she thought again about being able to sit down with her old friend.

Lord Rathbone offered his arm to her. "May I have the honor, Miss Worth?"

Little as she wished it, Verity was obliged to accept his escort. She laid her fingers on his elbow, murmuring polite thanks. They continued down the stairs at a leisurely pace that was dictated by the viscount.

Unexpectedly, he said, "You were surprised because you did not expect someone as top-lofty as I to recognize a mere acquaintance."

Verity was disconcerted by his uncanny reading of her thoughts and was betrayed into indiscretion. "Yes—no. Of course not."

When he laughed, she realized that she had been neatly trapped into being discourteous. She regarded the viscount with a kindling gaze. "You have succeeded in putting me firmly in the wrong, my lord. I must apologize."

"No, do not do so. I beg of you to serve me my just desserts," he said.

"What a very odd creature you are," she murmured, her slim brows drawing together in puzzlement as she stared up at his profile.

Lord Rathbone glanced at her. He said almost apologetically, "You see, I am trying so very hard to enliven what promises to be a respectable and very dull evening."

"I cannot imagine that this is precisely your sort of entertainment," agreed Verity, emboldened by the sardonic gleam in his eyes.

"That is much better, Miss Worth," he said approvingly. "You have managed to set me neatly in my place, implying that I am something of a frippery fellow. I allow you that much wit, at least."

They had by this time descended from the stairs and crossed the hall to the drawing room. Lord Rathbone paused to allow her to proceed him through the door. Verity glanced over her shoulder at the viscount, wondering at his singular attitude. There was a smile on his lordship's face that she found to be vaguely disquieting. But as their eyes met, she was disturbed even more at what passed between them. The strong magnetic pull startled and shocked her. She looked hastily away and stepped into the drawing room.

Verity knew that her color was considerably heightened, for warmth had suffused her cheeks. Fortunately for her peace of mind, those who had already gathered in the drawing room were all laughing at some joke or other that had been told, so that her moment of discomposure went unnoticed.

Verity at once moved away from the viscount and sought a seat beside another lady on the settee. Much to her relief, Lord Rathbone did not pursue her, but instead joined the group of gentlemen standing before the blaze in the fireplace.

Replying to her companion's friendly greeting, Verity entered into a genteel conversation that allowed her ample time for private reflection over the viscount's extraordinary behavior. Lord Rathbone had actually seemed to be flirting with her, but surely that was ridiculous. She was the least of consequence among the ladies.

There was a stir among the gentlemen and they turned almost as one to the door. Miss Pettiforth had made her entrance. She stood just inside the doorway, her charming pouting smile emphasizing the loveliness of her face. She was enjoying the admiration, and when her father stepped forward to draw her into the room, she at once broke into vivacious speech as she greeted the guests. Almost lost to notice was the entrance behind her of Mrs. Pettiforth and Mrs. Arnold.

"The girl is such a beauty. It is no wonder that the gentlemen flock about her. Why, even my Dudley, who is a veritable slow-top over anything that does not use gunpowder, is completely bowled out," said the lady seated beside Verity. She seemed to be highly amused at the sight of her portly husband making such sport of himself.

"Yes, Miss Pettiforth is very beautiful," said Verity, her eyes going to the viscount's tall figure. He, also, was amongst those paying court to the beauty, but whereas others were eager to catch her ear, his lordship merely stood on the periphery with a faintly mocking smile upon his face. She wondered what he was thinking.

Almost as though her thoughts had been heard by him, his eyes lifted and met hers. A heartbeat only, and then the viscount's gaze wandered back to Miss Pettiforth's winsome face.

Her heart beating ludicously quick, Verity shook her head at herself. If Lord Rathbone had been indulging in light flirtation with her on the stairs, it was but a momentary aberration.

No doubt it was simply habit for someone whose reputation for cutting a rakish dash was well-established.

The remainder of the guests soon gathered. Mrs. Pettiforth gave the nod to the butler to announce dinner. The company paired off, each of the ladies given escort into the dining room and seated at table.

With a smile, Verity thanked the gentleman who had seated her and then turned her eyes on the party. She had noted that Lord Rathbone had taken Mrs. Pettiforth in on his arm and she acknowledged that his lordship, whether or not his interest was in the daughter of the house, had impeccable manners. Now she was amused to see that Miss Pettiforth had maneuvered herself into a seat beside the viscount.

Verity suspected that the beauty meant to monopolize his lordship, but the attempt would probably fall short of expectation. Verity had already seen that Lord Rathbone's company manners were of the best. He would address himself equally to the ladies on either side of him. Unless Miss Pettiforth was so lost to place as to throw herself into a tantrum, she would have to bear the frustration of her purpose with smiling fortitude.

A gurgle of laughter escaped Verity. Hearing it, the gentleman on her right smiled and addressed a civil question. Verity responded and abandoned all thoughts of Miss Pettiforth as she gave herself up to enjoyment of the dinner.

Verity's complacency lasted only until the ladies had left the gentlemen to their after-dinner wine and retreated to the drawing room. She saw at once that Miss Pettiforth's sapphire eyes were bright with anger and that the girl was on the edge of ripping out. Verity sighed, wishing not for the first time that she did not have the responsibility for heading off the beauty's worst impulses. But there was no point repining, for she had agreed to do just that when she had accepted Mr. Pettiforth's offer.

Verity walked over to Miss Pettiforth, who stood at the window. The girl was staring out at the night while her slim fingers twitched the edge of the drape in short jerks. Verity regarded that sign of agitation with wary misgivings. She devoutly hoped that what she said would defuse the girl's obvious fury. "Miss Pettiforth, you did exceedingly well with the viscount at dinner," she said in a low voice.

Lord Rathbone's Flirt 87

As she had meant it to, her statement at once arrested the beauty's attention. Miss Pettiforth turned her head. Sparks of anger shot from the beautiful eyes. "What do you mean? He hardly spoke to me at all! And he escorted Mama into dinner, not me!"

"Yes, it was very wise not to be seen as too eager or to demand his lordship's undivided attention," said Verity, nodding. "A peer prizes good breeding and manners above all else. He wants a lady who can play a gracious hostess." She paused, as though she had made the most casual of observations, and pretended to glance about the company.

The gentlemen had come into the drawing room to join the ladies while Verity stood talking to Miss Pettiforth. The coffee urn was being brought in and Verity seized upon the opportunity it represented. "Excuse me, Miss Pettiforth. I believe that I see your mother signaling to me. Perhaps she wishes me to serve coffee this evening."

Verity walked away, but not before she had seen the thoughtful look that crossed Miss Pettiforth's face. Congratulating herself upon her success, she crossed over to Mrs. Pettiforth and offered her services in serving the coffee.

"Of course, Verity. I certainly have no objection," said Mrs. Pettiforth with a superior smile. She addressed her companion, saying, "Miss Worth is such a help to me, you can have no notion."

Verity turned away, hiding a smile. She knew that Mrs. Pettiforth had very expertly catalogued her offer, not as the gracious gesture that it was, but as a service to be expected of a hired companion.

As she went over to the coffee urn, Mrs. Arnold came up to her. The lady's expression was quizzical. "Really, Verity, how do you stand such nonsense?" she asked quietly. "You are scarcely to be thought of as a servant."

"I suspect that if Mrs. Pettiforth had her way, I would be relegated to an attic garret and only allowed the light of day when she needed me to draw off Miss Pettiforth's ill humors," said Verity, her eyes dancing.

"I think it detestable the way that woman puts you down. Why, you have more breeding in your little finger than—oh, very well! Laugh at me if you must, Verity. Just be sure that I shall show you the respect that you deserve. At least, I shall in company. I hope we are still good enough friends that I might tease you now and again," said Mrs. Arnold, also laughing.

"I am so looking forward to a comfortable cose with you, Betsy!" exclaimed Verity. "It seems like just yesterday that we had our heads together wondering what gentlemen would come to steal away our hearts."

"I daresay," said Mrs. Arnold, rolling her eyes. "But in all truth, I shall be glad to sit down and talk with you. I shall scold you a little, too, for neglecting me so shamelessly. I have not seen nor heard from you in months except for that single short note. You were in mourning, of course, so I was not greatly surprised when I did not see you in London. How in the world did you ever come to be here?"

Mrs. Arnold's gesture in Miss Pettiforth's direction was expressive. Once more Miss Pettiforth was the object of attention and her bright chatter overlaid more staid conversations. Lord Rathbone was standing close to the beauty. Her face was tilted up to his and her fingers rested upon his lordship's sleeve. The viscount's dark head was inclined to Miss Pettiforth's pretty confidences and he appeared to be amused.

Verity laughed. "Give me a few moments, Betsy, and then I shall be free to explain it all to you." The coffee was quickly served and she was able to slip away to a corner with Mrs. Arnold.

The tale was quickly told and at its conclusion, Mrs. Arnold shook her head in wonder. "I would not have had the courage to do the same in your place, Verity. And really, I am mildly insulted that you did not feel able to appeal to me, at least. You should have known that I would not have turned you away, nor begrudged the least expense even if Charles never returned."

"That is just like you, Betsy, and well I knew it to be true of you and, indeed, of one or two of my other friends. But my scruples forbade me to attach myself to anyone's charitable sleeve. Besides, it was the only way I knew to meet Elizabeth's needs. And fortunately, I was not forced to interview for some detestable post," said Verity.

"No, you fell into a veritable outpost of heaven with the Pettiforths," said Mrs. Arnold, quizzing her.

Verity laughed, shaking her head. "Perhaps not quite that, no. But I go on very tolerably, I assure you. I admit this house party did raise up awful spectres for me, but thus far it seems to be going better than one might have expected."

"I shouldn't place too much reliance upon Miss Pettiforth's continued good behavior, Verity. If I do not mistake the matter, she has the look of a banked volcano," said Mrs. Arnold, looking over at the beauty.

Miss Pettiforth was no longer hanging on Lord Rathbone's sleeve. Instead she was flirting outrageously with every gentleman within reach. At odd moments her eyes would cut to the viscount's tall form, where he stood conversing quietly with Mr. Pettiforth and Mr. Arnold.

"I have the most lowering feeling that you have the right of it, Betsy," said Verity with a sigh.

Mrs. Arnold's prediction was proven out over the next few days. Miss Pettiforth exhibited by turns her best and worst behaviors. Even Mrs. Pettiforth was driven to exclaim once, "Cecily, do leave off these vapors! Pray, do you wish to give his lordship an exceedingly odd notion of you?"

Miss Pettiforth had burst into stormy tears and raced from her mother's private salon. Mrs. Pettiforth turned to Verity. Her mouth was set in a grim line. "Verity, something really must be done. Surely you must know of a way to settle my dearest Cecily's nerves. I do not wish her to give Lord Rathbone a disgust of her, which is precisely what will happen if he should chance to see her in one of these miffs."

Verity said slowly, "I can see only one way, ma'am. Miss Pettiforth attends to you on most occasions. Perhaps if you were to hint that she might have to forgo some of the treats in store for her or even to go on a repairing lease, it would prove to steady her. If she goes on as she is, she will be completely burnt to the socket before your guests make their departures."

Mrs. Pettiforth's eyes narrowed, her expression sharply introspective. "Yes, you are quite right. Lord Rathbone might even leave before—why, it is not to be thought of." She nodded at Verity. "Very well! I shall speak to her just as you say."

Mrs. Pettiforth was apparently as good as her word. Miss Pettiforth emerged from her interview with a much subdued air. For several days the beauty's behavior was painstakingly correct, whether in her own home or out in the neighborhood. The entertainments went forward much more pleasantly for Verity, who did not feel called upon as often to divert Miss Pettiforth's quick temper.

Nevertheless, the days were fraught with stress for Verity. For some inexplicable reason known best by himself, Lord Rathbone showed her small partialities. Once he retrieved for her the book that she had forgotten. He strolled with her in the walking gallery, ostensibly in the company of Miss Tibbs and the girls; but since he had steered her away from the others, Verity knew it for a particular attention. On numerous occasions he spoke to her and smiled at her in such a way that her heart quickened.

Then, just when she was beginning to feel easy with him, he treated her to a formal bow or his eyes passed indifferently over her when he entered a room. The viscount blew hot and cold, until Verity felt herself to be so off-balance that she scarcely knew what to think. In addition, she sensed that Lord Rathbone's gestures of partiality had not gone entirely unnoted. She caught certain speculative glances from some of the house guests that made her uncomfortable. Altogether it was a confusing time.

The rumor of a grand ball that was being planned by the Squire and Mrs. Passenby, to which the whole neighborhood was to be invited, could scarcely be reflected upon by Verity with anything but a shudder. She thought of it only as an opportunity for Miss Pettiforth to somehow disgrace herself, or for Lord Rathbone to further his campaign with her.

Twelve

Before the invitation to the ball reached the Pettiforth manor, Miss Pettiforth was in a fever of impatience. It had been she who had first heard rumors of the ball. When the invitation was at last received, she was thrown into a transport of joy, for she had received indulgent permission from her mother to attend. For two weeks she could talk of little else. A new gown had been commissioned and was waiting to be worn to the event that evening.

"My first grown-up ball!" she exclaimed. "I shall dance every dance. *And* I shall be the prettiest girl there. Isn't it fortunate that Camilla Redding has taken the spots? I vow, I am quite in charity with her just now. I shall send her a nice basket of fruit."

Verity looked across the sitting room at the girl. Miss Pettiforth had jumped up and begun primping herself in front of the mantel mirror. "Cecily, you would do well to guard your tongue. Such catty remarks will not win you many friends."

Sophronia, with all the awkward frankness of her fifteen years, said, "Much she cares for that! She knows Camilla Redding can take the shine right out of her and Camilla is popular, besides! Cecily hasn't any friends."

"How dare you!" exclaimed Miss Pettiforth, angry color

flooding her face. "I shall box your ears for that impertinence!" She advanced on the younger girl, but Sophronia prudently whisked herself out of reach behind a settee.

Dorothy gleefully chanted, "Camilla's the belle! Camilla's the belle!"

Miss Pettiforth exploded with rage. She made a swipe at the younger girl, but missed. Dorothy stuck out her tongue. Sophronia laughed.

"Girls, girls!" expostulated Miss Tibbs. "I must insist upon order."

"As must I. Cecily, sit down!"

There was such a whipcrack in Miss Worth's voice that Miss Pettiforth instinctively started to obey. When she realized it, she leaped up again, bursting into a storm of tears. "You are mean and cruel, all of you! I shall have something to say to Mama, I promise you."

"Undoubtedly you shall. But so shall I," said Verity coolly. "I do not believe that a young woman who starts up in such a fiendish temper toward her sisters can be trusted to conduct herself properly in society. Mrs. Pettiforth has charged me with imparting to you the points of conduct expected of a young miss emerging from the schoolroom. She has high hopes for your come out. If you choose to toss aside your opportunities by behaving like a spoiled baby, then I can only recommend that you remain for another year in the schoolroom!"

Miss Pettiforth stared at Miss Worth, her tears suspended with shock. She was suddenly made uncertain. Her mentor's calm declaration put her forcibly in mind of her mother's warnings. Her bosom heaved of a sudden with strong feeling. "I detest you! I detest you all!" She swung round on her heel and ran out of the sitting room.

"Oh, well done, Miss Worth," exclaimed Sophronia.

"I fear that you have made a poisonous enemy in Miss Pettiforth," said Miss Tibbs quietly, not once faltering in her embroidery.

"Miss Pettiforth has never liked me," observed Verity with a small laugh.

"Cecily is a mean old cat," said Dorothy, giving a decided nod. "I don't like her, not one bit. And neither does Sophy."

Lord Rathbone's Flirt

"Sophronia, Dorothy, you will go up to the schoolroom at once. There you will work on your copybooks until I come for you," said Miss Tibbs sternly.

Dorothy cried out at the injustice, but Sophronia only tossed her head. She took her sister's hand. "Never you mind, Doro. It is worth it for having got a little of our own back at Cecily. And I'll help you with your copying."

The smaller girl brightened. "Yes, she was very angry, wasn't she? I am glad. I shall be ever so glad, too, when she weds Lord Rathbone like she keeps saying she will. Then she'll have to leave, the mean old thing, and we shall be comfortable."

"Dorothy." Miss Tibbs looked over the edge of her spectacles at the younger girl and a half-scared, half-ashamed expression settled on Dorothy's face.

Sophronia tugged at her sister's hand, anxious to be gone before either of them incurred further displeasure. "Come along, then, Doro. We shall go up to visit Rebecca, too. Poor thing, she has been so bored with just Nurse to talk to her. It must be horrid to have a head cold."

"Yes, and if we see Cecily on the stairs we shan't say a word to her just as though we don't see her. That will put her in a proper flame," said the incorrigible Dorothy.

The girls left arm in arm, their heads together as they whispered.

Miss Tibbs sighed and shook her head. "One cannot altogether blame the girls. I have tried to instill a proper respect in them for their elders, but in this one glaring exception it has been difficult."

"And I know precisely where the difficulty lies," said Verity.

Miss Tibbs glanced over at her, a speaking expression on her face. "I am afraid so. As I have told you, I could do nothing with Miss Pettiforth and she succeeded in upsetting the others so badly that carrying forward my duties became next to impossible."

"That I call well imagine," said Verity. "It is a wonder that you were able to accomplish anything at all."

Miss Tibbs sighed. "There has been a string of governesses that have come and gone in this house. Miss Pettiforth would have none of them, and because of the resulting chaos, they were let go. Sophronia and Dorothy, and little Rebecca, too, are good girls, though their conduct may not always reflect it. They possess quick and eager minds. That is unusual and very welcome. I did not want to be forced to leave a post where I had pupils with such possibility. But Miss Pettiforth posed a problem which I could not solve. At last I approached Mr. Pettiforth and suggested that a different sort of female would be more advantageous to his daughter, given Miss Pettiforth's lack of interest in lessons. Mr. Pettiforth at once seized on the practicality of my suggestion. He is perhaps more aware that anyone that Miss Pettiforth's assets are completely wasted in the schoolroom."

"So it was completely at your good offices that I came to be part of this household," said Verity, plying her needle.

"Indirectly, yes. I was quite glad when you came." Miss Tibbs smiled. "However, now I almost regret that it was upon you whom Mr. Pettiforth's choice fell."

Verity looked up, startled. "I beg your pardon?"

Miss Tibbs got up, folding her bit of handiwork. "I like you very well, Miss Worth. It is a thankless, difficult task that you have been set, bringing that spoiled beauty into line. You have already exceeded my expectations, I must confess. I do wish you well in your continued care for Miss Pettiforth." She hesitated, then said, "But have a care for yourself, too, my dear. A lady's reputation is a fragile commodity and once wasted can never be regained."

A swift tide of color rose in Verity's face. The older woman smiled again, perhaps a little sadly, and left the sitting room. Verity bent her head again to the embroidery that she was working on. Her thoughts naturally turned on the governess's quiet warning. For warning it most certainly was, she knew.

Miss Tibbs was a very observant, intelligent woman. She heard perhaps more than she was thought to, due to her ambiguous position, belonging neither to the family circle nor to the servants' hall. The governess in a household was nearly always ignored except in the discharge of her duties, and people spoke in front of her as though she did not exist. That would be even more true with a party of guests in the house. Undoubtedly Miss Tibbs had overhead things uttered by some of the houseguests or that had been said by some of their servants. She had thought the gossip sufficiently grave to drop that word of caution.

Verity sighed. The embroidery dropped to her lap as she stared in the direction of the window where the rain lashed. The past few weeks had proven to be more and more difficult. Lord Rathbone's attentions toward her had become increasingly marked and now, obviously, others were becoming aware that she was the object of his gallantries.

Not for a moment did Verity believe that Lord Rathbone had any serious intentions toward her. It was scarcely conceivable that it could be so. His lordship was a landed peer, wealthy and sought after as one of the most eligible gentlemen in England. Lord Rathbone could literally take his choice from amongst the young ladies of the realm.

Verity knew, for Mrs. Pettiforth had confided it to her ears, that Lord Rathbone had come down from London to make one of the house party for the express purpose of looking over his cousin, Miss Cecily Pettiforth, as a possible bride. His lordship had apparently decided that it was time to think of setting up his own nursery and had been advised by his mother to cast his sights at this member of their own family. Since fortune was not a consideration for Lord Rathbone, the suggestion that he meet Miss Pettiforth had been met with a shrug and a tepid acceptance, according to the letter sent to Mrs. Pettiforth.

All this and somewhat more had Mrs. Pettiforth confided bit by bit to Verity during the times when she was considered by her employer in the light of an ally. Mrs. Pettiforth had several times trotted out speculations about her daughter's chances at snaring such a rich matrimonial prize. Verity had tried diplomatically to avoid voicing her own opinions. She could only assure Mrs. Pettiforth that she would do all in her power to steer Miss Pettiforth into showing off her best side.

Mrs. Pettiforth had been immensely satisfied. "That will do the thing, indeed, Verity. I am certain that nothing more can be needed, for my darling Cecily is quite a catch for any young man, so pretty as she is."

Verity had murmured her agreement, reserving her own judgment that any gentleman of sense would hardly wish to be saddled with a wife who was every bit as selfish and self-centered as she was lovely. Of course, if all that was wanted was a pretty ornament, then the gentleman in question would not need to look any further, for Miss Pettiforth suited the qualifications admirably. That was an unkind thought, Verity knew, and she should be ashamed of it, but she was too much of a realist to obscure any such truth with platitudes.

"I know that I may rely upon you, Verity, not to repeat any word of this matter," Mrs. Pettiforth had said. "But I wished to impress upon you how very important it is that Cecily show her best face while Lord Rathbone is with us."

Verity had tried to carry out her commission. She had tried to curb Miss Pettiforth's impulsive vulgarities of phrase. She had tried to smooth away the beauty's all too frequent crotchets. She had gently but firmly pointed out to her charge the proper way of a lady aspiring to a great position. All efforts had met with but moderate success.

Miss Pettiforth, with the uncanny instinct possessed by one totally self-centered, had known without a word spoken to her the reason behind Lord Rathbone's visit. Her mother had only confirmed what she had already divined. She had been inordinately pleased to have such a prestigious gentlemen upon whom to practice her wiles and she was supremely confident that she could turn his lordship round her little finger at any moment that she chose to do so.

Verity knew what her charge thought. Miss Pettiforth had boasted too often to allow for misconstruction, and had proceeded with cunning to prove that she could snap up a plum of a peer before her eighteenth birthday.

However, Lord Rathbone had not fallen quite so easily at Miss Pettiforth's feet as that damsel had anticipated. He had been annoyingly elusive. Miss Pettiforth had early begun to fall away from her pattern-card behavior and to show more of her true colors.

Verity felt that she had done her best to spike the worst of Miss Pettiforth's impulses, but it had been a harrowing time. Coupled with her problems with the spoiled beauty was the ever-present anxiety that had been added to her burden through Lord Rathbone's strange bent in her own direction. Verity dreaded the day that his lordship's attentions became so obvious that Miss Pettiforth noticed them. There would be the devil to pay and no mistake, for the girl had a raging temper when she was crossed.

As for herself, Verity felt that his lordship's attentions were at once disconcerting and dangerous to her. She had been quite aware from the first that he represented a twofold danger.

Verity had foreseen that Lord Rathbone's seeming preference for her company would occasion gossip. She had tried to repulse him without giving offense. It had not served. He had continued his erratic flirtation with her. Taking her courage in her hands, she had flatly rebuffed him. She had seen by his expression that he had been both astonished and angered. He had bowed stiffly and walked away.

Perhaps it might have sufficed and her life would have returned to normal, except that it had come too late. The consequences of Lord Rathbone's attentions had already had their inevitable result. She and his lordship had become the subject of talk. She knew it to be so, for more than once lately when she had entered a room, the conversation had broken off and she had become the object of speculative scrutiny.

The second danger, of course, had been far more insidious. She had felt an overwhelming, shocking attraction to Lord Rathbone the day that he had opened his flirtation with her on the stairs.

Verity was a practical creature. She knew that situated as she presently was, she could not hope to aspire to honorable estate with a gentleman such as Lord Rathbone and she had resigned herself to that reality. Then Lord Rathbone had inexplicably insisted upon making her the object of his attentions. Verity had not dared to trust in his overtures. Despite her defenses, however, he had somehow come to occupy much of her thoughts.

She thought dispassionately that she was in a fair way to falling in love with his lordship, and that would never do.

"What will never do, Miss Worth?"

Thirteen

Verity looked round, startled. When she met Lord Rathbone's cool, amused gaze, the color rose into her face. She had not heard the door open, nor had she been aware that she had spoken her last thought aloud.

"My lord! I did not hear you come in," she stammered, embarrassed, but clutching at some semblance of composure.

"I recalled that I had left a newspaper here earlier. I came to retrieve it," said Lord Rathbone, smiling a little. He still stood in the open doorway, his hand on the knob.

She was inordinately aware that he had entered the sitting room unaccompanied and that they were alone. Her heart was set to racing. Her one coherent thought amongst the whirl in her mind was that she had to exercise prudence, and at once.

Verity gathered up her embroidery hoop and rose from the settee. "Pray excuse me, my lord. I have quite lost sight of the time. I was expected upstairs a quarter hour past."

"Do not run away on my account," he said softly.

Verity had started to step past him, but he shifted slightly so that she would have had to press against him to go through the doorway. She lifted her eyes to meet his gaze. His eyes were glinting with laughter and a disturbing warmth. Her color rose once more. "Pray let me pass, my lord."

"Will you not grant me a few moments of your time, Miss Worth? It has been very flat since the rain started. I am certain that a taste of your wit would enliven this dull day for me," he said, smiling.

The inclement weather had ensured that the houseguests had been forced to seek their entertainment indoors. Verity was acutely cognizant that at any moment someone might come down the stairs or exit the library or the billiards room. She and the viscount were in plain view from any one of these vantage points. It would do nothing but damage if they were discovered in this intimate pose.

In a low voice, Verity said, "You choose to make game of me, my lord. I beg of you, do so no longer. Consider what you are about and the consequences. Already we have been remarked."

Lord Rathbone leaned a broad shoulder against the doorjamb, effectively blocking the doorway altogether. "I choose when the game is over, my dear Miss Worth. But have no fear that I shall exact a cruel price for the pleasure of our mutual acquaintance."

"It has been of no pleasure to me, my lord," she retorted, his arrogant manner finally driving her to expose more fully the extent of her anger and frustration.

"Has it not, Miss Worth? Strange, I have found it far otherwise," he said.

Verity realized that his lordship was in a capricious mood and that there would be no reasoning with him. "Pray let me pass," she said coldly.

Lord Rathbone straightened and stepped aside. As she made to sweep past him without a second glance, he caught her elbow. She was perforce obliged to halt and look up at him. "Yes, my lord? You wished something else?" she asked with such elaborate civility that it was an insult.

Twin devils danced in his eyes. "I shall expect you to save a dance for me at the ball," he murmured.

"Chaperones do not dance, as well you know, my lord. And even if it was condoned, I still would not dance with you," said Verity evenly. The blood was racing in her veins. She did not understand why he affected her so.

"I think that you would, Miss Worth," said Lord Rathbone

with a slow grin lighting his face. His gaze had dropped to the quickened pulse in the hollow of her throat. He raised his narrowed eyes once more to meet hers. "Yes, I rather think that you would."

A mewl of inarticulate anger sounded in her throat. If Verity had believed that she could have gotten away with it, she would have slapped him then and there. But she could not. Their separate social positions in this house would not allow her even that much latitude. Her eyes expressed everything that she felt. "You are insulting, my lord!"

He laughed, very softly.

Verity snatched herself from his detaining hand. It was all part of his persecution of her. She had no idea why his lordship was so intent on oversetting her, but that he was succeeding far better than he should was galling.

Verity crossed the entry hall quickly to the stairs and mounted them at speed. She scarcely noticed one of the houseguests who was paused on the landing.

But the lady noticed Miss Worth. Her sharp eyes took particular note of the high color in Miss Worth's face. The lady's glance returned to Lord Rathbone, who was turning back into the sitting room with a satisfied smile on his face.

The lady pursed her mouth. She had been too distant to have been able to hear what had been said, of course, but Miss Worth's flight was quite telling, she thought, as had been Lord Rathbone's obvious interest. It was all very intriguing and no doubt would prove even more piquant in the telling.

The rain stopped a few hours before dinner. It was felt by all to be a good omen for the success of the ball. Spirits rose in anticipation, even the keenest of sporting gentlemen grumbling less than usual at the prospect of putting on fancy dress. After all, the morrow promised to be cold and clear, and they would be able to get out in the fields with their guns and dogs. It was a simple thing, therefore, to cater to the wishes of the ladies tonight.

In light of Lord Rathbone's arrogant assumption that she would stand up with him, Verity was reluctant to attend the ball. She was anxious that his lordship might continue his importunities at the function. It would be difficult to rebuff him without causing an abhorrent scene, she thought.

However, she also felt that to cry off because of her own foolish fears was cowardly. So she dressed with care and put in her diamond earrings and a matching diamond-studded comb in her upswept hair. She wore a gown that had been made up from a blue satin discovered in a trunk at Crofthouse. It was one of three new gowns sent to her by her mother. The gown looked exceedingly well on her and she reflected that she need not be anxious for her appearance, at least.

The coach was called for and Mrs. Pettiforth set forth with Miss Pettiforth and Verity. They were without benefit of male escort, Mr. Pettiforth having cried off at the last moment. The rest of the house party also took to their coaches, most with every expectation of being well-entertained.

Lord Rathbone was among those who set out to enjoy the squire's hospitality. He did not, however, anticipate the evening as thoroughly as his companions. As he stepped down from the carriage he glanced up at the clear night sky. It was the full moon and chilly.

Lord Rathbone sighed. It was perfect steeplechasing weather. How unfortunate that for the next several hours he would be cooped up in a too-hot ballroom doing the pretty with a crowd of ladies who held not the least fraction of interest for him. The only reason that he had come was on the chance that Miss Worth meant to make one of the company.

His boredom quickly dropped away when he turned in time to see his aunt and Miss Pettiforth descend from their carriage, followed by Miss Worth.

Miss Worth's eyes chanced to meet his own as she stepped down to the walk. She turned quickly away and accompanied the Pettiforths into the manor house.

""So you came, after all," murmured Lord Rathbone, looking after her appreciatively. All of a sudden the evening had taken on a pleasant aspect.

"What was that, Rathbone?" inquired Mr. Herbert Arnold, emerging from the same carriage that his lordship had used.

Lord Rathbone shook his head. "I was but admiring the night, sir. I was thinking what a pity it is that we do not have a steeplechase."

"By Jove! That is a capital notion. I shall bruit it about and we shall see whether we do not get one up. Good fellow, Rathbone! You are a gentleman after my own heart," exclaimed Mr. Arnold jovially. He turned then to give his hand to his wife, saying, "What do you think, my love? Lord Rathbone wishes to get up a steeplechase."

Mrs. Arnold descended gracefully to the walk. She said laughingly, "I shall hold it against you, my lord, if this neck-or-nothing man of mine takes a tumble."

Lord Rathbone returned some sally, and in the company of the Arnolds, walked up the steps. When they had entered the manor and been divested of their cloaks, they were directed to the ballroom. Lord Rathbone moved up the stairs with the others to the ballroom, where they were greeted by the squire and his lady and their two daughters. Having said everything that was polite, Lord Rathbone moved on past the receiving line. He paused to survey the bright, laughing company in the ballroom. None could have guessed from his lordship's demeanor that he was searching for a particular lady's figure.

The ball was situated in a suite of rooms opening one into another. A crumb cloth had been stretched over the carpets. Mrs. Passenby had made certain as she greeted each of her guests that the gentlemen were made aware that more than dancing was offered. "At the other end of the room is the card room and a refreshment room is nearby so that the ladies will not get chilled passing down a staircase on their way for tea or lemonade. The supper room is downstairs," she had said.

Coming up beside Lord Rathbone, Mr. Arnold rubbed his palms together in contentment. "It is not steeplechasing, but it shapes up to be a jolly good function for all that," he said.

Mrs. Arnold put her hand through her husband's arm. "I don't mean to allow you to run off to the refreshment table until you have danced with me," she said.

"You see how a married man cannot call himself his own," said Mr. Arnold with a broad wink.

Lord Rathbone smiled and politely concurred. He moved away as soon as it was civil to do so. He had espied the Pettiforth party, but instead of immediately approaching the ladies, he sauntered about talking to various personages.

The squire had a liking for punctuality and the ball had

begun promptly at eight o'clock. A grand piano, a cello, and a violin constituted the orchestra and were placed at the end farthest from the door where the hostess and her daughters still greeted incoming guests.

Lord Rathbone, as one of the gentlemen of highest rank, led out the eldest of the squire's sandy-haired daughters. The opening minuet was followed by several country dances. Before many sets had formed, the ball was already accounted a huge success by the guests. The entire neighborhood appeared to have turned out, with every expectation of enjoyment, and not one young lady was left without a partner.

The ballroom had been warm to begin with, but with the energetic exercise, the heat steadily climbed to nearly an unbearable degree. Wax began to drip from the melting candles in the chandeliers onto the dancers below. Several gowns were ripped when the hems were trod upon by male boots, and the ladies discreetly retired to the small cloakroom which had been supplied for this very purpose, to have the tears swiftly mended by waiting maids. It was all part and parcel of a successful function.

Lord Rathbone had been patient in achieving his object for that evening. He had dutifully squired every maiden and every matron onto the dance floor. He had fetched lemonade and tea and, in general, made himself agreeable. Satisfied that he had left nothing undone, he then approached Miss Worth to claim her hand for a dance.

As he had expected, she at once declined. There was a decided spark in her eyes as she said, "You should take out Miss Pettiforth, my lord. She is quite the belle tonight."

"I have already squired Miss Pettiforth twice, Miss Worth. I do not intend for the gossips to have us engaged by doing so for a third time," said Lord Rathbone.

"Oh! Of course, how silly of me. I suppose that I did not count properly," said Verity, feeling all sorts of fool. Of course he would not transgress the unwritten rule. A third dance in one evening with a particular gentleman meant that it was in a fair way to being understood that the young lady had accepted a flattering offer. As she knew very well, if there had been any such offer in the wind, Mrs. Pettiforth would have shouted it from the rooftops.

"What an odd companion you are, to be sure," he said quizzingly.

She started to retort, but caught back her hasty words when she saw the anticipatory gleam in his eyes. She laughed instead. "No, you shall not have ground to accuse me of discourtesy so easily, my lord. I have learned my lesson at that."

"Good. Then dance with me," he said.

Verity looked around, rather helplessly. "Surely there is someone else, my lord. You must know that it will occasion talk if I should leave the matrons' side and accept."

"Do you care so much? I confess that I do not." He held out his hand peremptorily. "Come. I wish to dance with you. I shan't stop importuning you until you accept."

Verity saw that he was perfectly serious. He wore that twisted smile that conveyed an obstinance and arrogance that could not be easily gainsaid. If she did not accept, his lordship was perfectly capable of seating himself down beside her and devoting himself so assiduously to her that it would occasion far more notice than a single turn about the dance floor.

"It is only a round dance, Miss Worth. Surely your reputation will survive," he said softly.

"Oh, very well," she said crossly, rising from her chair.

Taking her hand, he led her onto the floor and escorted her into their place in the set. Verity's misgivings over being singled out by Lord Rathbone were strong, but the lively steps and music made shadows of her lingering doubts. She became buoyed also by the reflection that he had indeed danced with every other lady; surely just this once his attention toward her would go relatively unnoticed.

Verity managed to enjoy herself enough that she almost regretted it when the set ended. Smiling, she said, "Thank you, my lord. That was indeed pleasant."

He stared down at her. Her gray eyes sparkled, and her face was warmed with rose. He had retained her hand and now, as he heard the strains of a waltz, his fingers tightened. The light of deviltry entered his eyes. "We are not done yet, Miss Worth!"

At once she understood his intention. "No—pray!" But he did not yield to her instinctive recoil. His arm swept about her waist and he swung her gracefully into the waltz.

Lord Rathbone glanced down at his partner, amused by the rigidness of her body beneath his guiding hand. Her face was white and she stared straight at his cravat. "What, Miss Worth? Do you not delight in the waltz? I quite thought you might, as light as you are on your feet."

Her eyes rose to his face, humiliation and anger in their bright depths. "How could you, my lord? You expose me to the worst sort of scrutiny by this deed. Surely the sport is cruel, even for you."

Lord Rathbone's hold tightened on her fingers so that she winced. "I told you once, Miss Worth, that the game will be over when I will it so. Do not look so despairing, my dear. Your fears are unfounded, believe me. I have yet to play fast and loose with a lady's reputation."

She averted her face. "Then I can only suppose that you do not deem me worthy of respect."

"Miss Worth, were I to tell you what I thought of you, it would most assuredly astonish you."

There was something in his tone that made her startled gaze sweep up to meet his. He laughed a shade grimly. "I did not much like you in the beginning, Miss Worth. I shall leave to you to decide my feelings at this moment."

Verity felt no hesitation in doing so. She said hastily, "Surely you despise me, then, for you have done your utmost to overset my peace and to make a byword of me. You have persecuted me unmercifully, my lord!"

Lord Rathbone was astonished by the shaking timbre of her voice and the glimpse of tears in her eyes. His conscience was dealt an uncomfortable check. What was he doing in forcing his attention on a female who had made it plain from the outset that she wanted nothing of him? But he knew the answer to his own question. It had been his pride, and that damnable taste for revenge that he had inherited from his mother, that led him to this abhorrent pass.

The last strains of the waltz had scarcely died away when Lord Rathbone abruptly stopped and led Miss Worth back to her chair. He stepped back. "You are right, Miss Worth. It was ignoble of me to take advantage of you. I shall stay at a distance for the remainder of my sojourn here," he said quietly.

Fourteen

~

Lord Rathbone walked away to the refreshment room. His thoughts were in turmoil. His objectivity seemed to have been blasted. With hindsight he saw that what Miss Worth had said was true. He had persecuted her and for no other reason than to extort much the sort of confession that he had just wrung from her.

Lord Rathbone picked up a wineglass. He moved into the shadows of a draped window embrasure. His position was such that he could watch the company and yet be far enough removed from the refreshment table that he would not be immediately noticed. The last thing that he wanted was to be drawn into idle conversation. Almost absently, he tasted of the wine.

A small group of ladies approached the refreshment table, chattering brightly among themselves. Upon their drawing near, Lord Rathbone had further withdrawn into the window embrasure. He paid not the slightest attention to the ladies' conversation until he heard his own name.

His brows drew together in irritation, even as he shrugged in contempt. He should be inured to discovering himself to be a topic of gossip. He would have ignored the remainder of the conversation, but at the next statement he stiffened.

"I wonder that Lord Rathbone would keep her on the dance floor in such a blatant way," said Mrs. Passenby, mild disapproval shading her voice.

"Oh, have you not heard?" There was a brittle laugh from one of her companions. "Our trusty Miss Worth is his lordship's latest flirt!"

Mrs. Passenby gasped. "Well! I should never have expected it of Miss Worth. I have always considered her to be exceptionally pretty-behaved. And certainly what she has accomplished with Miss Pettiforth is close to prodigious. We have all remarked upon it."

"Miss Worth is a sly one, indeed," commented the other woman. "It has been obvious from the beginning of our house visit that there has been something odd taking place. There is Mrs. Pettiforth pinning her faith in the woman to make something of that spoiled child, Cecily. You speak of Miss Worth's efforts with admiration, ma'am, but I assure you that her actions covered a dark motive of her own. I believe that she used her influence with Miss Pettiforth to draw herself to the viscount's notice."

"Surely you do not truly believe that. Why, even if it were true that was what Miss Worth intended, how could she dream of enticing a gentleman such as Lord Rathbone away from that beautiful child? I have two daughters of my own and I know how the gentlemen are. When Cecily Pettiforth is in the room, every one of them looks at her in the most besotted way imaginable," said Mrs. Passenby, with pardonable bitterness.

"Nevertheless, dear ma'am, you must believe me when I tell you that I have observed any number of instances when his lordship expressed a clear preference for Miss Worth's company. And he did not do so without active encouragement, for just as you say, every other woman pales in the light of Miss Pettiforth's beauty."

"It is preposterous! I do not mean to say that Miss Worth is ill-looking. On the contrary, I consider her to be a most handsome female with a great deal of countenance. But to say that she put herself up to compete against Miss Pettiforth is ridiculous," said Mrs. Passenby forthrightly.

"Mrs. Passenby, this very afternoon I saw her practically *encouraging* Lord Rathbone's advances!"

"Oh, dear!"

The first lady had listened in avid silence, but now she took a hand. 'So encroaching of her, to be sure, when everyone knows she hasn't a feather to fly with. Mrs. Pettiforth has confided it all to me. It was only the Pettiforths' generosity that led them to make her a salary. She should know where her loyalties lie and be properly grateful."

"How true! But that wasn't enough for the woman. She must try to snatch one of the richest peers in the realm right from under all of our noses. The effrontry of it all is what is most particularly galling."

"Poor Alice Pettiforth! One cannot but feel for her, and for Mr. Pettiforth, too, of course. There was his lordship primed to make an offer for Cecily and it is all vanished like smoke!"

Mrs. Passenby had listened with appalled disbelief to the poisonous exchange. "Are you certain? I had not heard it was at all a done thing. If Lord Rathbone was set to make an offer, he would surely have done so by now."

"Oh, as to that!" One of the gossips lifted her shoulders in an expressive shrug. "What other explanation can there be for the viscount's continued presence in the neighborhood? It is too well-known that Lord Rathbone positively detests the country. Why, he is in London for every Season. I have it as a fact from Mrs. Arnold, who is on intimate footing with his lordship, that he scarcely ever leaves town."

"I feel for Alice Pettiforth, indeed. It would have been the coup of the year to bring Rathbone to heel. Then the Worth woman makes an object of herself and all is fair lost."

The women moved away, still exclaiming with their heads together, never having noticed that they had been overheard.

Lord Rathbone had stood quite still, unable either to quietly retreat or to make his presence known. As the ladies at last withdrew, the wineglass he had been holding disintegrated. Glass splintered on the carpet at his feet. He glanced down at the sharp stinging in his hand. His fingers were bloody. Coolly, he noted that the stem of the wineglass had snapped in two.

He took out a handkerchief and wrapped the linen square around the bleeding digits. Then he thrust the injured hand into his coat pocket. It was his left hand, fortunately, so that he would not be required to bring it out when he was offered someone's hand to shake.

It was time to make his adieus to his hostess, which he lost no time in doing. Mrs. Passenby expressed polite regret that he was retiring early, but he rather suspected that he read condemnation in her eyes.

Lord Rathbone started toward the exit of the ballroom. His progress was not as swift as he would have liked as he was hailed by various acquaintances and forced to respond.

At one point Mr. Arnold caught hold of his sleeve. "Here, Rathbone! I say, have you heard? The squire has promised to mount a few of us for a steeplechase. We are not even staying to put off ball-dress. You are joining us, are you not?"

"No, no, I think not, Arnold." Lord Rathbone forced a stiff smile to his lips. "I'm afraid that I've rather lost interest in the notion."

"Oh, very sorry to hear that. Your inspiration and all that," said Mr. Arnold, disappointed.

"Pray do not let my doldrums keep you from your own enjoyment," said Lord Rathbone.

"No, I should think not! Jolly good of you, Rathbone. Well, shan't keep you any longer," said Mr. Arnold, giving a good-natured wave.

Lord Rathbone saw that he was already forgotten as Mr. Arnold hurried over to join a small group of waiting gentlemen. A sardonic smile emphasizing his stern features, he turned once more toward the door of the ballroom. As he did so, he saw Miss Worth sitting by herself to one side of the dance floor.

There was a pocket of empty space around her, though people stood all about in witty conversation and laughter. Miss Worth was pale of face, but composed. Her upright posture spoke of pride.

Lord Rathbone understood in a flash. She knew or had already heard the talk, then. Something twisted inside of him.

Lord Rathbone started to cross over to her, but he stopped himself in midstride. It would only make matters worse for her if he were to approach her so publicly.

He turned on his heel and strode away, leaving the elegant ballroom behind.

Verity watched the viscount go. She felt wretched and angry all at one time. Though she did not acknowledge them, she could see the glances thrown in her direction and the whispered confidences behind lifted hands. It did not do a bit of good to tell herself that she had known what the outcome would be and that she had been wise to try to prepare herself for it. The reality was so much more hideous than she had anticipated.

There was no escape from the bright, cold stares. She could not leave the ballroom on any pretext without underscoring just the sort of ugly speculations that were running rife through the company.

She could only hope that the Pettiforth party would soon return home. Her only recourse of the moment was to bear herself with pride. It would never do to betray a quiver of weakness, or even to show awareness that she was the object of malicious gossip. How she was to endure it, she did not know, but endure it she must.

A whisper of fabric warned her of someone's approach. Steeling herself, Verity turned her head. She met the sympathetic expression of her friend, Betsy Arnold. Tears stung her eyes. She could have met a malicious smile and a stinging reproach with fortitude, but she had no defense against kindness.

Mrs. Arnold sat down in the chair beside Verity, her fingers giving Verity a warning nip. There were a score of interested gazes directed toward the two women. "Verity, I was just telling Mrs. Pettiforth that I have been struck with the most monstrous headache. As I had no wish to interrupt her pleasure, I begged that you might be allowed to bear me company back to the manor. Would you be so kind?"

"Of course, I shall do so," said Verity, rising. Her eyes communicated her heartfelt gratitude, though there was nothing else in her expression or her demeanor to indicate her relief.

Mrs. Arnold put her arm through Verity's in a companionable way and gave her a comforting squeeze. "Thank you, my dear. I know that I am a sad trial to take you away so early in the evening."

Maintaining a light discourse, to which Verity had only to smile and to reply at appropriate intervals, Mrs. Arnold eased her past the cold stares and out of the house.

The ladies stepped outside, their wraps about their shoulders. Verity put back her head, her eyes closed, to take a deep breath of the crisp cold air. On a note of relief, she said, "I was stifling in there."

"I do not doubt it in the least. The heat was positively horrendous. I felt it most acutely myself." The words were accompanied by a sharp pinch and a meaningful glance at the manservant holding a lantern for them as the carriage was brought round. "It is no wonder that I should have developed the headache. You are so kind to have come with me."

The ladies stepped up into the carriage. The door was shut, the whip cracked. As the carriage bolted forward, Verity said in a low, trembling voice, "Thank you, Betsy. I do not know that I could have borne it much longer."

"Nonsense. I know you too well," said Mrs. Arnold bracingly, not at all as though she had a headache. She paused for a a long moment, as though not quite certain how best to phrase what she wished to convey. Finally, and very quietly, she ventured, "Verity, I shall stand your friend whatever is said. You have but to tell me what I can do for you."

Verity gave a shaking laugh. "I doubt that anything can be done at this juncture."

There was enough truth in the flat words that Mrs. Arnold was left with nothing to say. She could only cover her friend's cold hand with hers and press Verity's fingers in mute sympathy. The remainder of the drive was completed in silence.

When the ladies disembarked from the carriage onto the gravel to go inside, Mrs. Arnold turned impulsively to Verity. She said urgently, "Come up to my room whenever you wish to unburden yourself, my dear. I shall be available to you whatever the hour."

"Thank you, Betsy. I shall remember." Verity managed a credible smile as they trod up the steps and entered the manor. The porter closed the front door and the ladies traversed the hall in silence.

At the bottom of the staircase, Mrs. Arnold paused. She spoke quietly so that the sleepy porter would not be alerted to their conversation. "Will you come sit with me now, Verity?"

Verity shook her head. "I-I would prefer to have time alone to reflect. My mind is in such a whirl."

"I understand, of course. Then I must wish you goodnight, my dear." Mrs. Arnold offered her a quick embrace. Verity clung to her friend for a moment, then laughed. "Don't make me cry, Betsy."

"Oh, bother! What a goose you are, Verity!" said Mrs. Arnold, also laughing with the glint of tears in her own eyes.

As they parted, they heard a quick, hard step. Both turned, and Mrs. Arnold gave a soft exclamation.

Fifteen

Lord Rathbone had come out of the library and he stood in the doorway, regarding them. His hand was still on the knob. He swept a cursory bow of acknowledgment to Mrs. Arnold, but his eyes immediately returned to Miss Worth's whitening face. "Mrs. Arnold, I would like a private word with Miss Worth."

Mrs. Arnold gasped in sheer indignation. She forgot the presence of the porter or the possibility of any other servants being about. "My lord! After tonight I wonder how you can dare!"

Verity touched her friend's arm. Her wide gray eyes were shadowed but calm. "Please, Betsy. I believe it is perhaps for the best that I grant his lordship's request."

Mrs. Arnold wavered, her expression one of doubt and misgiving. She faltered. "You must do as you think best, of course." She rounded on Lord Rathbone, flaring up once more. With awful sarcasm, she said, "I trust that his lordship shall act the gentleman!"

A little white about the mouth, Lord Rathbone bowed.

Mrs. Arnold accepted this assurance with obvious reluctance. She turned to Verity and kissed her cheek. "I shall wait for you in my room," she said meaningfully. With that, she turned and mounted the stairs.

"The sitting room, I think," said Lord Rathbone shortly. "I had just snuffed the candles in the library when I heard your voices, but I believe that a branch is still burning in the sitting room." He gestured politely and, without speaking or glancing up at his face as she passed, Verity preceded him into the room. Lord Rathbone entered and closed the door, shutting out the porter's sleepy curiosity.

A fire was still crackling lazily on the hearth in front of the heavy wooden settle. But neither Lord Rathbone nor Verity sought out the warmth. Instead they faced each other like enemies wary of one another's motives.

Verity felt color rise in her face under his lordship's intense scrutiny, but she did not drop her own gaze. It cost her a little to present a proud front, yet somehow she managed to still the shaking sensation she felt in all her limbs. She would not be the first to break silence, she thought rebelliously, for it was he who had requested this interview.

Finally, Lord Rathbone said, "I can do little more than apologize to you, Miss Worth. It was never my intention to make you the butt of ill-bred, malicious gossip."

"Was it not?" Verity's voice conveyed a sort of ironic curiosity that made him stiffen. "Then what was your intention, my lord? For your behavior these last weeks has certainly led me to that very conclusion."

"Miss Worth—Verity!"

He had taken a hasty step forward, his hand lifting toward her.

But at her raised palm, he stopped. He held himself very stiffly, not trusting himself nor his rapidly slipping control. "Believe me, my dear lady, not once did I entertain any such motive. I cannot explain to you why I—no! I can be honest enough with myself, and with you, to voice the truth."

He smiled then, but it was not the mocking, amused expression that was characteristic of him. His face was stern. "In all truth, my vanity was pricked, Miss Worth. I overheard a few scathing words uttered against my character that I could not let go nor forget. You brought yourself very firmly to my notice through your disapproval of my frippery person."

"And so you thought to teach me a lesson," said Verity

calmly. Her hands were now clasped tightly in front of her as though she would fly apart without the contact.

Lord Rathbone winced. It was noticeable even in the uncertain firelight that he had gone pale beneath his tan. "Yes."

"What was your object, my lord? That I should make a fool of myself over you, perhaps even to form a passion for you!" she asked. Her eyes were huge in her face, wide, fathomless gray pools that demanded the truth.

The admission was strangled in his throat. Nevertheless, he forced it out. "Yes."

"How much you must have hated me," she said, averting her head. She could no longer bear to look into his face. Her chest felt as though it would burst.

"No!"

The denial was explosive, immediate. She was so shocked by the violence inherent in his voice that her eyes snapped up to meet his. There was an intensity in his gaze that scorched her and she involuntarily took a backward step.

Recognizing the shadow of fear in her eyes, Lord Rathbone mastered his emotions. Very controlled, he said, "It was not hate. I have never felt that toward you."

Verity made a weary gesture. "Revenge, then. It is all one, is it not?" She started to turn away from him to the door.

He stepped swiftly forward and caught her arm before she could leave him. He spoke quickly, urgently. "It was I who has ended by making a fool of myself. Verity, I have used you abominably, I know. I swear to you that once I realized what I was doing to you in the eyes of the world, I never regretted anything more in my life."

"Regret?" She laughed then, disbelievingly.

She shook off his fingers as she rounded on him. Despair and fury alike blazed in her expression. "I am my lord's flirt. That is what they called me tonight. I could scarcely look anywhere for the shame that was thrust upon me." She was visibly trembling. She passed a hand over her eyes as though dazed. "Dear God. You have ruined me as surely as though I had been your mistress."

He rocked back as though he had suffered a body blow, as perhaps he had. "I . . . I infinitely regret—"

"Of what possible use it that to me, my lord?"

Verity shook her head violently, tears glittering in her eyes. "I have no patience for such selfish feeling. No, my lord! You would deny your self-centered motive in making your apologies to me tonight. But we both know better, do we not? I begged you to have a care toward me, for I knew what the outcome must be. You would not listen and now when it has all come to pass, you have finally come to your senses."

A nerve jumped in Lord Rathbone's tightly held jaw. "I know that I deserve your condemnation. Believe me, it could be not harsher than that which I hold for myself! I desire nothing more than to wipe the slate clean. You must believe that, Miss Worth."

Verity stared at him. She shook her head. "Your apologies are completely meaningless, my lord, for they arise out of guilt, not fellow feeling. You care for nothing and for no one but yourself and your own self-consequence."

He reached out for her hand, but at her gesture of revulsion, his own hand dropped. The hoarseness of his voice was strange to his own ears. "Verity, I care for you. I offer you my name. If you will accept me, you will do me greater honor than I deserve."

Astonishment held her still, but only for a moment. Then all of the despair and anger within welled up with such force that she felt suffocated. He dared—dared!—to mouth the lie. With all the strength at her command, she swung her hand. Her palm cracked against his face, leaving behind a reddened imprint.

Lord Rathbone stood as though turned to stone.

Verity did not wait for him to regain his self-possession. She brushed past him and opened the door. She swiftly crossed the hall to the staircase. She did not hesitate nor look back, but ran up the stairs.

Lord Rathbone stood where she had left him, shocked and sick. He had not even turned his head upon her exit. Now he turned slowly to the open door, about to leave the sitting room, when a stir of movement came to his ears. He swung around to face the shadowed room, alarmed that there should have been any witness to the encounter. He would not have any further mischief spread that would hurt Miss Worth.

"Who's there?" he called sharply, taking a step forward.

A portly figure rose and came round the end of the tall settle. Lord Rathbone pulled himself up sharply as he recognized his uncle by marriage. "Mr. Pettiforth!"

Mr. Pettiforth gravely regarded the viscount for a long, uncomfortable moment. He said finally, "Perhaps you would be so good as to close the door, my lord."

Lord Rathbone did as he was requested, feeling that he had somehow strayed into an unending nightmare that was turning darker and deeper with each passing moment.

He squared his shoulders as he turned back around to face the gentleman. His voice grating, he said, "You have overheard what passed between myself and Miss Worth."

Mr. Pettiforth nodded. "Aye. I had dozed off, you see, and by the time I had my wits about me again, I was in no mind to declare myself. The conversation that just took place explained much that has puzzled me of late. I wondered at the sly glances and the innuendos that were directed at Miss Worth, but she never confided in me. I had hoped that she would; now I regret that I did not press the matter."

Lord Rathbone felt his hands clench into hard fists. He said tightly, "I have behaved badly, sir. I have trespassed upon your hospitality and I have done a grave disservice to a member of your household. I hold myself solely responsible."

"Well said, my lord. It is a pity that pretty words cannot mend what has been so carelessly trampled. Slander is an insidious thing, my lord. Once established, it is difficult to eradicate," said Mr. Pettiforth.

"I would have done my best to mend the damage, but she would not grant me the right," said Lord Rathbone in a low voice. "As my wife, she would have had the protection of my name."

"But what else would she have, my lord?"

At the viscount's startled comprehension, Mr. Pettiforth slowly shook his head. "I think that under the circumstances this visit would best be terminated at once."

Lord Rathbone swallowed. He had never suffered such humiliation on top of humiliation. He bowed, maintaining his expressionless composure with difficulty. "Of course. I shall make arrangements for my immediate departure at first light."

He turned to go and had dropped his hand to the doorknob when Mr. Pettiforth's voice stopped him.

"Miss Worth is a distant relation of mine. She is of good family. `Tis a pity that you chose to trifle with one of her quality. Nephew you may be, Rathbone, but I shall not welcome you again to my home. I'll not have a libertine under my roof."

Without looking around, his pride and sense of honor completely stripped from him, Lord Rathbone left the sitting room.

Mr. Pettiforth glanced around the empty room and sighed. It had not been easy to order the viscount out of the house. But he had done so and he did not regret it. The unpleasant necessity was done.

He did not know what could be done for Miss Worth. He felt wholly to blame for the path that matters had taken for her under his roof. Her father had been a cherished friend and, in the beginning, he had been prepared to accept Miss Worth unconditionally on that account. But now he had come to treasure her as much for herself. It pained him that he had not had either the foresight or the fortitude to do something about the ugly tide that he had perceived to be gathering.

Mr. Pettiforth well knew that there was more unpleasantness to weather. It would be wonderful indeed if his spouse did not have something to say to him. She had never truly liked having Miss Worth brought into the house. He had known that, but he had hoped that she would eventually become reconciled. He had been encouraged that was in a fair way to happening, as Miss Worth had proved herself to be as diplomatic with Mrs. Pettiforth as she had been effective with his daughter.

Now that there had been talk coupling Miss Worth's name with that of the viscount, however, he doubted very much that Mrs. Pettiforth's grudging respect for Miss Worth would survive. She would not hold her tongue upon the matter, either. As for his daughter, Cecily, he was fairly certain that the girl would be enraged to hear that the gentleman whom she had considered hers to conquer had had his sights set on another lady.

Mr. Pettiforth knew himself for a man who disliked confrontation and contention. It was a failing in him, he saw now, that had eroded his authority in his own home. Rather than endure constant bickerings over what he had perceived as an ill-judged coddling of his eldest daughter, he had chosen to bite back all objections and allow Mrs. Pettiforth a free hand in the girl's upbringing. Only once had he stood firm and that had been in bringing Miss Worth into the household.

It had been a desperate measure, borne out of his pained awareness of his daughter's lack of character and the ruinous road that she was so firmly set upon. As much as he detested his daughter's spoiled ways and her tantrums, he had nevertheless loved her throughout.

His wish had been that Miss Worth's example and influence would make a difference in Cecily, but he had felt little actual hope. His surprise had been sharp when he saw that his daughter could actually be handled, even under the limitations that Mrs. Pettiforth's prerogatives had dictated.

Now, as he regretfully thought over all that had gone before, he wondered idly whether his daughter under different circumstances might yet be salvageable.

His mild visage became unexpectedly strengthened by the grim light of determination that entered his eyes. Yes, if he had learned nothing else through this unpleasant experience, it was that he must take an active role in his eldest daughter's life.

Mrs. Pettiforth would strenuously object to having her unchallenged authority curtailed. That was to be expected. He disliked very much the thought of the scene that would follow.

Nonetheless, he would do his best to rectify the matter. The sooner it was accomplished and his position understood, the sooner he would be comfortable again.

He would start the campaign to claim back his prerogatives as head of the household in the morning.

Sixteen

Verity longed for nothing more than to be able to throw herself across her bed and give in to a hearty bout of tears. But she was not allowed that indulgence. The maid who did up her fire had earlier offered to help her out of her finery and Verity had accepted with gratitude. The servantwoman had waited up to undress her and Verity felt it would be capricious to send the woman off. She had no choice but to submit to the maid's ministrations. Verity choked back her emotions, holding herself under the strictest control, and though she spoke with less than her usual warmth, she did not betray herself in front of the maid.

She was returning the maid's goodnight when there was a knock on the door. The maid opened the door and Mrs. Arnold came into the bedroom. "Verity, I am sorry to bother you at such a late hour. I hope that I may sit with you a few minutes?"

Verity sighed. She should have expected this visit, for she had known how reluctant Mrs. Arnold had been to leave her to a private conference with Lord Rathbone. She signaled the maid to leave them and then turned to her friend. "It was not necessary to come to me, Betsy. I am perfectly all right, as you can see."

"No, you are not," said Mrs. Arnold roundly. She put her arm about Verity and led her to the settee in front of the fire. "Why, your hands are like ice! I will not pry, dear one, but I am here if you wish to confide in me."

Verity sank down on the settee, Mrs. Arnold sitting down beside her. Verity shook her head, staring down at her hands in her lap. "Oh, Betsy. There is not much to tell, truly there is not. Lord Rathbone wished only to apologize."

There was a short silence in which Verity did not dare to look up, for fear that her friend would see the tears that stung her eyes. At last, Mrs. Arnold said in a carefully controlled voice, "And so he should have. Verity, my dear."

There was such tender sympathy in Mrs. Arnold's voice that Verity's tears slipped free. She buried her face in her hands and wept, while Mrs. Arnold held her in her arms and murmured soothing words.

It was several minutes before Verity regained control of herself. She straightened, avoiding her friend's anxious gaze, and dashed her hand across her eyes. "I am sorry, Betsy."

Mrs. Arnold produced a handkerchief so that Verity could dry her face. "Nonsense, dearest. A good cry was just the thing you needed. Now, what is to be done?"

Verity shook her head. She gave a feeble tickle of laughter. "I have no notion. I fear that I am quite sunk beyond reproach. Certainly whatever influence I once exerted over Miss Pettiforth is blasted. The girl is of such a jealous nature that the gossip shall set her into a foaming rage and she will set her face against me at every turn. Even beside that, my credit in this neighborhood is beyond repair, so either way my position here cannot now be one of long duration." Her voice thickened. "Nor would I wish it to be. I do not want to endure this injustice, Betsy!"

"Very proper sentiments," approved Mrs. Arnold. "Shall you return to Crofthouse, then?"

Verity stared at her companion in horror and dismay. "Why, I cannot. As I told you before, we shut up the house until Charles should return to England, for things were in such a state after Papa died that we could not maintain ourselves. Betsy, I—I am not certain what I shall do."

"Then you shall come home with me," said Mrs. Arnold

firmly. "no, listen to me for a moment, I pray you. You are quite correct in your assessment of your reputation. You have been ruined, at least in the eyes of most in this neighborhood. However, most of these personages are provincials. They have little influence and very likely few acquaintances in London circles, whereas I have a superfluity of both."

Mrs. Arnold took Verity's hands in hers, grasping them with the intensity of her feelings. "Verity, you mustn't flee and hide away in some out-of-the-way hole. I want you to hold your head high. I want you to stare down anyone who should dare question your integrity. I promise you, I shall be right there beside you. With my support and influence, any whispers that might follow us to London shall simply wither away."

"And what of Lord Rathbone? What shall I say when I meet his lordship?" asked Verity, closing her eyes despairingly.

"You shall give him a polite nod. You shall comment on the pleasant weather or . . . or the latest offering at the theater," said Mrs. Arnold fiercely. "You shall not wear your heart on your sleeve!"

Verity's eyes flew open. Startled, she stared at her friend. "How did you know?" she whispered.

Mrs. Arnold's eyes held an expression that was older than her years. "My dear. You are not the first woman to ever love a gentleman who is unworthy of you."

"Betsy, you?"

Mrs. Arnold shook her head. A smile teased at her lips and the sad expression vanished as though it had never been. "Perhaps there was a time. But not now. Now we are speaking of you. Verity, will you come? You must see that it would be for the best. You cannot go back to any of your family with Crofthouse closed and especially with this pall hanging over your head."

"No, no, I cannot," agreed Verity, as she thought how difficult it would be to hide away the hurt she felt from those who loved her best. "Very well, Betsy. I shall go to London with you. I only trust that neither of us shall regret it."

"I promise you that I shan't. And I mean to see that you do not," said Mrs. Arnold, rising from the settee. "Now you must go to bed and rest. I shall inform Mrs. Pettiforth in the morning that Herbert and I must take leave of her at last. I shall tell her, also, that I have invited you to return to London with me for an extended visit. I shall leave to you how you shall manage your own affairs, of course."

Verity rose and embraced her friend quickly. "Thank you, Betsy . . . for everything. I do not know what I would have done without you tonight, dearest of friends."

Mrs. Arnold smiled and crossed to the bedroom door. But before she quite reached it, it flew open with a crash. Mrs. Arnold was thrust back by a flying fury. She stumbled and fell to the floor, crying out more in surprise than from injury.

"Betsy!" Verity rushed forward, her hand outstretched, quick concern coming into her face.

Cecily Pettiforth had rushed into the bedroom, uncaring that she had knocked Mrs. Arnold aside. Her eyes glittered with rage. High spots of color stained her cheeks and her nose and mouth were pinched. When her darting eyes lighted on Verity, her bosom heaved. "You! You—you *hussy*! I shall scratch your eyes out this instant!"

With astonishment, Verity fell back as the girl flew at her. "Miss Pettiforth! *Cecily!*" She caught the girl's wrists as the girl's fingers raked at her eyes. "Cecily, pray get control of yourself!"

Mrs. Pettiforth had followed shortly on her daughter's heels and now added her pleas to Verity's, but to no avail. Miss Pettiforth was in the throes of the most furious passion of her life and no ordinary power could have turned her from her course. Her shrieks were heard throughout the wing and an audience quickly formed at the open door.

Miss Tibbs did not hesitate in the doorway, but marched across the bedroom. Taking hold of Miss Pettiforth's shoulder, she spun her around and smartly smacked the girl across the cheek. Miss Pettiforth's furious tirade was stopped in midstream as she stared in shock at her former governess.

"That will be enough of that, Cecily. We will have no more of your nonsense this night, if you please," said Miss Tibbs quellingly.

"Miss Tibbs!" exclaimed Mrs. Pettiforth, shocked. Miss Pettiforth dissolved into racking sobs and at once turned into her mother's protective arms. "There, there, dearest one. Mama is here."

Miss Tibbs looked at an obviously badly shaken Verity. "Are you quite all right, Miss Worth?"

Verity straightened, saying uncertainly, "I believe so. But Mrs. Arnold! I must see to her!"

However, Mrs. Arnold was already back on her feet. Some of the other ladies who had stood about the doorway had come forward to help her up, all the while questioning her on what had happened. Most had obviously just returned to the house, their ball gowns sadly crushed. Some had already put off their finery and were attired in dressing gowns. The contrast spoke volumes of the keen interest generated by Miss Pettiforth's hysterical screams.

As Verity joined them, Mrs. Arnold was repeating again what she had already said. "I was wishing Miss Worth good night. She had been good enough to see me back here when I was taken with the headache. Miss Pettiforth attacked me and then she flew after Miss Worth, who had remonstrated with her and tried to help me to my feet."

Several of the ladies gasped and all shook their heads. "How extraordinary! The girl must be touched in her upper works," said one, and others nodded.

"Oh no, no!" exclaimed Verity. "Of course, she is not. Miss Pettiforth is high-strung certainly, but—"

"It is good of you to defend her, Miss Worth. But I for one have heard and seen enough tonight to quite decide me that the girl wants schooling," pronounced an older dame. A full sleeping cap covered her head and the laces that trimmed it quivered with the lady's indignation. "Why, my dear Miss Worth, it was that baggage that precipitated the most monstrous tale concerning you this very evening."

"I do not think the girl was the first to set it about," objected one lady judiciously. "Though I will say this, once she had hold of the tale she could not stop talking about it!"

"Tale?" faltered Verity. She was suddenly the focus of several pairs of eyes and felt ready to sink.

"Indeed! Did nothing of it come to your ears, Miss Worth?" asked one lady rather maliciously.

"As point of fact, I informed Miss Worth of the details myself when I came to visit her," said Mrs. Arnold. "I assure you, she was just as shocked by it as I was. There is not a bit of truth in it, of course."

"Miss Pettiforth has always been a somewhat jealous and capricious young lady," interjected Miss Tibbs. "In the past, her nature has led her to believe even those things of her own making." Miss Tibbs had spoken as though only to herself, but her words were heard by several of those standing about. Sharp glances were sent her way, but the governess seemed quite insensitive to them.

"I have heard before much the same thing from my sister, Lady Redding," said one lady thoughtfully to her companion. "You know her, of course, Tilly. We attended a small turtle dinner at her invitation not two weeks past. It seems that my niece, Camilla, and a few other young ladies of the surrounding county have often been the object of Miss Pettiforth's little jealousies."

The lady's companion frowned and nodded. "Yes, I seem to recall that there was an expression of relief that Miss Worth had been able to curb Miss Pettiforth to a small extent. How extraordinary!"

"If there is anything that one might do—"

"Thank you, ma'am," said Miss Tibbs firmly. "However, I believe that Mrs. Pettiforth and I shall be well able to handle the matter. I know that Mrs. Pettiforth would not wish to burden any one of you. And indeed, I would be remiss in upholding her standard of hospitality if I did not urge you to return to your beds."

Murmuring, their heads together, the ladies began to reluctantly disperse. One or two bid Verity good night, a courtesy that she was amazed to receive.

When all had gone, Mrs. Arnold said cynically, "And thus it goes. You may not need to leave the vicinity after all, my dear. Before the night is over, this entire unpleasantness will be seen simply as the work of a thoughtless, spoiled little beauty."

"Not entirely," said Miss Tibbs softly with a significant glance. Mrs. Arnold and Verity, following the direction of her gaze, took the governess's meaning. The lady of the house was still attempting to soothe her wildly weeping daughter and had paid no attention to what else had happened during the past several minutes.

"I had forgotten that small detail. Never mind, Verity. We shall simply go on as we had decided," said Mrs. Arnold, sighing.

Miss Tibbs saw that her three young charges had crept to the door and were all staring, wide-eyed, at their elder sister, who was still carrying on with almost unabated unrestraint. "Come, my dears. Say your good nights to Mrs. Arnold and Miss Worth. I am certain that they shall be very glad to have all of this excitement done with so that they may also return to their beds."

"You are an intelligent woman, Miss Tibbs," said Mrs. Arnold dryly.

"Miss Tibbs!"

The imperative stopped both the governess and Mrs. Arnold from exiting. Mrs. Pettiforth had at last emerged from her absorption with her eldest daughter. She said coldly, "You will take my poor Cecily to her bedroom and see that she is comfortably settled, Miss Tibbs."

Mrs. Pettiforth then turned a full glare on Verity. "I have a few choice words that I wish to say to Miss Worth which will not wait for morning."

"Now you are in for it, my dear."

Verity did not know which of her friends had uttered the soft conviction, but she very much agreed with its sentiments. She thought wearily that it would be a wonder if she managed to survive the remainder of this awful nightmarish night.

"Certainly, Mrs. Pettiforth," said Miss Tibbs coolly. "I must trust that the other daughters of the house will manage without me."

Mrs. Arnold took charge of the younger girls. "Come along, girls. You shall show me the nursery. It will be very much a nostalgic treat for me, you know, for I am quite ancient."

"Are you really? You don't at all show it," said Dorothy frankly, looking the lady over very carefully.

"What a precious your are! I quite think that we shall be the best of friends," said Mrs. Arnold, leading the girls away.

Meanwhile Miss Tibbs had persuaded Miss Pettiforth to let go of her clutching hold on her parent and was forthrightly guiding that sobbing damsel from the bedroom. Miss Tibbs nodded to Verity as she passed her, but said not a word.

"Pray close the door, Miss Worth," said Mrs. Pettiforth in freezing accents.

Verity did as she was bid and then turned to go over to one of the chairs before the fire. She gestured politely to the settee as might a gracious hostess.

High color flew up into Mrs. Pettiforth's face and she flounced over to the settee with ill grace. "Now, Miss Worth! We come to it, you and I," she said awfully.

Verity looked at her employer. Nothing showed in her expression but polite interest. "Do we, ma'am?"

"Do not play the innocent with me, miss! *I* heard the whispers tonight, as did my poor baby. It is no wonder that she went into hysterics! You have betrayed my trust, Miss Worth!"

"That I have not. I have endeavored to encourage Miss Pettiforth to put forward her best manner," said Verity.

Mrs. Pettiforth flung up her hand. "Pray spare me, Miss Worth! If it was not for you, my dearest lamb would at this moment be celebrating her engagement to Viscount Rathbone! But you had to ruin all! Spinning your wiles and casting sheep's eyes at his lordship, I do not doubt! Well, you have been found out, my dear Miss Worth, and now you must pay the piper. The consequences shall be dire, I promise you!"

Verity shook her head. "If only you would listen to me, ma'am. Your daughter is undisciplined and completely uncaring of what it means to be the lady of a grand house. Pray believe me when I say that Lord Rathbone would never have offered for Miss Pettiforth regardless of—"

"How dare you!" Mrs. Pettiforth rose abruptly and glared down at Verity. "You dare to cast aspersions upon my innocent dear whilst you went about seducing his lordship. I shall have you out of my house, Miss Worth. Do you hear me?"

Verity found that she also was standing. She was trembling with the strength of her feelings. "I hear you very well, Mrs. Pettiforth! And believe me, nothing could gratify me more than to shake the dust of this place from my feet. I have suffered unjust persecution and slander in this house. Unfortunately, I am too well-bred to throw at your head a few home truths, but know this much, cousin! Your ambition has poisoned your eldest daughter. Unless she is curbed and brought under rein, you will never realize the advantageous marriage that you so desire for her."

"I have heard quite enough." Mrs. Pettiforth surged toward the door. She turned. "You will pack your bags and leave within the hour. I will give orders to have a carriage readied to convey you to the village."

"Do you not intend to set me afoot, madame?" asked Verity, her eyes glittering, holding herself proudly.

Mrs. Pettiforth drew herself up, affronted. "I hope that I am not a vengeful person, Miss Worth!" She wrenched open the door and exited, slamming the door behind her.

Seventeen

Verity sank down on the chair, numbed by what had passed. She could scarcely think, except that it seemed imperative that she rise and dress and collect her belongings. But still she stared about the bedroom, apparently unable to put herself into motion.

At length, she rose. How much later, she did not know. Slowly, she changed her attire. Her fingers were fumbling and it was difficult to do up the tiny buttons on the back of her dress, but she managed most of them. Then she pulled out of the wardrobe her portmanteau and her bandboxes.

The task of packing seemed insurmountable to her in her shocked state. But as she started, it seemed that the very activity warmed her mind and limbs and she began working faster and faster. Yes, she would leave this house! As quickly as possible. She would leave the Pettiforths far behind. And Lord Rathbone, as well!

Her mind was filled with all that had gone before and every word, every action, loomed ever larger in her recollection. By the end, she was throwing garments and possessions into her baggage almost in a frenzied manner. Tears streamed down her face, but no sound issued forth from her mouth for she would not allow the pain that squeezed up through her chest to announce itself to the rest of the house.

As she tightened the last strap on her luggage, there came a soft scratching at the door. Verity stilled. She swiped swiftly at her face. She still had her pride. No one must know the depth of her pain.

She went to the door and opened it a crack.

A footman stood outside. "I am to carry down your baggage, miss," he said woodenly.

Without a word, Verity opened the door wide. She watched the man pick up her small chest and bandboxes. Then she put on her pelisse and followed him out of the bedroom without a backward glance.

The house was darkened except for the branch of candles that the butler held high over his head for the footman and the young woman so that they would not stumble on the stairs.

As Miss Worth passed him, the butler glanced sharply at her pale, composed face. Miss Worth had been popular with the staff. The butler had had his orders and, even misliking them, he would carry them out. The butler had a shrewd notion that the master of the house did not have an inkling of what was taking place that night. A pity, that. Perhaps in the morning when he saw the master, it would not be beyond the scope of his duties to let drop a word about the strange happenings of this night.

Verity was ushered outside. A carriage stood waiting. Her baggage was strapped to the back and she climbed up into the body. At once the carriage jerked forward.

Verity shut her eyes. She was glad for the dark interior. Not that there was anyone to observe her, for which she was most thankful. But what she felt was more akin to the darkness than it would ever have been to the light of day.

The drive into the village was accomplished in what seemed a very short time. She was set down at the inn, her baggage was placed beside her, and the Pettiforth carriage turned around and drove away.

The innkeeper had come sleepily from his bed upon hearing the rattle of wheels in the yard and now he regarded the young lady standing alone at the door of his inn with not a little curiosity. He had recognized the Pettiforth carriage, as he did the young lady. She had arrived on the mail, to his recollection, and had been collected by that same carriage.

Rumor had it that a companion had been engaged for that pesky Miss Pettiforth, and now here the young lady stood. The innkeeper shook his head regretfully. That was the way of it. Hired one day and let go the next.

"May I help ye, miss?"

Verity turned a startled face. She blinked and passed a hand before her eyes, as though coming awake. "Yes. Yes, you can. Is there a room available?"

The realization suddenly burst upon her that she had very little in her purse. She had not yet been paid by Mr. Pettiforth that quarter and most of last quarter's salary had been sent to her mother for Elizabeth's care. "At least . . . no, perhaps it would be best to ask instead when the next coach comes through?"

"Not until six of the clock, miss," said the innkeeper. He saw the dismay and the shadow of fear and uncertainty in her eyes. "Perhaps you would be wanting to sit on the settle in front of the fire for a bit, miss? Just until you decide what you will be doing?"

"Yes, thank you. It-it is quite cold tonight, is it not?"

The innkeeper murmured agreement. "Just go right in, miss. I'll be bringing your things." As the young lady passed into the inn, the innkeeper picked up her pitifully few belongings. He weighed the boxes and portmanteau in his hands and swore softly. He misdoubted that he was too kindhearted for his own good, but he would allow the young lady to sleep on the settle for free. She was obviously quality and from all that he had heard in recent weeks, she had gone a fair way to curbing that testy Miss Pettiforth's distempered freaks. A pity, it was. A real pity, he thought, shaking his head as he stumped into the inn.

Verity was roused by a gentle shaking of her shoulder. She opened her eyes, confused by what she saw. A great hearth was directly before her gaze and a large woman was blowing the fire into existence. Verity frowned. Then memory came rushing back and she sat up abruptly.

"There ye be, miss. I thought ye should be wakened, seeing

as how the coach will be getting here in half an hour," said a female voice.

Verity looked up. Automatically her hands rose to smooth her hair. A short-dumpy woman stood over her, regarding her with mingled curiosity and pity. "Would ye be wanting a cup of hot tea, miss? To take the chill off, like." The woman held out a teacup and saucer.

"Thank-thank you," Verity stammered, flushing. She realized that she had fallen asleep and slept the night through on the bare wooden settle. The hard bench had left aches where she had not known before that she had muscles.

As she sipped the hot tea, she took stock of her surroundings. The inn was somewhat shabby in appearance, but had obviously at one time enjoyed quite a custom. Her predicament was much like that. She had very little money and nowhere to go.

Verity realized for the first time that she had not even thought of appealing to Mrs. Arnold before she had been driven off in the Pettiforth's carriage. She knew that if Mrs. Arnold had been made aware of her eviction, she could have counted upon Betsy to help her. But that was past. What mattered more was what she was to do now.

Verity thought about it for several minutes. Her brain seemed to be working with unusual clarity. Verity decided that what she had done was for the best, after all. She should not expect Mrs. Arnold to burden herself with her problems. No, it would even be best if she did not seek to join Mrs. Arnold on the road to London.

Verity asked for paper and pen and ink. When they were brought to her, she penned a short note to Mrs. Arnold to briefly explain her feelings. Then she hesitated, wondering what to put down next.

But if she was not to go to London, then where? Verity soon had the answer to that, as well, and she scrawled it down swiftly. Crofthouse. True, it had been closed up and the servants discharged, but there were still the retainers in residence and one room could be opened again for her use. She would go home.

As she sanded the sheet, she reflected that she would have hours while she rode in the coach to think of a way to solve the dilemma of how she was now going to take care of the expense of her sister's seminary.

Her mind made up at last, Verity rose and shook out her wrinkled skirts. She went over to the short dumpy woman to return the emptied cup. "How much do I owe for the use of the settle and the tea, please?"

The short dumpy woman cocked her head. "Why, as to that, I'm sure I don't know. And I haven't time to figure it none, either, for there is the coach. Now ye best be getting the ticket, miss. Me husband is already handing up ye're bags. Good luck to ye, miss."

Verity thanked the woman and the innkeeper for the unexpected kindness and gave her note into their care to be delivered that same morning to Mrs. Arnold at the Pettiforths. Then she climbed into the mail coach. She squeezed past two farmers' wives, who did not interrupt their conversation about prime egg layers one jot as she did so.

Verity closed her eyes and her ears, sighing. It would be a long, long ride. How very glad she was that she was going home. She could not understand in the least why she was choking back tears.

Lord Rathbone did not breakfast at the Pettiforths'. He left at first light, driving himself away in his own vehicle, his valet up beside him. He did not glance back at the manor.

Somewhat later a boy on a broken-down cob trotted up to the manor and put into the hands of a footman the note from Miss Worth. Miss Pettiforth happened to be passing through the hall when she overheard the footman report the note to the butler, and that it was from Miss Worth to Mrs. Arnold.

Miss Pettiforth turned instantly round to the servants. She held out an imperious hand. "Give it to me, please. I shall see that it is properly disposed of."

The butler hesitated for a fraction of a second. He did not care for the hard look in the miss's eyes, nor the white line about her mouth, both signs that she was in a proper temper. But he had little choice except to do as he was ordered. He gave the note into Miss Pettiforth's hand, whereupon she dismissed him and the footman to attend to their duties.

Miss Pettiforth waited until the servants had left the hall.

Then she tore the note across, and across again, before dropping the ragged pieces into the wastebasket. Without a backward glance, she went on into the breakfast room.

If she had looked back, she might have realized that she had not been as alone as she had thought. Sophronia had watched her sister's odd behavior from the landing. When Miss Pettiforth had disappeared into the breakfast room, Sophronia ran lightly down the stairs and retrieved the torn pieces out of the wastebasket. She escaped back upstairs with her treasure to the nursery, where she could examine it without running the risk of being discovered by her eldest sister.

When Mrs. Arnold came down to breakfast, she found her host and hostess, Miss Pettiforth, and a few others already at the table. She greeted them all, her eyes sweeping the breakfast room for one particular face.

"I do not see Miss Worth. Did she breakfast earlier?" she asked.

Mrs. Pettiforth's expression stiffened. "Miss Worth has left us, Mrs. Arnold. She will not soon be returning."

Mr. Pettiforth looked across at his wife, a frown coming into his face.

"But—!" Mrs. Arnold bit back the remainder of her exclamation. She could well read the malicious satisfaction in her hostess's eyes and the sudden flare of curiosity that ran around the breakfast room. The scene played out in Miss Worth's bedroom had been witnessed by nearly a dozen women, some of whom had conveyed the details to their spouses. Quite a number of people had gone to bed trading speculations on just what had been transpiring the last few weeks in the Pettiforth house. Angered, and having guessed correctly that Mrs. Pettiforth had given Verity her marching orders, Mrs. Arnold yet did not wish to create just the sort of scene guaranteed to be memorable.

She smiled and shook her head. "I see that Miss Worth has stolen a march on me. She had mentioned to me, of course, that she had a few things she wished to attend to before joining me in London. Mr. Arnold and I must leave for London this morning, so I shall take leave of you now, Mrs. Pettiforth."

A stupefied expression came over Mrs. Pettiforth's face. She made a feeble attempt to dissuade, but Mrs. Arnold overrode all protest with a charming manner that was nevertheless inexorable.

As she placed her napkin on the table, having consumed a light repast of biscuits and tea, Mrs. Arnold commented, "I shall be so glad to have Miss Worth make an extended visit with me. We shall shop and go to the theater and have all manner of amusement. I vow it will be very like old times."

Miss Pettiforth looked green at the thought of her former mentor enjoying such high treats.

"Have you known Miss Worth long, then?" asked a dame with lifted brows.

"Oh yes. We were in seminary together and came out the same season. Miss Worth became engaged immediately, whilst I did not accept an offer until four months later," said Mrs. Arnold.

"Miss Worth was engaged? Then why has she never wed?" asked Mrs. Pettiforth, seemingly doing a reassessment of the lady in question.

"It was such a tragic thing. Her fiancé was killed in the Peninsular. He was Chard's heir. I believe that Verity is still on very good terms with the family, for she was a particular favorite of the earl and the countess," said Mrs. Arnold.

She saw that the information that she had deliberately let drop was having its inevitable effect. Several expressions reflected startled respect. In their minds, Miss Worth was going through a metamorphosis from being an unimportant individual of dependent gentility to that of a young lady with influential social connections. Satisfied that she had done much to undermine the validity of the slander that had so pained her friend, Mrs. Arnold rose from the table with the request that a message be sent round to the stables for her carriage to be made ready.

"Of course, Mrs. Arnold. I shall arrange it myself," said Mr. Pettiforth quietly. He also rose. "In fact, I will bear you company and attend to it now, for I should like to say good-bye to Mr. Arnold."

Mrs. Arnold was surprised, but she graciously assented. "That is very kind of you, Mr. Pettiforth. He is above stairs just now changing out of his hunting attire. He had gone out with his fowling piece quite early this morning."

"Yes, of course. A sportsman will make the most of the time," said Mr. Pettiforth. He escorted Mrs. Arnold out of the breakfast room and across the hall. At the bottom of the steps, he quietly requested a short word with her.

Mrs. Arnold, her foot already on the first step, looked up at him without undue surprise. "Of course, sir."

Mr. Pettiforth was frowning. "Mrs. Arnold, you are Miss Worth's friend. I know that she would not have left without a word to me or to anyone. Miss Worth is not a capricious young woman."

"No, she is not. Mr. Pettiforth, I am as puzzled as you. Yet, perhaps a little less so." Mrs. Arnold studied his face, wondering how much she could say without giving offense. "Mr. Arnold, you are aware of the rumors that were set about at the ball?"

His expression hardened, "Yes, indeed. I know also that those rumors were lies. Miss Worth was not to be held at fault."

"So I know, also. But others held quite a different opinion. Miss Pettiforth, in particular, was very much overcome by the things that were being bandied about," said Mrs. Arnold.

Mr. Pettiforth regarded her silently for a long moment. "Did something occur last night between my daughter and Miss Worth, ma'am?"

"I visited Miss Worth in her bedroom a few minutes after we returned from the ball. I had just bid her good night when Miss Pettiforth came into the room." Mrs. Arnold paused fractionally. "Miss Pettiforth was in the throes of hysterics."

"I see. And Mrs. Pettiforth?"

"She could do nothing with Miss Pettiforth. It was left to Miss Tibbs to calm the girl. Miss Tibbs, Miss Pettiforth, and I left Miss Worth's bedroom at your wife's request," said Mrs. Arnold. She looked searchingly into her host's face, hoping that he had understood all that she suspected and had left unsaid.

Apparently he had, for Mr. Pettiforth took hold of her hand and bowed over her fingers. "Thank you, Mrs. Arnold. You have perfectly explained exactly what I wished to know," said Mr. Pettiforth. "I will send word for your carriage to be brought round. Pray give my regards to your husband. If you would be so kind to join me in my library for a moment before you depart, I should like to entrust to your care a letter and a cheque for Miss Worth. Her departure was made so hurriedly that she neglected to collect the reimbursement I was to make to her for taking her away from Lady Worth at this difficult time."

"Of course, Mr. Pettiforth. I will be glad to be of such service to you," said Mrs. Arnold.

They parted on excellent terms.

Eighteen

Mr. Pettiforth sent word to the stable and then returned to the breakfast room. As he entered, the butler was in the act of handing a folded note to Mrs. Pettiforth.

Mrs. Pettiforth unfolded the sheet. She read the few penned words, her countenance growing ever more aghast. She fell back in her chair with an expression of disbelieving horror. "Lord Rathbone has gone!"

Miss Pettiforth shrieked. "What! I do not believe you! He could not possibly!" Miss Pettiforth snatched the note from her mother's limp fingers and read it in her turn. "No! He cannot have left. It is a horrid hoax. I shan't believe it! I shan't!"

Mr. Pettiforth had sat down again at the table and was calmly cutting his steak. Mrs. Pettiforth rounded on him, repeating the tidings in strident accents. "What do you think of that?" she demanded.

Mr. Pettiforth looked across the table at his wife, his expression one of mild surprise. "Why, nothing. Indeed, why should I? Lord Rathbone conveyed his intentions to me last night before you and our daughter had returned from the ball. He had formed the desire to return to London and informed me that he was taking immediate departure this morning."

Miss Pettiforth uttered another, more penetrating, shriek.

The others of the company began to furtively eye the door. "Never could abide a female given to distempered freaks," muttered one gentleman uncomfortably.

Mr. Pettiforth glanced at his daughter in patent disapproval. "If you cannot conduct yourself in a more moderate fashion, young lady, I shall request you to remove yourself to the schoolroom."

"Oh, well done!" exclaimed the gentleman. He than glanced around guiltily as he realized that he had spoken quite loud. But no one particularly noticed, being too interested in what was transpiring.

Upon her father's pronouncement, Miss Pettiforth's mouth had opened. No sound came forth, however, even though hot color surged into her cheeks. She stared at her father. Apparently comprehending that he meant what he had said, she subsided with uncharacteristic meekness.

"But why would dear Lord Rathbone rush off in such a precipitate manner?" wailed Mrs. Pettiforth. She had retrieved his lordship's curt note and had been rereading it with an effort to understand what might be between the lines.

"I fancy Rathbone remained longer than he intended. The hunting was excellent, of course," said one gentleman, nodding to Mr. Pettiforth.

"Indeed, I expected him to leave much earlier. It was my understanding that house parties in the country are not his lordship's usual fare," said a lady.

"No, by God! Nor mine, come to think of it," discovered one of the gentlemen. "Pettiforth, it has been a dashed good stay. Excellent country and all that. But I must cut my visit short. Other obligations, you know."

Mr. Pettiforth indicated that he understood perfectly. He wished his departing guest a pleasant journey. That seemed to signal the end of the house party and the other guests also extended their gratitude for the hospitality. Mrs. Pettiforth said all that was proper, though with a somewhat distracted air.

When the door shut behind the last personage, only the Pettiforths and their daughter remained in the breakfast room. "Well, my dear lady, it seems that our house party comes to an end at last," said Mr. Pettiforth happily.

"Yes, and how disappointing it has been, too. I had hopes that—"

Mrs. Pettiforth cast a glance at the footman who had entered to slowly clear some of the empty serving dishes on the sideboard and finished lamely, "Well, I mean to say it is all very odd. Lord Rathbone is, after all, my nephew and I should think I could have expected more of him." Mrs. Pettiforth held her silence for as long as she was able before exclaiming, "Leave them, man!"

The footman correctly interpreted his mistress's glare and quickly exited.

Mrs. Pettiforth leaned forward across the table, her eyes fixed on her husband's in an intent manner. "Dear Mr. Pettiforth, did his lordship say anything to *you* before he left?"

Miss Pettiforth had been sitting in a sullen posture, but at her mother's question she snapped upright, her expression alert and avid.

"Regarding what, my dear?" asked Mr. Pettiforth mildly.

"My hand, of course, Papa!" exclaimed Miss Pettiforth, contemptuous of her father's obtuseness.

Mr. Pettiforth bent a baleful look on her. "You want manners, my girl. Such disrespect toward an elder is uncomely in any young person. I see that I have allowed you to be too much spoiled. Every governess ever engaged for you failed to impress the importance of self-control upon you. Miss Worth was obviously unable to curb your willfulness, as well. I regret the necessity, of course, but I shall not ask Miss Worth to return to us at the end of her visit to Mrs. Arnold."

A swift tide of color rose in the beauty's face. Her bosom heaving with the force of her outraged emotions, she said stormily, "I am glad! I am glad to be rid of her. She tried to steal Lord Rathbone from me!" Her eyes flashed and it seemed certain that she was about to deliver herself of further opinions when her mother hastily spoke up.

"That is quite enough, Cecily. Not but what it might be altogether too true, but we shall not speak of it," said Mrs. Pettiforth, patting her daughter's arm. Miss Pettiforth pulled away with a petulant frown.

Satisfied that her daughter was, for the moment at least, unlikely to break into a tiresome tirade, Mrs. Pettiforth turned to her husband. "Indeed, Mr. Pettiforth, I think it best that Miss Worth is let go. She has stirred up considerable gossip, which I heard from any number of people last night, as I am sure you did, as well."

"I trust that you, too, are too intelligent to have been taken in by such jealousies, my dear wife," said Mr. Pettiforth with a straight look.

Mrs. Pettiforth stared. She stammered uncertainly, "Of course, Mr. Pettiforth. I trust I am not such a ninny to believe every tittle tattle."

Miss Pettiforth was astonished by her mother's inconsistency. "But you know that it was true, Mama! You agreed with me last night as we came home that it was all so very horrid and tawdry."

Mrs. Pettiforth was made acutely uncomfortable at what else might be let drop by her daughter's impulsive tongue. The previous night she had not seen any necessity in informing Mr. Pettiforth that she had ordered Miss Worth from the house, having made the sublime assumption that he would be thankful to have the focus of such gossip gone and would ask no questions. Now in the face of his grave declaration she realized that she was perilously close to offending him. Too late, she recalled that Miss Worth was the daughter of Mr. Pettiforth's favorite cousin and that Mr. Pettiforth had always displayed an inexplicable liking for the young woman. She frowned deeply at her daughter. "Enough, Cecily. You put me to the blush."

"It is plain to me that what Cecily lacks is a bit of polish," said Mr. Pettiforth.

At her mother's reproof a hasty retort had sprung to Miss Pettiforth's lips, but at her father's words, the anger in her narrowed gaze became suddenly arrested. Her eyes grew bright as she leaped to a welcome conclusion. The mutiny in her expression disappeared, to be replaced by a dazzling smile.

At last, she was going to be brought out in London.

Her lips parted as visions of dizzying prospects unfolded in her head. "Oh, dearest Papa! That *is* so! A little polish is precisely what I do need. Then I will know just how to go on and I won't displease you anymore."

"I am glad that you agree, daughter. I shall write to a most exclusive seminary this very morning to let the headmistress know when to expect you. As I understand, it is a strict establishment that guarantees to turn out well-behaved young ladies," said Mr. Pettiforth.

With one outraged glare of disbelief, Miss Pettiforth fell promptly into hysterics. She snatched up a plate and wildly slung it through the air, smashing it against the opposite wall.

"*Cecily!* Mr. Pettiforth, pray—! No, no, *not* the tea!"

Amidst the fury of screams and implorings and the smashing of flying crockery, Mr. Pettiforth got up from the table and calmly walked out of the breakfast room. It had gone very well, indeed, he thought contentedly. He was at last master in his own house.

Mr. Pettiforth repaired to his library. There he wrote out the letter and cheque for Miss Worth and enclosed them together. As he was engaged in this, a knock sounded upon the door. At his call, the door was opened. Mr. Pettiforth, rising from his chair and expecting to greet Mrs. Arnold, was surprised when Miss Tibbs and his second eldest daughter entered.

"Why, Miss Tibbs! And Sophronia. What is this?"

He walked around the desk and placed an affectionate hand upon his daughter's shoulder. She glanced up fleetingly, a shadow of anxiety in her eyes, and Mr. Pettiforth frowned. "Is there something that I should know about, Miss Tibbs?"

"Indeed there is, sir. Sophronia shall tell you about it herself," said Miss Tibbs.

The girl cast up another glance, this time at her governess. Miss Tibbs nodded encouragement. Sophronia circled the toe of her slipper on the carpet. "I found a note from Miss Worth, Papa."

"Did you, indeed! You must tell me about it. Have you got it now?"

Mr. Pettiforth was astonished when Miss Tibbs handed into his hand several shredded pieces of paper. Then as he listened to Sophronia's story, he turned to the desk and began to match the pieces together much in the manner of a puzzle. "Yes, it is from Miss Worth and it is addressed to Mrs. Arnold. There is no need to be in a quake, child. You did quite right, Sophronia. Now I shall see that Mrs. Arnold receives it. She is to come to see me presently."

"Then we shall not keep your further, sir," said Miss Tibbs. She and the girl started to leave.

"Miss Tibbs. A moment, if you please," said Mr. Pettiforth.

Sophronia looked up in question, but Miss Tibbs said, "You may wait for me outside in the hall, Sophronia."

Reluctantly, the girl did as she was bid. She knew very well that something of import was in the wind. Her father wore a most unusually grave expression.

When the door slowly closed, Mr. Pettiforth addressed the governess. "Miss Tibbs, my daughter Cecily will shortly be journeying to a seminary in the wilds of Yorkshire. I do not wish Mrs. Pettiforth to tire herself with such a trip. I hope that I may impose upon you to undertake that journey with Miss Pettiforth to see that she is safely ensconced in that establishment. In addition, I would like you to act as my deputy to the headmistress. I repose the fullest confidence in your ability to convey to that lady the particulars of Miss Pettiforth's character and upbringing, and my hopes for her education."

"I understand you perfectly, sir. I shall be happy to be of assistance, of course. I shall inform Nurse that all of the girls will be in her care until my return," said Miss Tibbs. She coughed delicately. "Er . . . when shall I expect to leave, sir?"

"I am writing the letter today. Miss Pettiforth will be ready to leave upon the return acknowledgment," said Mr. Pettiforth quietly.

Miss Tibb's light blue eyes rounded. There was a good deal of astonishment as well as respect in her expression. "Very good, sir."

There came a light tap on the door, followed immediately by its opening. Mrs. Arnold entered, but paused upon seeing the governess. "Forgive me, Mr. Pettiforth. I did not know that I was intruding."

"Not at all, Mrs. Arnold. Miss Tibbs has merely conveyed to my hand a note discovered to be from Miss Worth to you," said Mr. Pettiforth.

Upon Mrs. Arnold's exclamation and drawing nearer, Miss Tibbs quietly effaced herself from the room.

Mrs. Arnold stared down at the mutilated note, then turned her puzzled glance on Mr. Pettiforth. "But I do not understand."

"Perhaps I should explain that the note passed first through Miss Pettiforth's hands," said Mr. Pettiforth, his face flushing ruddily.

"Oh!" Mrs. Arnold understood, but she did not voice her sympathy for the gentleman. It would be more gracious not to do so. She turned her attention to the contents of the short note and exclaimed in astonishment. "Verity means to return to Crofthouse! But it is shut up and Lady Worth is gone from there. Oh, the foolish girl!"

"I was not aware of this. Surely Miss Worth would not place herself in such a spot," said Mr. Pettiforth, disturbed.

"Oh, would she not, indeed! I know just what it is. She has taken some prideful, silly notion into her head that she cannot bring her troubles to me. Well, I shall soon disabuse her of that," declared Mrs. Arnold, sweeping the shreds of the note into her reticule.

"What do you mean to do?"

"I shall follow her to Crofthouse. And once I have given her a thundering scold, I shall carry her off to London with me and make certain that she is positively raddled with amusements," said Mrs. Arnold in vigorous tones.

Mr. Pettiforth chuckled. "I believe that you will, indeed. Here is the letter and the cheque for Miss Worth that I promised to you earlier. Thank you, Mrs. Arnold."

"I shall see that she has them safely, sir."

Mr. Pettiforth gallantly escorted Mrs. Arnold to the front door and she took final leave of him on the outside steps.

Mr. Arnold was waiting to hand his wife up into the carriage, but he paused to say his good-byes to his host. "Must express my appreciation for a smashing time, Pettiforth. I got a brace this morning and I've left them with your cook."

Mr. Pettiforth was gratified and assured Mr. Arnold that he would be welcome to return at any time.

Mrs. Arnold shuddered at the prospect as she glanced toward the open front door. She saw nothing of Mrs. Pettiforth or the eldest daughter, for which she was thankful. She had waited tolerantly, her expression one of smiling good humor, during the exchange and her patience was soon rewarded.

"Ready, my dear?"

"Thank you, yes." With a brilliant smile, she gave one hand

into her husband's and with the other caught up her skirt. Mrs. Arnold climbed up into her carriage, followed by Mr. Arnold. The driver snapped his whip and the equipage rolled away down the drive.

Nineteen

It was a dismal homecoming for Verity. It was sleeting and cold when she descended from the mail coach. She was cold and hungry and tired, but she considered herself fortunate that the coach did make a regular stop in the village that she had known all of her life. Since she was well-known by the proprietor of the small inn, she was able to arrange for a carriage to Crofthouse on what little remained in her purse.

The innkeeper's curiosity was naturally large about what had brought Miss Worth back into the district when all knew that Crofthouse had been closed, but he was discreet enough not to inquire. It would undoubtedly all come plain in time. In the meantime, he would make it his business to provide whatever services were required of him, even if it meant taking a loss, for he was confident that when the new baronet finally arrived, his lordship would express suitable gratitude for such loyalty.

When the carriage driver set Verity down, along with her baggage, before the manor, she climbed the front steps of Crofthouse to pull on the bell. It was several long moments before she heard the grating of the bolt inside. The door was opened only a few inches and a suspicious eye studied her.

"'Tis I, Stafford," said Verity, summoning up the travesty of a smile.

"Miss! Well, I never!" The door was flung wide. "Come in, come in, Miss Worth! Whatever brings you home at such an odd time? Have you heard from Sir Charles, then, miss?" The butler had hurried out and picked up her baggage, his eyes trained on her all the while as the questions spilled from him.

Verity stepped inside, at the same time pulling off her gloves. She surveyed the front hall, which was lighted by the single branch of candles. The illumination scarcely pierced the deep shadows of the staircase and the far end of the hall. The gloom matched the dimness of her spirit. "No, I have heard nothing from my brother. Has there been any word left here?"

The butler had retrieved her baggage and now set the bandboxes and portmanteau inside. He frowned, closing the door, but in his abstraction neglecting to bolt it. "No, miss. We have heard nothing."

"Ah, well. Perhaps tomorrow or next week we shall do so," said Verity, sighing. "Stafford, I am very weary. I should like a cup of tea. Would it be possible?"

The butler's eyes sharpened. He noted for the first time the worn look on her face. It startled him, and his fatherly instincts were roused. "If you would care to enter the sitting room, miss, I shall inform Mrs. Stafford at once."

"Thank you, Stafford."

The butler picked up the branch of flickering candles and preceded Verity down the entry hall to the sitting room. Opening the door, he went inside and began to light some of the candles standing about on the mantel and sideboard. The flickering lights gathered, putting the dark into retreat.

Verity stood in the doorway, inexpressible feelings falling upon her at sight of the covered furniture and the cold, cheerless hearth. "It does not look very much like home," she murmured.

The butler heard her and, glancing in her direction, said, "No, miss. I suppose it doesn't. But once I have informed Mrs. Stafford of your arrival, I shall return to lay a fire. That will serve to dispel some of the gloom."

"Yes," agreed Verity, though without much conviction.

When the butler had gone on his errand, she took off her

damp pelisse and draped it neatly over one of the covered chairs. On top of it she laid her gloves and bonnet. Then she unshrouded one of the settees closest to the hearth from its holland cover.

The butler returned with the makings of a fire, which he laid on the hearth. Soon he had a brisk fire crackling in the grate. The warmth was immediately felt in the cold air of the room.

"That is immeasurably better, Stafford. Thank you," said Verity quietly.

The butler straightened and turned. He was struck by the picture presented by the daughter of the house. He knew that she was quite unconscious of the forlorn appearance she made in the midst of the holland covers—she was always one to shoulder the troubles of others, rather than burden others with her own.

"It was Mrs. Stafford's thought that you might want a bite of supper to go with your tea, miss. There are some slivers of mutton and the remains of a meat pie," Stafford offered.

Verity realized that the butler was anxious to please. She smiled her acquiescence even though she had no real appetite. "I should like that, Stafford."

The butler's anxious expression eased slightly. "Very good, miss." He exited the sitting room, carefully closing the door, leaving his mistress alone with her thoughts."

The clock on the hearth mantel ticked away the quiet minutes.

Verity did not care for her reflections. She was not naturally of a morose disposition and it was uncharacteristic of her to feel low; but there was no denying that for some hours past she had been feeling supremely sorry for herself.

"What a pitiful wretch you are, to be sure!" she mocked herself. But it was no simple matter, after all, to put aside the despair that threatened to overwhelm her—for she had lost something more precious to her than even her good reputation.

Verity desperately looked about for something to do that would change the direction of her thoughts. She found a basket of old piecework at the end of the settee and with relief took out the unfinished embroidery and some silks. The familiar task was soothing and she concentrated on the placement of her stitches to the exclusion of all else.

The door to the sitting room was thrust open and a quick step sounded. Verity did not look round, expecting that her supper was being brought in. "You may put the tray on the table there, Stafford. I shall serve myself."

But it was not the butler who had paused in the doorway. A tall young gentleman attired in a coat of military cut, his bearing that of one used to command, left the door and strode into the room. His rather hard blue eyes considered Verity, whose attention had remained fixed upon her embroidery. "Well, this is a fine welcome, I must say! The place is covered in hollands and not a servant to be had. It's a good thing I found the door unbolted or I daresay I would still be standing on the front step in the freezing rain! What the deuce is going on around here?"

Verity started up, the embroidery hoop and silks tumbling to the carpet. Her expression was one of startled disbelief. Then gladness swept her face. "Charles!"

She flew across the room to him and cast herself on his chest. "Oh, *Charles*!" She grasped his lapel, laughing and crying all at once.

Sir Charles Worth caught his sister close. He was somewhat alarmed and astonished by her show of emotion, for she perhaps more than the rest had always seemed particularly levelheaded. "Here, Verity, where's Mama? Why does the place look like a dashed morgue?"

He grasped her shoulders suddenly and set her away from him. There was apprehension in his eyes as he demanded, "Is Mama all right? Nothing has happened to her, has it?"

Verity shook her head, dashing tears from her face. She gave a gurgling laugh. "Oh no! Mama is in Brighton with our great-aunt. We shut up the house, you see."

"Thank God! For a moment I thought—" Sir Charles stopped, a frown descending between the line of his well-marked brows. "But why are you here, then? Why are you not with Mama?"

"I came home." Verity gently extricated herself from him and turned to retrieve her tumbled embroidery hoop and silks from the carpet.

"Came home?" It struck him as odd, and looking around the sitting room he thought that Verity must have been powerfully motivated to return to Crofthouse under these conditions. "Do not tell me that you have quarreled with Mama. I shan't believe it," said Sir Charles, narrowly watching his sister's face.

"Of course I did not. I have not been in Brighton at all," said Verity, resettling herself on the settee. She made a show of straightening her work, hoping that her brother would not query too deeply into her concerns.

She looked up, saying brightly, "It came as such a shock to see you just now when we have heard nothing from you. You must tell me about all that you have been doing and of your journey."

But Sir Charles knew his sister too well to be diverted by such tactics. He looked over at her, his still-narrowed eyes very keen and bright. "You have that expression that you always get when you are turning things over in your head. Come, Verity, cut line. Pray do not try to spin a farrago for me."

Verity considered her brother's unsmiling expression. He did not appear to her to be in a frame of mind that would be lightly diverted. With a sinking heart, she saw that she would have to own up to at least part of the truth. How she would have preferred to put off this discussion! Her emotions were so frayed that she did not feel equal to the certain confrontation that would result from her disclosure.

Verity had never been one to cry craven, however, and so she summoned up a smile. "You will no doubt laugh when I tell you."

She was quite certain that he would do no such thing, but her father had always said it was best to get over uneven ground as quickly as possible. She was about to prove or disprove her sire's assertion.

"Why do I have the disquieting feeling that I am about to be put into a flaming temper?" Sir Charles wondered aloud.

Verity lifted her chin. With only the slightest quiver in her voice, she said, "I have been at our cousins, the Pettiforths. You will recall that Papa corresponded with Mr. Pettiforth for many years."

"Yes, of course I do," said Sir Charles impatiently. Ignoring the holland cover, he dropped negligently into a chair. Throwing one leg over the arm, he swung his booted foot slowly to and fro. "I find it dashed odd that you should go to stay with cousins that we are hardly acquainted with."

"I went to the Pettiforths to become a paid companion and chaperon to their daughter," said Verity quietly.

She had abandoned her embroidery, quite unable to set a straight stitch while she felt such anxiety. Her hands were clasped tight in her lap. She had steeled herself, but nevertheless she winced at her brother's bellow of outrage.

Sir Charles leaped to his feet. "Paid companion! *You*, Verity! What were you thinking of? What was *Mama* thinking of? Yes, and August, too! I shall have a few choice words for our dear brother!" His hard blue eyes flashed while his lips tightened and thinned.

"That you shall not! You shall say nothing at all to August or to Mama, Charles. It was all my own notion and I would not listen to their objections. Indeed, it is all my own responsibility, every . . . every bit of it," said Verity. She had choked on the last words as thoughts of what she had left behind welled up in her. She shook her head quickly. "No, everything is quite my own fault. You mustn't blame anyone else, Charles."

"But why, Verity? I do not understand why you would insist upon doing such a thing," said Sir Charles, curbing his ire under a taut rein. There was more to this thing than had yet met his eye—he would stake his life on it. His instincts had been thoroughly aroused and he had learned to trust in their accuracy, for more than once they had saved his life. "Why did you take such a position, Verity? For I know that you are as aware as I what is due your name!"

"We had to shut up the house and let go most of the servants." Verity watched the altering of her brother's expression. "There was nothing to keep it up, you see. It was all tied up in the entail and Mama's portion just did not . . . suffice."

"Good God! Of course I should have realized how it would be, but it never occurred to me that—" Sir Charles bit off what else he meant to say. He shook his head. "That still does not explain why you did not go to Brighton with Mama."

Verity sighed tiredly. "I did not want Elizabeth to be obliged to leave the seminary. She has been so very happy there, you see. I thought that with what I could save I could enable Mama to keep her there."

She saw that her brother's expression was looking increasingly distressed, the weathered lines in his face from nose to mouth becoming more pronounced. She said gently, "It was only to be for a little while, Charles, only until you returned and set things right again."

"I see. Of course I had Mama's letter about Papa, but I had no notion that she would run aground so quickly." There was a tight look about Sir Charles's mouth. In a hard voice, he asked, "And the boys? What about Timothy and Bart? Were they forced to withdraw from school?"

"August took the boys back to Highcroft. He is tutoring them himself so that their education would not suffer. I imagine it is much like a holiday for them," said Verity.

Sir Charles gave a crack of laughter. The tense look in his eyes had vanished, giving place to an amused gleam. "That I doubt! I suspect our August is proving himself to be something of a taskmaster, as those impudent puppies have probably discovered. No, Timothy and Bart shall think themselves fortunate to return to school with their fellows! They'll be the better for it, however, and August will undoubtedly be elevated to awe-inspiring heights in their minds. I shall be quite eclipsed, I daresay."

Verity smiled up at her brother, her own eyes reflecting amusement. "Surely a soldier must always command the admiration of his young brothers."

"I daresay." Sir Charles turned his head to stare into the fire. His lids drooped over his eyes so that their expression could not be easily read. Abruptly, he swung his gaze back upon his sister, taking her by surprise. "Tell me the rest, Verity. What happened at the Pettiforths that sent you scrambling back here to a cold empty house? Were they unkind to you? Was that it?"

"Oh no, no! At least," amended Verity, "not dear Papa's cousin, Mr. Pettiforth. I liked him very much."

Sir Charles regarded her with a sardonic smile. "I take it that Mrs. Pettiforth did not stand as high in your regard."

She gave a rueful laugh. "I fear not. Mrs. Pettiforth is consumed by ambition for her favorite daughter. As for my charge, Cecily, I have never had the misfortune to be acquainted with a more disagreeable girl."

Sir Charles raised his brows, and sat down again. "That is a sweeping condemnation, coming as it does from you, dear sister. But none of this tells me why you have come back to Crofthouse with your tail tucked between your legs."

"Does it not?" asked Verity, keeping her smile in place. She avoided her brother's eyes by once more taking up her embroidery.

"Come, Verity! No dragoness or her spoiled pet is the equal of you and well I know it!" His voice was impatient. "I told you before, cut line with me. I shan't be satisfied until you tell me the whole."

"Will you not? Even when I tell you that I would prefer not to do so?" asked Verity with a shaking laugh. She dashed a hand across her eyes.

"Verity!" He came out of his chair in a shot and sat beside her on the settee. Putting a strong arm about her shoulders, he commanded, "Now tell me the whole, my poor girl."

Verity struggled to retain her self-control even as all the evils of her situation rushed in upon her again. Her voice trembled. "I am all to blame, Charles, for it was my idiocy that placed me in such unhappy circumstances. Oh, I made such wretched work of it, Charles! I should have known how it would be. But I didn't, not at first. Then, when I began to realize what was happening and how everyone was beginning to talk, I could not make him see that he was destroying me. Oh, Charles! How I wish that I had never said what I did, for it was all done for revenge! All of it!"

At some point Verity had turned to hide her face against her brother's shoulder. Her fingers clutched tightly at his lapel. Her last words came muffled to his ears, but their meaning was appallingly clear.

Sir Charles's face tightened. His eyes became deep pools of pale blue fury. He said thickly, "Never mind, Verity. It is all right now, for I am here."

"Oh, Charles! I am such a *stupid* fool!"

A sob escaped Verity. She tried to swallow it back, but it burned so in her throat and chest that she could not contain it. The one was followed by others and she cried at last, held safe in her brother's arms. His embrace was inexpressibly comforting in its unstinting acceptance.

It was as well that she could not see her brother's expression, for it would have frightened her.

Twenty

The butler chose that moment to enter the sitting room. The sight of his young master made him start so badly that the tray in his hands was in danger of sliding from his hands. He steadied it, even as he exclaimed joyfully, "Sir Charles!"

"Yes, it is I," said Sir Charles with a singular lack of appreciation for his servant's effusive tone. "Is that supper for my sister? I shall have a tray of the same, if you please."

"Yes, my lord! I shall return in a trice."

Stafford set the tray on the table, sending a swift glance at Miss Worth, who had straightened and was attempting to mop her eyes. It was not at all wonderful that Miss Worth's emotions had overcome her with the shock of Sir Charles's sudden appearance, reflected the butler. He was himself still recovering. "I will be but a moment, my lord. Shall I bring a bottle of the madeira?"

"Yes, yes. And go about it quick, man," said Sir Charles, impatient for the butler to be gone. There were a number of questions he still wished to put to his sister, which he could not while the butler was fussing about the room.

The butler bowed and exited, but he had not gone many steps down the hall before he heard the impatient pull of the front bell. "Now what is toward, I wonder?" he muttered to himself.

Straightening his shoulders as though bracing for another surprise, he opened the door. He was forced to step aside before the forceful entry of a lady. In her train followed a thin, respectably garbed female of scowling demeanor that the butler at once recognized as a dresser of superior talent.

The unexpected visitor was obviously of some standing to afford such a henchwoman. Nevertheless, it was his domain that had been trespassed without a byword or courtesy. Drawing himself up with all the affront and frosty mien of his station, Stafford inquired, "Madame?! May I help you?"

The lady barely glanced at the butler as she pulled off her gloves. "I am Mrs. Arnold. I am a friend of Miss Worth's and I have come to speak with her. Is she still downstairs?"

Stafford was startled and bewildered by the lady's knowledge that his mistress was in residence. It was a certainty that few as yet knew of her return, so this lady was undoubtedly in Miss Worth's confidence. However, he considered that the lady's timing could not have been worse. The high hour of Sir Charles's return should be a private one. "In the sitting room, ma'am. But I hardly think—"

Mrs. Arnold brushed aside any subtle objections that might have been put forward. "Never mind, I can find my own way. Meek, we shall stay the night here."

"Very good, ma'am," said the hatchet-faced female. She fixed a baleful glare on the butler. "I shall inquire where we are to be housed, ma'am."

Stafford's uppermost thought was that he had never seen a woman who so little resembled her name. He appealed to the mistress. "Ma'am, we are terribly understaffed. If you will but permit me to make arrangements—"

Mrs. Arnold had finished drawing off her gloves. She glanced at the butler. "Tell my man where the stables are, I pray you. It is hideous weather and I do not wish my cattle to be kept out any longer then necessary."

Without waiting for the butler's reluctant offices, Mrs. Arnold swept down the hall to the one doorway through which light was visible.

*   *   *

When Mrs. Arnold entered the room, Verity, who had recognized her friend's imperious voice, had already started to her feet. She stepped forward. "Betsy! Whatever are you doing here?"

Mrs. Arnold crossed over and met her in a quick embrace, retorting, "I might ask you the same, mightn't I?"

She did not wait for an answer, for her glance had fallen upon the tall, harsh-faced gentleman who was slowly rising from the settee. Mrs. Arnold's brows rose in swift surprise. "And who is this fine gentleman? No, allow me to guess, for there is a certain resemblance. This must be the missing brother, Sir Charles Worth!"

Swift color had surged into Verity's face at her friend's tart rebuke, but she recovered sufficiently to make the proper introductions. Indeed, it was the necessity of observing the civilities that enabled her to regain her balance. Her manner and expression would have seemed completely normal to anyone not thoroughly acquainted with her.

"Charles, this is Mrs. Betsy Arnold. She and I were at seminary together and we came out the same Season."

"Yes, and we have been good friends ever since. Though perhaps we have not been living in one another's pockets as much as we should have been, since I stay much in London while Verity merely visits in town. I have missed your sister dreadfully. That was brought home to me when I ran into Verity at a recent house party," said Mrs. Arnold, offering her hand in a friendly way to the baronet. "I am so very pleased to meet you at last, Sir Charles, for Verity has told me a great deal about you. I know that she is most pleased that you have come home."

"I am pleased to make your acquaintance also, Mrs. Arnold," said Sir Charles, amusement touching his face and relieving the stern visage he had worn when the visitor had first come into the sitting room.

Mrs. Arnold tilted her head, assaying his hawklike features and superb physique. He was not a gentleman one could easily forget, she thought, as she said, "I cannot think why we have never come into one another's way before."

"Doubtless it was because I had already gone into the army

before Verity left the schoolroom," said Sir Charles. "I am a few years older than my sister."

"That is probably the reason," agreed Mrs. Arnold, nodding.

"Betsy, where is Herbert? Is he not with you?" asked Verity, as she realized that her friend's spouse was conspicuously absent.

"I sent him on to London without me. He grumbled a good deal about it, too, since he had counted upon me to make things comfortable for him when we arrived. He wished me to convey his disgruntlement at having his placid habits upset by what he called your 'pesky start,' Verity," said Mrs. Arnold.

Verity's color rose once again, especially as she felt her brother's curious gaze upon her. "I shall certainly apologize when next I see him."

"Oh, Herbert is such a dear that he will have forgotten all about it already. I, however, am quite a different species altogether," said Mrs. Arnold.

"Betsy, please!" said Verity, smiling, trying to turn it all into an amusing pass. "Must you continue to scold?"

Mrs. Arnold ignored her friend's plea. She smiled at the silent baronet and said confidingly, "I hope that you do not think me rude, Sir Charles. But obviously I have a bit of a bone to pick with your sister, which I intend to pursue. It is the entire reason behind my abrupt arrival."

"Not at all," murmured Sir Charles.

He saw his sister's quick shake of the head at Mrs. Arnold, obviously made to warn her friend against speaking out of turn. He was made very curious. He had been quick to note Mrs. Arnold's reference to a house party. It seemed very probable that the house party in question had been held at the Pettiforths, for he knew that Verity had not been in London. And now Mrs. Arnold had rushed to follow Verity back to Crofthouse.

It seemed that his sister had something that she wished to keep secret from him. He was equally determined that he would learn the whole. He had gathered enough from Verity's unguarded hasty words to have considerably alarmed him. Now that he knew that Mrs. Arnold was in possession of that same secret, he was not about to leave the two alone as courtesy demanded of him. "I trust that my presence will not be a hindrance to you, Mrs. Arnold."

"Charles!" exclaimed Verity quietly, glaring reproachfully at her brother.

He ignored her look and spread his hands in a deprecating gesture. "You see, Mrs. Arnold, this is the only room in the house which appears to have been opened. Apparently Verity, like myself, arrived only a short time ago. Forgive me, but I have no wish to substitute a draughty parlor for the well-established warmth in this room. In addition, Verity was just relating some of her experiences while I have been away. I am certain that you will recognize my reluctance to miss any subsequent details."

Mrs. Arnold leveled a stare upon him, weighing the advantages and disadvantages, her quick brain having already absorbed Verity's reluctance to have her brother present. Verity had not, then, divulged anything of importance to her brother. Mrs. Arnold decided upon the instant to honor her friend's desires, and she smiled. "I do not mind in the least, Sir Charles. And I cannot conceive that Verity would have any objections, either, for nothing can be tamer than my own contribution." She looked meaningfully at her friend.

The renewed protest on Verity's lips died before it was spoken. She realized at once, and with gratitude, that Mrs. Arnold did not intend to betray her.

She had done quite well at that task for herself, she thought, bitterly regretting already the words that had poured out of her several minutes before. She had never meant to say so much to her brother. She only hoped that he would dismiss the major portion of it as feminine nonsense. She meant to do her utmost in fostering that impression with him as soon as she possibly could. Meanwhile she must play the role of the unconcerned.

"Pray let me remove that holland cover, Betsy, so that you may be comfortable. You must be famished. Charles, pray ring for Stafford."

"Oh no, I supped earlier. I need nothing else, I assure you. Unless you are taking tea?" Mrs. Arnold sat down in a wingback chair, smoothing her gloves on her lap.

"We shall send for it," promised Verity, smiling.

"While we are waiting for Stafford, perhaps you will relieve my lamentable curiosity, Mrs. Arnold, and reveal why you are so displeased with my sister," said Sir Charles.

Mrs. Arnold exchanged a look with Verity. She said coolly, "it is no great matter after all, Sir Charles. It was only that I had thought we might travel to London together, but Verity stole away before we had quite settled our plans. I have hopes of persuading Verity to come to me for a long visit in town."

"Certainly that would seem to hold out more possibility of entertainment than keeping company with the holland covers," said Sir Charles with a glance about the sitting room.

"Just so, my lord," said Mrs. Arnold.

The butler appeared then and it was seen that he had anticipated the visitor's preferences. He had brought a pot of tea, cream, and a selection of bisquits. There was also the madeira for Sir Charles and a plate of sandwiches.

Sir Charles was appreciative. "Thank you, Stafford. You know to a nicety my tastes."

"Verity, I have for you a letter from Mr. Pettiforth. You had left so very unexpectedly that he had not had an opportunity to convey his sentiments and since he understood that I was going to call upon you, he entrusted the letter to my charge," said Mrs. Arnold, handing over the packet.

"Did he?" Verity did not dare to meet her brother's eyes. She could feel his thoughtful gaze upon her and a slow flush rose into her face. She knew that her brother had taken notice of Mrs. Arnold's artless reference to the hurried manner in which she had quit the Pettiforths. "Thank you, Betsy. I shall read it later at my leisure."

"Why do you not read it now?" suggested Sir Charles quietly. "Stafford has not quite finished setting out the refreshments. You are such good friends that I feel certain Mrs. Arnold will not feel that you are neglecting your duty toward her."

"No, indeed. Of course you must not stand on ceremony with me, Verity. I quite feel that I am amongst family. In point of fact, I shall be happy to pour out the tea," said Mrs. Arnold.

"As you wish, Mrs. Arnold," agreed Sir Charles, inclining his head.

Mrs. Arnold quietly dismissed the butler and proceeded to

carry out her self-appointed task. "I know that Verity takes only a little cream and sugar. Do you also, my lord?"

Sir Charles indicated that he did, but his polite attentiveness was soon returned to his sister. "Pray do not allow us to keep you any longer in suspense, Verity. Mrs. Arnold and I shall manage without you for the few moments that your letter shall take to read."

"Very well." Verity felt that she had little choice but to break the seal on the missive. There was really no reason for such reluctance to glance over her own correspondence, except that she was so aware of her brother's lazy smile. It seemed to hide some thought behind it.

As Verity unfolded the missive, a cheque fell out onto her lap. Before she realized what he was about, her brother had leaned over and retrieved it.

"What is this?" He glanced at the front of the cheque and his brows lifted. "Generous, indeed! It appears that our cousin truly valued your services, Verity."

"Yes, Mr. Pettiforth was most generous. He understood that Mama was making a sacrifice in letting me go to them," said Verity quietly. She wondered at the unacknowledged depth of her brother's interest.

"How odd, then, that you felt obligated to flee his hospitality so precipitously," Sir Charles remarked.

His mouth hardened suddenly and when he lifted his gaze to his sister's face, she was startled by the ugly expression in his eyes.

"Was it Pettiforth, Verity?" he demanded harshly. "Was it he who forced his attentions upon you?"

Twenty-one

The teapot clattered onto the tray. "Oh, my word!" Mrs. Arnold gasped. She snatched up a napkin to clean up the drops of splattered liquid. "I am so sorry. So very clumsy of me, to be sure," she said, attempting to pass over her violent start.

But neither of her companions was paying the least attention to her words. Brother and sister were locked in tableau. Sir Charles's expression was measuring and cold, while Verity's face had whitened.

"No! Of course not, Charles! Don't be absurd!" exclaimed Verity.

Sir Charles reached out and ungently grasped her wrist. Very quietly, he said, "You are to tell me the truth now, my girl. I shall wait no longer."

For a moment, Verity met her brother's implacable gaze. Then she averted her face.

Mrs. Arnold took one look at Verity's pale expression and hurriedly said, "I can assure you that it was not Burton Pettiforth, Sir Charles. And whatever was said was an absolute parcel of lies, to be quickly discounted and forgotten."

Sir Charles turned his head and thoughtfully regarded Mrs. Arnold's anxious countenance. He would have his answer, indeed. But still he did not release his sister's wrist, being fully aware from the tension that he sensed in her that Verity wanted passionately to flee from the sitting room and so escape from his prying. "Will you be so good as to identify the gentleman, Mrs. Arnold?"

"Betsy!"

Mrs. Arnold glanced quickly at Verity's face, then dropped her gaze away from her friend's pleading eyes. "I am sorry, my dear. I meant to honor your confidence, truly I did. But since Sir Charles already knows so much—"

"He knows nothing except that I was made a fool," said Verity hastily. "It is over and I simply wish to forget it all!"

"Verity, you must recognize that as head of your family, Sir Charles has every right to know! It is his duty to protect your honor," said Mrs. Arnold.

"But I don't wish a question of my honor to be upheld to the public. It is above all things the one most repugnant to me!" Verity cried, feeling her spirit to be lacerated. "Have I not suffered humiliation enough?"

"Pray do not be an idiot!" said Sir Charles, almost indifferently. Without ever glancing at his sister, he said, "Mrs. Arnold, if you please."

"It was the Viscount Rathbone. He showed Verity such pointed interest that she became the object of malicious gossip," said Mrs. Arnold firmly.

"I see. And precisely what form did this . . . interest take, Mrs. Arnold?" asked Sir Charles. He smiled slightly, his eyes very cold and hard. "You must be painfully honest with me, Mrs. Arnold."

It was Mrs. Arnold's turn to grow pale. It was clear to her that Sir Charles desired to know whether his sister had been seduced. She shot a swift glance at Verity and hoped that there was nothing more to be revealed. She was already involved too deeply for comfort. "You must not think that your sister behaved in any way reprehensibly, my lord! Indeed, I believe that she did try to warn Lord Rathbone away. But—but still she was labeled Lord Rathbone's flirt."

Verity gave a low cry and covered her face with her free hand.

Mrs. Arnold was moved by her distress. She said helplessly, "I am so very sorry, Verity. But what else can I do? You must see that it is better for your brother to be told what actually took place rather than to leave him to imagine worse things."

Verity let drop her hand. Her riotous emotions were such that she felt ready to sink through the floor. In a low, trembling voice, she said, "Now you know the whole, Charles. Will you please release me?"

Sir Charles let go of her wrist. At her quick movement toward escape, he said, "Pray do not go just yet, dear sister. I feel certain that you would far rather put me in possession of the full details rather than leave it to poor Mrs. Arnold to repeat whatever she might have heard or seen."

At that, Verity's head came up. Her gray eyes blazed, sparkling like diamonds behind unshed tears. "I would infinitely prefer it!"

The touch of a smile flitted over his face. "So I thought. But I think that we shall have Mrs. Arnold remain so that she may prompt you if you chance to forget some small detail."

"Really, I would much rather not, Sir Charles," began Mrs. Arnold, starting to rise. She had rarely been put in the position of such discomfort.

"You have little choice, ma'am. You have chosen to make yourself privy to my sister's affairs. I am not likely to excuse you now," said Sir Charles in a hard voice. He waited while she sank down once more on the settee. Then he turned toward his sister. "Well, Verity?"

"How utterly detestable you are! I had quite forgotten," she shot at him.

He laughed. "Yes, I think that you must have. But never mind trying to bludgeon my sensibilities. I have been at war too long to pay much heed to anything that *you* may throw at my head. Now the round tale, if you please."

"Very well. I hope that it may edify you, brother," said Verity coldly.

She began at the first, relating the fatal words that she had spoken to Mrs. Arnold without realizing that she had been overheard. She spoken concisely, calmly, as though she was commenting on another's ill-fortune in becoming the object of gossip and slander. Her voice betrayed her only once, toward the last, when she related how Lord Rathbone had admitted he'd brought ruin upon her out of a desire to teach her a salutary lesson.

"I threw his lordship's apology in his teeth and left to go up to my bedroom. A few minutes later Betsy knocked on my door and she had not yet left when I sustained a visit from Miss Pettiforth and her mother."

Verity paused, reliving that horrible scene and the interview afterwards. "The upshot of it all was that Mrs. Pettiforth accused me of stealing Lord Rathbone from her daughter and drove me out of the house."

"My dear!" exclaimed Mrs. Arnold, greatly distressed. "I guessed at breakfast that something of the sort had happened, of course. But whyever did you not come to me? I would not have allowed her to treat you so. Or why did you not appeal to Mr. Pettiforth, for you must have known that he would have stood your champion."

"It did not even occur to me, Betsy. I believe I was in a state of shock by then. I wanted only to be away from that woman and her dreadful daughter and . . . and everything! So I left just as I had been ordered. It did not dawn on me until I had been let off in the village that it was the small hours of the morning and that there would not be a coach to buy passage on," said Verity.

"But what did you do? I know from what Mr. Pettiforth confided to me that you had very little in the way of funds with you," said Mrs. Arnold, appalled and yet fascinated.

"The innkeeper allowed me to sleep on the settle in the parlor and he saw that I got onto the mail coach in the morning. I suspect that he pitied me, rather, for he did not charge me for the night or for the tea that I drank," said Verity reflectively.

She was startled by a sharp curse. When she realized how grim was her brother's expression, she laid her hand upon his knee. Even through the remaining anger that she felt toward him, she could sympathize with his feelings. She knew that he genuinely cared for her and it had pained him to hear her narrative. "I came home safely, Charles."

"Yes, we must be truly thankful for that," said Mrs. Arnold, shuddering. "It could have gone so very wrong, could it not? If the innkeeper had not taken compassion upon you, why, you would have been out in the weather and prey to-to—"

Sir Charles leaped up from the settee, unable to contain his feelings any longer. He exclaimed harshly, "Indeed! It could have been far worse."

With deliberation he smashed his fist down on the top of the mantel. The ladies jumped, horrified by the expression of violence, yet dimly recognizing that the very control that he exhibited in executing the blow emphasized the depth of his fury.

His expression was terrible; when he spoke, however, his voice was remarkably even. "Rathbone has much to answer for, I believe. You have suffered extraordinarily at his lordship's hands. But I promise you that he shall answer to me for it."

"Charles, no!" Verity jumped up from her seat. She clutched her brother's unyielding arm. He glanced down at her with hard eyes and she felt herself quail before the foreign emotion in their depths. She spoke quickly, urgently, "Pray do not confront the viscount, Charles. There is not the least use in it. I said all that mattered, pray believe that! As for my reputation, Betsy has assured me that since most of the house party were provincials, there will be little said in London circles among my real friends, and that it wants only some resolution and boldness to put to death any wayward rumors."

"That is quite true, Sir Charles. I added a few brilliant strokes of my own at the Pettiforths before I left. Even those who might have continued to believe ill of Verity somewhat revised their opinions when it was revealed that she is a favorite of the Earl and Countess of Chard," added Mrs. Arnold.

Verity turned an incredulous stare on her. "What a bouncer, Betsy! We exchange cordialities, nothing more."

Mrs. Arnold shrugged, smiling a little. "Perhaps I exaggerated. But I do not believe that it was bad of me to do so when the connection so neatly fit the purpose."

"I appreciate your efforts on Verity's behalf, Mrs. Arnold." Charles's voice was polite, but there was a vein of steel underlying it that hardened as he continued. "However, my sister's situation requires more than the whitewash bestowed by the name of a noble acquaintance. Nor am I so sanguine as to trust that it shall all blow over so very neatly. No, I shall seek out Lord Rathbone."

"No, Charles! Pray do not!" exclaimed Verity.

"No, Verity. You cannot persuade me otherwise! I intend to demand satisfaction. Lord Rathbone shall meet me." A peculiar smile lit Sir Charles's eyes, though his mouth remained hard. "Or his lordship shall put his wedding band upon your finger."

"Charles, you cannot possibly do this!" exclaimed Verity, horrified, stepping back and staring up at him as though she had never truly seen him before.

"Can I not? I promise you, this time next week Lord Rathbone will either lie dead on the green at my feet, or he will have offered you an honorable estate. My own preference is to make a quick end of him." Sir Charles regarded his sister's pale face with detached interest. "Come, Verity, can you harbor fellow feeling for a gentleman who with such callous indifference stole your honor?"

Verity turned away sharply, one hand going to her mouth.

Sir Charles frowned. He stepped after her, catching her elbow and turning her to face him. She would not meet his eyes. "Verity."

With his other hand he forced up her chin. Still she refused to look at him, her lashes hiding her expression. "What is this? Do you actually care for the blackguard?"

There was a long, strained silence. It proved his answer. Sir Charles let go of her and sighed. "Very well. I shall do my best to curb my more violent instincts."

"I do not wish to be forced into wedlock," said Verity in a low, intense voice. Her hands were clasped tightly in front of her.

"You shall wed Rathbone, or not, as you please," said Sir Charles.

She looked up quickly, meeting his eyes. "You mean to kill him otherwise, do you not?"

Her brother shrugged. "Our place in this world is established, Verity. There are rules of conduct that we must all follow. Transgressions are not forgiven, nor forgotten. You must know that. Though your own conduct may have been entirely blameless, and should all fall out entirely as Mrs. Arnold has predicted, yet you would still be forever haunted by an ugly cloud of speculation. That is not what I wish for you. Therefore I must defend your honor as best I know how."

"He is right, my dear," said Mrs. Arnold softly, her gaze compassionate.

The enormity of the trap in which she found herself was stunning. Her mind reeled under the impact. She could either agree to her brother's decree of death for Lord Rathbone, or she could bow to his pronouncement of her future lot. Oddly enough, it did not enter her mind that it might be her brother who would find death in a duel with Lord Rathbone. She was altogether focused on the viscount and how his destiny—and hers—hung in the balance.

Verity's shoulders sagged. "I have no choice then, have I?"

Sir Charles did not answer what was, after all, a rhetorical question. "I shall leave for London in the morning. Mrs. Arnold, I would consider it a favor if you would allow Verity to accompany you to London and stay with you until this matter is happily resolved."

"Of course, Sir Charles. Verity knows that she is always welcome," said Mrs. Arnold. She rose and shook out her skirts. "I discover that I have lost my interest in taking tea. I hope that you will excuse me, Sir Charles. Verity, why do we not go up to bed? I am certain that your good Stafford has made some arrangement for us abovestairs."

"Yes, of course. You must be tired," said Verity mechanically. Taking up a branch of lit candles, she ushered her friend toward the door of the sitting room. Without looking around, she said, "Good night, Charles."

He watched his sister and Mrs. Arnold exit, an expressionless mask concealing his emotions. Turning to the fireplace, he poked at a smoldering log with the toe of his boot. "What a thoroughly damnable homecoming," he muttered.

The following morning, Verity and Mrs. Arnold left Crofthouse for London. They drove away in the Arnold carriage. Sir Charles, who professed his preference for the freedom and fresh air of riding, accompanied the carriage on horseback.

Mrs. Arnold's maid and Sir Charles's attendant followed in one of the carriages from Crofthouse with all of the baggage.

Several times in the course of the journey, Mrs. Arnold attempted to engage Verity in conversation. She suffered a singular lack of success. At last, Mrs. Arnold said contritely, "I am sorry, Verity. Perhaps I was wrong to reveal Lord Rathbone's identity against your wishes."

"It is all right, Betsy. You meant it for the best," said Verity. It was the most she had said all day.

Silence fell again, broken once more by Mrs. Arnold. "You do love him, Verity. Since that is true, it is not such a bad bargain. Eventually Lord Rathbone must come to love you as well."

"I tell myself that must be true, Betsy. But how can it be so when I know what his feelings are for me? He despises me, Betsy."

Verity did not look at Mrs. Arnold, but there was such flat conviction in her voice that Mrs. Arnold realized the depth of the despair that gripped her. Not for the first time, Mrs. Arnold was left with nothing to say.

Twenty-two

Lord Rathbone returned to his town house at an unusually early hour.

The porter who opened the front door to his lordship was astounded to see his master before midnight. Casting a furtive glance at his lordship's closed visage, however, the servant-man thought it prudent to stay his greeting. His lordship appeared to be in a rare tweek, he thought.

Indeed, Lord Rathbone might have agreed with his henchman's assessment if he had been at all aware of it. He passed into the house, tossing his hat and gloves to the porter. "Send a bottle of brandy up to me," he ordered. Without glancing round or waiting for acknowledgment of his order, he swiftly climbed the stairs.

A fire had been prepared in the sitting room. Lord Rathbone cast himself into the wingback chair and put back his head, his eyes closing. His thoughts were not pleasant ones. Despite the round of entertainments that he had plunged himself into upon his return to London, he had been unable to banish from his mind the Pettiforth house party.

The day following his return, he had gone to call on his mother, wanting to have the unpleasant duty over quickly.

Lady Rathbone had listened without comment to his curt,

abridged report of what he had found at the Pettiforths. He had not mentioned Miss Worth even in passing; but he had told her ladyship about his aunt and his cousin. At the end, Lady Rathbone said only, "'Tis a pity that you took such an aversion to the connection."

Lord Rathbone had stared grimly at his mother. "I do not intend to hasten off to find another candidate, ma'am."

"I have not suggested it, George," Lady Rathbone had said.

Lord Rathbone had entered her ladyship's sitting room prepared for a battle of wills. Lady Rathbone's inexplicable complacency had denied him an emotional release that he badly needed, and it angered him to an insensible degree. He had given a jerky bow and strode out of the room, seething.

The white-hot anger and resentment had inevitably cooled, leaving exposed the true underlying emotions that now racked him. Lord Rathbone sighed, passing his hand wearily over his face. He bitterly regretted all that had happened. It could all be laid to the door of his damnable pride and self-consequence.

If he had it to do over again, he would have shrugged off Miss Worth's assessment of his character. What had she meant to the scheme of his world, after all? Miss Worth had stood in the capacity of a hired companion. She should never have attained such prominence in his thoughts nor such total focus in his attentions.

He knew now that at some point he had crossed a line, all unknowingly, when what had begun as sport had become of utmost seriousness.

It was only by slow degrees that he had begun to understand what he felt toward Miss Worth. By the time he had, it had become too late, either to draw back from the precipice, or to speak the glimmerings of his heart.

The night of the ball had spelled the end of anything that he might otherwise have hoped for, because he had made of Miss Worth a public spectacle.

The whisperings of his conscience continued to haunt him. He, who had endured all manner of slander and backbiting from the time of his infancy, had inflicted like torment upon another fellow creature.

Lord Rathbone uttered a bark of harsh laughter. He had sworn with revulsion that he would never beget a bastard because he would not watch another subjected to the same treatment that had been his portion. Instead, he had destroyed a young woman's reputation and her right to self-respect. He was no better than those others had been—in fact, he was worse, for he had continued in his chosen path despite having realized what he felt toward her.

The servant entered, carrying a bottle of brandy and glasses on a tray. As he set down the tray, he said, "My lord, there is a gentleman wishing to see you."

"Send whoever it is away. I don't care to see anyone," snapped Lord Rathbone, rising from the chair. He crossed to the occasional table and took hold of the bottle.

The servantman watched, perturbed, as a generous amount of brandy was splashed into the glass. It was not like his lordship to drink alone or in such quantity, as he had for some nights past. Perhaps a diversion would be just the thing to turn his lordship from what were obviously unpleasant, brooding thoughts. "The gentleman was quite insistent. Adamantly so, I might say, my lord. He sent up his card."

With an impatient scowl, Lord Rathbone sharply set down the bottle so that he could take the calling card. His eyes fell on the inscription. He was very still for a long moment, then slowly raised his head to stare unseeing at the wall opposite.

"My lord? Shall I tell the gentleman to go?"

Lord Rathbone turned his head. There was such a grim expression on his face that his serving man was startled. "No. No, send him up."

Not at all certain that he had done the right thing after all, the servant went away to carry out his lordship's order. Presently he returned, accompanied by a tall, well-built gentleman attired in riding dress.

The visitor strode into the room with the self-assurance of a man completely aware of his own capabilities. His sharp gaze traveled the sitting room before settling upon the lone occupant.

Lord Rathbone had been leaning on his hands upon the occasional table. Now he straightened, his eyes meeting and clashing with his visitor's hard stare. "That will be all, Booker," said Lord Rathbone quietly.

When the servant had withdrawn, Lord Rathbone indicated

a wingback chair. "Pray make yourself at ease, Sir Charles. May I offer you a brandy?"

"I shall stand, my lord. I have not come on a social call," said Sir Charles Worth in a clipped voice.

Lord Rathbone corked the brandy bottle. "I had not thought you had. You have come on your sister's behalf. I am correct, am I not? You are Miss Verity Worth's brother?"

Sir Charles smiled, but the expression did not lighten the hard look in his eyes or about his mouth. "You do not seem surprised to see me, my lord."

"Once I had your card in my hand, it seemed to me inevitable that this interview would take place." A muscle jumped in Lord Rathbone's taut jaw. With suppressed violence, he said, "Since the moment I had the misfortune to meet your sister, Sir Charles, the fates have been damnable!"

Sir Charles narrowly regarded the viscount for a moment. He came to a decision. "I'll take that brandy, my lord."

"Will you, indeed? Then you do not mean to run me through just yet," said Lord Rathbone, throwing a challenging glance over his shoulder as he turned to the serving tray.

Sir Charles gave a short laugh. His teeth flashed in a grin, yet when he spoke his voice was very cold. "Not just yet," he agreed.

Sir Charles accepted the glass that the viscount held out to him. At his host's grave gesture, he walked over to a wingback chair and sat down. Sir Charles waited until Lord Rathbone was seated opposite him before speaking again. Then he said, "I arrived home yesterday to discover my sister sitting amongst the holland covers in an empty house. It was a pretty tale that I bullied out of her and she still would have kept back from me any mention of your name except for the timely intervention of a friend."

"That would be Betsy Arnold," interposed Lord Rathbone coolly. He swirled the brandy in his glass, watching the amber liquid with a detached air.

"As you say, my lord." Sir Charles tossed off his measure of brandy. He set the glass down with a distinct clink. The gaze that he leveled on his lordship was glittering. "Now we come to it, my lord."

"You mean to call me out," stated Lord Rathbone.

"I mean to kill you," corrected Sir Charles.

At the flat words, Lord Rathbone raised his brows, somewhat nettled. "That might perhaps be more difficult than you anticipate, Sir Charles. I am accounted a fair shot and a dangerous swordsman."

"Whilst I have made it my business to cut down my enemies with the least said or done," said Sir Charles softly. There was a menace in the very way he held himself. He was still seated in the wingback, but he gave the impression of being on a tightly coiled spring.

Lord Rathbone laughed, suddenly and genuinely amused. "You have the advantage of me there, I fear. You are a soldier to the bone, no doubt, and will prove a ferocious fighter. Very well, then; I own to it. Perhaps after all you *will* kill me."

"Or I shall see to it that you are wed to my sister." The quiet words were said with a devilish grin.

Lord Rathbone was startled. His black brows snapped together in a heavy frown. "What do you mean? Miss Worth could not possibly wish to wed me. She holds me in the strongest aversion. That was made abundantly clear to me, believe me! Nor do I hold it against her, for I do not like myself very much. What I did was unpardonable, unforgivable!"

He had risen sharply to his feet as he spoke. He discovered the wine glass was clenched in his hand, the brandy still untasted. He crossed to the occasional table where he rid himself of it. He did not immediately turn. When he did, Sir Charles was startled by the blazing look in his eyes.

Lord Rathbone stared challengingly across the room at Sir Charles. "Very well!" he snapped. "You have the right to call me to account. Which form is it to take, sir? I am completely at your disposal."

Sir Charles was swift of thought and he had had time to reflect. He had been startled and dismayed by the terms with which Lord Rathbone had castigated himself. He had believed the censure that his sister had come under to be grave, but in light of the viscount's obvious self-loathing, he suspected that he had not been told the whole after all.

With a sinking feeling he wondered whether his sister had actually been seduced. Neither his sister nor Mrs. Arnold had admitted to more than that Lord Rathbone had caused Verity to become the object of gossip.

Deadly calm stole over him as he reviewed all that had been said and how Verity had exhibited some sort of strangled emotion over the question of the viscount's fate. He recalled, too, that Mrs. Arnold had seemed torn between her loyalty to Verity and her sense of what was right.

Sir Charles credited Mrs. Arnold with the good sense to have revealed all that she was privy to, but perhaps that lady had feared that she had not been wholly in Verity's confidence.

The military life had taught him many lessons, not the least of which was to be prepared for any eventuality. For Verity's sake, he could not let the question of her honor to be concluded with a duel.

"I should like very much to kill you, Rathbone," he said softly. As a result of his thoughts, his eyes were very cold, very hard. "But I don't mean to. At least, I will not before you have been wed to my sister. Then we shall see how matters fall out."

Lord Rathbone stood quite still. His stone-carved face did not betray his feelings, except for the white line about his mouth. "I understand you perfectly. I have said that it was for you to choose how justice was to be executed. Now I give you my word. Miss Worth shall not take any harm through her marriage to me."

Sir Charles stood up. "I think we understand one another tolerably well, my lord. I will take my leave of you now. There are matters that I must attend to in the morning. By the by, my sister has posted up to London with Mrs. Arnold and shall be staying with the Arnolds until I can bring my mother to town. You will wish to convey your respects to your intended as soon as possible, I imagine."

"I feel quite certain that you are right, Sir Charles," said Lord Rathbone ironically. "Forgive me for my lapse in good manners, but I will not show you out. You know the way."

Sir Charles nodded. He could well appreciate his lordship's feelings at that moment and could almost sympathize. If it had been anyone else but his sister, he sensed that he could have liked the viscount very well. They were much alike, he and Lord Rathbone.

A grim expression suddenly shadowed his eyes. There was one vast difference between them, however. He would not have offered a lady of quality a slip on the shoulder.

Sir Charles had opened the door when the viscount called out sharply to him. Sir Charles turned. Lord Rathbone was standing at the mantel. The firelight cast flickering shadows over his lordship's countenance, and for a moment, Sir Charles had a clear window to the depths of the viscount's torment.

Lord Rathbone's smile was twisted. "I am not quite the blackguard you think me, Sir Charles. I did offer to marry your sister."

Seeing the swift change in his visitor's expression, Lord Rathbone shrugged. "She did not tell you, then. I did not think so. She spurned me. I wonder, if she refuses again, will you try to spit me on a sword?"

"She will not refuse you again, my lord. I will see to that," said Sir Charles quietly.

His antagonism toward the viscount had lessened to a degree with the gentleman's admission. Lord Rathbone had at least attempted to make reparation. It was yet to be discovered what maggot had taken possession of Verity's brain to have induced her refusal. Sir Charles could have sworn that she cared for the viscount. However, when all was told, it scarcely mattered. The viscount had agreed to marriage. Wed him she would.

Sir Charles stepped through the door and closed it firmly behind him.

Lord Rathbone laughed to himself. It was a harsh, derisive sound in the empty room. "A reluctant bride who finds me repugnant! Lord, I have made a rare mull of it." He stirred the fire with the toe of his boot.

Brooding, it occurred suddenly to Lord Rathbone to wonder why he had thrown the decision of how justice was to be meted out to Sir Charles. It had not been through fear of facing the gentleman. He had lived recklessly too long to quake now at the mortal danger posed by a duel. It would not have been his first such meeting, after all.

Lord Rathbone frowned abstractedly, then straightened abruptly. He had had enough of introspection for the night. Striding across the sitting room, he yanked open the door. He set up a call for his valet. "I'm to bed, Barrow!"

Twenty-three

Lord Rathbone made a formal visit to the Arnold residence that same week. Having sent up his card, he restlessly paced in the sitting room for word that he was to be received by the lady of the house and her guest. Eventually the butler returned and escorted his lordship into the drawing room where Mrs. Arnold and Verity awaited him.

Mrs. Arnold rose to meet his lordship's bow. "My lord, this is a pleasant surprise. I am positive that Miss Worth must share my feelings."

Lord Rathbone glanced at the lady in question, and thought grimly that it did not appear from her expression that she entered completely into Mrs. Arnold's assurances. After one fleeting glance at him when he had stepped into the room, she had not looked directly at him. "I hope that I am not regarded wholly as an enemy, Miss Worth," he said quietly.

She did meet his eyes then, her own gray gaze steady and considering. "No, my lord. You are not."

Quickly glancing from one to the other, Mrs. Arnold interposed, "It is early yet, my lord, but I trust that you will not object to taking tea with us."

Lord Rathbone indicated his willingness. The social nicety would guarantee that his visit would be an extended one.

Above all else, he desired the chance to speak with Miss Worth, and the odds of doing so lengthened the longer his stay.

He knew that because of what had happened between them, it would be difficult to articulate what he needed to say to her. Lord Rathbone discovered that his courage was not so deep as he would have liked. He could not contemplate the necessity of referring to what he only wished to forget without inwardly flinching. In that short period of time, he had been stripped of everything that mattered to him.

Nevertheless, there were things that had to be aired. So he bowed to the maudling of his insides with tea and biscuits and hoped that his courage would not desert him before the end of his visit.

Tea was duly partaken and all of the civilities observed in commonplace conversation. The part that Miss Worth took was scarcely encouraging to a gentleman already apprehensive.

At last, Lord Rathbone seized upon his destiny and said, "Mrs. Arnold, if it is at all possible, I beg of you the favor of a few private words with Miss Worth."

Mrs. Arnold turned her head, her expression inquiring. "Well, Verity?"

Verity felt an instant of panic. Mastering her reluctance, she nodded. "Of course. I am at his lordship's disposal."

She felt that she had been given no choice in allowing Lord Rathbone to have his say. Her brother had informed her briefly of his interview with the viscount. He had made it perfectly clear how matters stood: either she entertained Lord Rathbone's suit or he would be obliged to call out the viscount. It had been no less than blackmail on his part, as he had willingly acknowledged.

"However, I am not an ogre, Verity," he had said. "I want only what is in your best interests."

"And a marriage of convenience is what you consider to be best for me? Charles, I beg you! Do not force me to do this," she had said.

Sir Charles's blue eyes had been quite hard. "I leave it to you, Verity. It is your choice. I will naturally abide by your decision."

"You know very well that I do not wish you to meet him," said Verity in a low voice. "Not when you are determined to destroy him."

Sir Charles had been unmoved. "Your decision, Verity."

And so she had acquiesced.

Mrs. Arnold rose with a swish of her skirts. "Very well, then. I shall leave you now, my lord. I shall grant you a quarter hour."

"Thank you, ma'am. I am grateful to you," said Lord Rathbone. He had also risen and now accompanied the lady to the drawing room door. He opened it for her and Mrs. Arnold, with a last backward glance in Verity's direction, exited.

Lord Rathbone closed the door. He did not immediately leave it, but stood quite still as he gravely considered his intended bride from across the expanse of the room. She met his regard with calm, her head held high, her hands folded neatly in her lap.

Lord Rathbone abandoned his position and moved across the room. He sat down in a wing chair opposite that of his companion. He wanted to give her no reason to feel intimidated, either by standing over her or by coming too near her. Nevertheless, the tension that shot between them was palpable.

For a long moment Lord Rathbone cast about in his mind for the best way to disclose what was uppermost in his thoughts. He realized that there was no phrasing that could possibly answer the purpose. He would simply have to plunge in and hope for the best.

Lord Rathbone cleared his throat. "Miss Worth, I wish first to apologize to you once again. Pray accept my humblest assurances that I am genuinely repentant for the pain that my words and actions brought you."

"There is no need to say more on that score, my lord. I am fully aware that you are here under what you feel to be an obligation to me. I do not think it, nor have I desired it of you," said Verity quietly.

Lord Rathbone inclined his head in polite acknowledgment of her rebuff. It did not surprise him that she held him in aversion. Grimly, he pressed onward. "Nevertheless, I do have an obligation toward you, ma'am. I felt it at the time, as you will recall. Sir Charles's visit only led me to feel it more strongly. I shall be perfectly plain, Miss Worth. To do less than to offer you once more the protection of my name would be permanent dishonor, both to you and to myself."

Upon his words, Verity had risen from her chair. She walked to an occasional table and aimlessly picked up a figurine. She turned it this way and that, watching the sunlight strike off its smooth patina. "I, too, have heard my brother's view of the matter. I do not altogether share it. However, his argument was vastly convincing."

"Then what is your answer?" he asked tautly.

Verity carefully set down the figurine. She turned. Placing her hands on either side of her on the edges of the table, she looked directly into Lord Rathbone's eyes. "Very well, my lord. I accept your offer for my hand."

Lord Rathbone rose from his chair. He stepped toward her, holding out his hand. She laid hers in his palm. His fingers closed over hers. He felt the tremor that ran through her and his own tension increased. His thoughts were shaded equally by despair and resignation. Dear God, she could scarcely bear his touch.

Without expression, he raised her hand to his lips. The salute was brief, without passion. Releasing her hand, he said, "You have made me the happiest of men, Miss Worth."

Verity raised her eyes to his unfathomable gaze. She felt stifled suddenly. He despised her. He had been forced into declaring for her. It was all a travesty. She could not go through with it, whatever the consequences to him. She wanted to tell him so, but the words stuck in her throat.

Instead, her glance dropped away before his. She said, colorlessly, "You do me great honor, my lord."

The door to the drawing room opened. Mrs. Arnold sailed in, her eyes going from Lord Rathbone's grave expression to Verity's pale face. "It has been a quarter hour, my lord. I trust that was sufficient time?"

Verity spoke up. There was no smile in her eyes or on her face. In a cool, remote voice, she said, "You may congratulate me, Betsy. I have accepted Lord Rathbone's very obliging offer."

"My dear!" Mrs. Arnold advanced to embrace Verity and

whispered, "I know that Sir Charles will be awfully pleased." She kissed Verity on the cheek.

Turning then to Lord Rathbone, Mrs. Arnold extended her hand to him. With a smile, she said, "I am glad of this news, my lord. Allow me to be the first to extend my heartfelt felicitations to you. I know that you will give Verity all that she could possibly wish or desire."

Lord Rathbone responded with a twist of his lips. He sensed the questioning note in the lady's voice and knew that Mrs. Arnold had unspoken reservations. He glanced at his intended bride, who averted her face from his scrutiny. He wished with all of his being that he could reassure her. "Indeed, ma'am, it is my hope that I am able to do so."

"I am so glad. Herbert is not at home or I would instantly call him in to share with us this momentous occasion," said Mrs. Arnold.

"There will be another time," said Lord Rathbone. "I shall take my leave of you, ma'am. There are naturally matters that I must now attend. Miss Worth, if you have no objection, I shall take it upon myself to insert an immediate notice into the *Gazette*."

Verity shook her head, tracing with her finger a pattern on the top of a chair. "No, I have no objection, my lord."

Lord Rathbone bowed. "I will leave you now, then. Pray convey my respects to Sir Charles and inform him that I shall call upon him at his earliest convenience to discuss the settlements."

"Of course, my lord," said Verity, quite coolly. She lifted her eyes briefly to his as she gave her hand to him. The merest brush of his lordship's lips across her knuckles was all the salute he vouchsafed her before he turned and exited the drawing room.

The door closed behind the viscount. Mrs. Arnold turned to Verity. "Well, it is done, my dear. I know it has not chanced as you would have liked. I hope that you are not too disappointed."

"Disappointed, Betsy?" Verity gave an angry little laugh. It ended on what sounded suspiciously like a sob. She blazed up. "How should I be disappointed when I have managed to snare one of the most eligible *partis* in England? I shall be envied by every other unattached female. Oh, no, I am in fine feather. Can you not tell?" She dashed her hand across her tearing eyes and flew out of the room.

"Oh, my poor dear!" exclaimed Mrs. Arnold. She started to hurry after Verity, but then she paused as the thought struck her. It would no doubt do Verity good to indulge in a good cry.

Verity's emotions had been perilously strained. Mrs. Arnold had even expressed private concern to Sir Charles. But that gentleman had been remarkably unmoved. "Yes, no doubt. However, Verity is pluck to the backbone. She'll come around once she has squalled a bit."

Mrs. Arnold had thought Sir Charles to be singularly unfeeling, but now she wondered whether there had not been a good deal of wisdom in his assessment. And so she did not go after Verity after all. Instead, she hoped that with the passing of the storm, her friend would be better able to support her fate.

The quiet announcement of the betrothal of Miss Verity Worth, daughter of a mere baronet, to Lord Henry Alan George Sandidge, Viscount Rathbone, one of the most eligible bachelors in England, went out in due course. The intelligence was felt in some corners with far-reaching and electrifying force.

Various friends and acquaintances of Miss Worth's felt that she had done very well by herself, and either sent to her or called upon her with their sincere compliments. Lord Rathbone was variously roasted and congratulated by his friends upon his commitment to the marriage altar.

Mr. Pettiforth and Miss Tibbs were as one in their quiet satisfaction. They were happily unaware that somewhere in the wilds of Yorkshire, a spoiled young beauty was laid by the heels with hysterics when she heard of Miss Worth's good fortune.

As for Mrs. Pettiforth, she read the news item with appalled fury. She laid the blame squarely at Miss Worth's door that her darling daughter had not only lost a wealthy peerage, but also had been banished to a select and very strict seminary. She instantly dashed off a bitter and abusive denunciation of Miss Worth to her sister, Lady Rathbone.

Lady Rathbone read Mrs. Pettiforth's communication with

great interest and discernment. Upon her son's visit to her to report the result of his stay at the Pettiforths, she had been struck by his lack of objectivity. His usual indifferent cynicism had been conspicuously absent in his curt account. She had known then that there was more to the tale and that was why the viscount had found her to be so frustratingly unruffled.

She had bided her time, waiting upon her sister Pettiforth's account. Now that Lady Rathborne had it in her hands, a smile started to play about her thin mouth. Very deliberately, she refolded her sister's missive. Lady Rathbone had an almost overwhelming desire to meet her son's betrothed.

That desire was swiftly satisfied. Lord Rathbone took it upon himself to call upon his mother and engaged to escort her to the Arnolds' residence for an interview.

The butler revealed that Miss Worth was in to visitors. When the callers were shown up to the drawing room, Verity set aside her embroidery and rose from the settee to make Lady Rathbone's acquaintance. Her manner did not hint at the ill-ease that she felt. Instead, her smile and her gracious words of welcome showed all the proper respect that must be shown to one's prospective mother-in-law. "Pray will you not be seated, my lady? I have already rung for refreshments."

Lady Rathbone sat down. Her eyes swept over the younger lady's face and form. She was pleased with what she saw. Miss Worth was not in the first bloom of youth, nor was she a great beauty. But she possessed a natural air of poise and in her dress displayed excellent taste.

Lady Rathbone began to loosen her gloves. "Thank you, my dear Verity. I hope that I may call you that?"

"Of course, ma'am. My lord, will you not also be seated?" said Verity quietly as she resumed her seat.

Lord Rathbone took a chair opposite her. As Verity turned to address Lady Rathbone, she was acutely aware of his gaze on her face.

The refreshments were brought in then and a few minutes passed in determining her lady's preferences. Lord Rathbone refused all of the tempting offerings. Verity herself chose a single biscuit, and that only out of deference to Lady Rathbone's own expression of acceptance.

Lady Rathbone declined a second slice of the excellent

plum cake. After conveying her compliments to be passed on to the cook, Lady Rathbone touched her lips with her napkin and laid it aside. She said abruptly, "My son has perhaps told you that I am a formidable dame. I can be, indeed, especially with those whom I consider to be fools. Nevertheless, Verity, my hope is that we shall come to know one another to a degree that will allow us to rub along tolerably well."

"Miss Worth is scarcely a fool, dear ma'am," said Lord Rathbone, softy, his mouth hardened. He had straightened in the chair, his easy posture abandoned.

Lady Rathbone threw a measuring glance at the viscount. She was mildly surprised at how quickly he had taken up the cudgels on his betrothed's behalf. It would be interesting to see whether he would expose himself further.

Lady Rathbone smiled, but her eyes did not perceptibly warm. With deliberate calculation, she replied, "Indeed. We shall see. I do not wish her to be lulled into a false sense of romantic nonsense through her betrothal to you, my son. Verity must understand that you will no doubt make the very devil of a husband. You will probably continue in all of your extravagances and keep a mistress or two along the way. She will have your name, access to your wealth, and will bear your heirs. That must necessarily be enough."

Verity stared, her lips parting slightly with astonishment.

"I will thank you to keep a civil tongue in your head, my lady," snapped Lord Rathbone. His eyes glittered with wrath. "I did not bring you here today so that you might insult Miss Worth."

Lady Rathbone raised her brows. Her smooth expression effectively hid whatever thoughts she harbored. "Nonsense. I have not insulted Miss Worth in the least. On the contrary, I have done her the honor of considering her to be a rational creature."

Twenty-four

Lord Rathbone stared across the short space between himself and her ladyship, his own brows snapped together in a tight fashion. He ground out, "I do not know what you are about, ma'am. But I warn you that I shall not sit idly by if you mean to deal in abuse and insult."

Attempting to overcome her astonishment, Verity made a graceful gesture of dismissal. "I am not so easily insulted, my lord. On the contrary, I am grateful for her ladyship's plain speaking. It makes it so much easier, does it not?"

Lord Rathbone scowled, but he settled back into his chair.

Verity turned her head then and looked at Lady Rathbone. Her gray eyes held a hint of anger. "You choose to take off the gloves, ma'am, and so shall I. I have few illusions regarding this bargain that has been struck between myself and Lord Rathbone. You need not fear that I shall be shocked or disappointed with my lot. Nor, I should think, should you be anxious on his lordship's behalf. We both of us go into this marriage with our eyes wide open. It is a marriage of convenience, and we shall treat it so."

"You are not a fool, then. Very well, Verity. I shall lay aside whatever reservations that I might have held. Indeed, I suspect that you and George will deal very well together," said Lady Rathbone suavely.

Altogether she was immensely satisfied with Miss Worth. The young woman was obviously made of resilient stuff, not easily overset nor of a foolish turn of mind. And if she was not mistaken, she detected signs that Miss Worth was not altogether indifferent to her son. It showed in the pains that the young lady had taken in not glancing at the viscount any more often than civility demanded.

As for her son, Lady Rathbone had been pleasantly surprised to discover that he was himself not quite without feeling toward Miss Worth.

Lady Rathbone pulled on her gloves, signaling the end of her visit. She glanced over at Verity with the faintest of smiles. "I shall give a small party in your honor, my dear. You will thus be able to meet several personages that in your position as Lady Rathbone will not ordinarily come in your way."

Lord Rathbone narrowed his gaze upon his mother. He snapped, "Have you in mind what I suspect, ma'am?"

Lady Rathbone glanced at the viscount. "Not knowing what you suspect, George, how can I say?"

She rose to her feet, Verity following her example. Giving her hand to Verity, Lady Rathbone said, "I am glad to have made your acquaintance, Verity. Perhaps we shall even come to like one another." She turned. "George, you may escort me downstairs to the carriage, if you please."

Lord Rathbone bowed, his expression saturnine. "Of course, dear ma'am. I am yours to command."

Lady Rathbone uttered a deep-throated chuckle. For the first time since she had entered the drawing room, some expression other than cool appraisal crossed her face. "No doubt, my dear. Perhaps you will explain to me how that is so."

Upon the departure of the Rathbones, Mr. Arnold entered the drawing room looking for his wife. Verity had resumed her embroidery, a slight frown drawing her brows. She was glad of the interruption. Her expression lightened. "Betsy has gone shopping for a particular gauze to compliment her Italian silk. I expect her to return within the hour, however."

"What, Verity, you remained tamely at home when there was frivolous female frippery to be bought? You are not the lively young miss to whom I once paid court," he said teasingly.

Verity laughed a trifle ruefully. "No, I suppose that I am not," she agreed. "But it is just as well that I did not go shopping today. Lord Rathbone brought his mother to call upon me."

"Yes, I met them going out. The viscount spoke civilly enough, I thought." Mr. Arnold grimaced. "However, her ladyship could freeze a pheasant to death with but one of those frosted glances of hers. I daresay you have done well for yourself with Rathbone, Verity, but I do not envy you *that* connection!"

Verity laughed again, this time with genuine amusement. "I have the most lowering feeling that you may have the right of it, Herbert. However, one cannot repine too much. Lady Rathbone did me the honor of informing me that she does not think me to be a fool, at least."

Mr. Arnold stared at her. With a good deal of affront, he exclaimed, "Well, I say! That's mighty handsome of her, indeed!"

Verity saw that he had not quite entered into what she had felt to be a joke. "Never mind, Herbert. I didn't take it to heart. Have you by chance seen Charles since we breakfasted? I wished to ask him whether he had yet heard anything from my mother."

"I should think that he has! I ran into him just as I was coming out of my club. He was off to some agent or other to rent a house for Lady Worth and your sister and some aunt. What the deuce he wants to rent a house for at this time of year, I can't fathom. Told him that they were welcome to my roof for as long as they wished," said Mr. Arnold, vague hurt replacing the placidity of his expression.

Verity tried to excuse what was obviously seen as the lapse in her brother's manners. "I expect that he was thinking of my Great-aunt Mary, who is something of a semi-invalid and can be hard to manage on occasion."

"Peckish, is she?" said Mr. Arnold knowledgeably. "Had a grandmother once who was a regular tartar. She was bedridden, but wore her household to flinders. Shouldn't like that in my house. I shall thank Sir Charles when next I see him."

He started to withdraw through the door, then paused. "By the by, I asked Sir Charles how the settlements were coming. He said he met with Rathbone this morning. His lordship came down handsomely with nary an objection. It is all made tidy. That must relieve your mind, I don't doubt."

"Yes, of course it does," said Verity, managing a smile.

Mr. Arnold nodded and went his way, whistling, confident that he had done all in his power to support Verity's spirits.

Verity's feelings were mixed upon learning that the settlements had been completed. She felt at once strangely resigned and rebellious. It was a curious thing. If she had given any thought at all to examining her emotions, she might have discovered the courage to defy her brother's decree.

Perhaps sensing his sister's wavering acquiescence, Sir Charles did not allow her time for introspection. He commissioned Mrs. Arnold to see that his sister had a proper trousseau. Mrs. Arnold, always a firm believer that shopping raised even the most recalcitrant of spirits, enthusiastically embraced the task of bullying and badgering Verity into a constant round of fittings and trips to the shops.

Verity's life began to take on a whirling aspect. Town was virtually emptied of polite company, but there were still a number of souls who would not dream of leaving the metropolis. Those who remained for the winter season sent out a stream of invitations. A heavy abundance of them found their way to the Arnolds.

Verity and Lord Rathbone saw much of each other during these social functions. His lordship invariably made up the foursome when the Arnolds and Verity went out. Hostesses made certain that she and the viscount were always seated together. In the minds of everyone, Verity and Lord Rathbone had become an established couple.

Verity alone questioned the truth of the appearance that she and Lord Rathbone made to the world.

Lady Worth came up to London accompanied by her daughter, Elizabeth, and her aunt, Mrs. Moffet. Lady Worth rejected all of Sir Charles's efforts to ensconce them in a town house. She insisted instead that they could do very well with apartments in a respectable hotel.

"For we mean to make only a short stay, Verity. Elizabeth

must be gotten back to the seminary and dear Aunt Mary will fret if she is kept too long away from her home. I wished only to assure myself of your happiness and well-being," said Lady Worth. She looked closely at her daughter's face. "You appear somewhat pulled, Verity. Is there aught that I should know?"

Verity summoned up a laugh. Not for worlds would she make her mother anxious by disclosing her misgivings over her betrothal. "Nothing, dear ma'am. I am fagged to death, if you must know. I have been in a positive whirl to get my trousseau made up. Betsy is forever dragging me off to another round of shopping or out to enjoy some frivolous dissipation. You would scarcely credit how in demand we are, Mama. I never dreamed that so many personages remain in London over the winter."

"No doubt Lord Rathbone is particularly fond of London," said Lady Worth. She smiled and laid her hand over her daughter's. "But you shall come down to Crofthouse over Christmas, I hope? Charles has made everything comfortable again. In fact, once I have seen Aunt Mary back at home and settled Elizabeth again, I shall be returning to Crofthouse to oversee the preparations for the holiday."

"I do not know. That is, it never occurred to me, so I have not spoken of it to Lord Rathbone," said Verity.

"Well, you must do so. I should like all of my children with me over the holiday. August and Sally mean to come and of course there will be Timothy and Bart and Elizabeth. It will be exceedingly jolly," said Lady Worth.

"I shall speak to Lord Rathbone," Verity promised, smiling. Nostalgia was a welcome pain in her heart. The thought of being reunited with all of her family made her spirits rise. "Perhaps I shall do so this very evening, if there is opportunity. You will be at Lady Rathbone's tonight?"

"Of course, my dear. I would not miss a soirée given in my own daughter's honor," said Lady Worth. She rose from the settee. "You must convey my respects to Mrs. Arnold and tell her that I was sorry to find her out. Now I must run. I promised Elizabeth that if she sat with Aunt Mary while I was out, I would take her to Gunther's for an ice as a reward for being so good."

Verity laughed as she walked arm in arm with her mother

toward the door. "Poor Elizabeth! I hope that her ingenuity will not be taxed too greatly in entertaining my great-aunt."

They reached the door, which the porter quickly opened.

"Oh no," said Lady Worth, turning to her daughter. She smoothed her gloves over her wrists. "I told her to read the latest *on-dits* from the newspapers to Aunt Mary. That will stir the old lady's memories and you know what a positively *wicked* lady your great-aunt was in her heyday. I imagine that I shall find Elizabeth sitting wide-eyed absorbing it all. It would not astonish me to discover that she will have quite forgotten all about our outing."

Lady Worth took her leave with a last wave and Verity turned back into the hall. A swift glance at the standing clock showed her that it would soon be time for dinner and she went upstairs to change.

The Arnold household sat down to dinner at their own table, each resplendent in formal dress. Mr. Herbert tugged restlessly at his tight waistcoat. He sucked in his comfortable girth, only to let it out again in defeat. "I do not wish to complain, my dear, but I find this rig devilish uncomfortable."

"It is only for tonight, Herbert," soothed Mrs. Arnold. "Then you may go down to Crofthouse. Sir Charles told me only today that he has made all the arrangements for your enjoyment."

Mr. Herbert brightened. "Yes, by Jove! And dashed good of him it is, too, since he will remain stuck here in London. Not to say that I am not glad for all the notice you and the viscount have been enjoying, Verity. But all this fol-de-rol makes a man pine for a good gun and a hunting dog."

"I understand perfectly, Herbert," said Verity. "If I had my preferences, I would also be going down to Crofthouse in the morning."

Mrs. Arnold glanced over at Verity quickly, but Mr. Arnold was the one who responded. "Would you indeed! I always thought you were a sensible one, Verity."

Satisfied with his world, Mr. Arnold applied himself to his repast. When dinner was finished, he pronounced himself ready to escort the ladies to the evening's entertainment.

They had stepped out of the door and were about to enter

the carriage when Lord Rathbone arrived. After exchanging greetings all around, Lord Rathbone turned to Verity. He arranged her cloak more closely about her shoulders. The lamplight spilling down from the open door of the town house glimmered in her wide eyes and drew sparks from the diamonds she wore in her ears and about her slender throat. His hands rested briefly on her shoulders. "You look well this evening, Verity. I have rarely seen you lovelier," he said quietly.

Verity cast a startled glance up at him. His face was in shadow and she could read nothing in his expression. Heat had risen to her face and she was grateful for the uncertain light. "Thank you, my Lord. It is a pretty compliment."

His hands tightened on her shoulders, then slid away. Politely he offered his hand to her so that she could climb up into the carriage. When she was seated, Lord Rathbone entered and took the place beside her. He pulled the door closed and rapped their readiness to the driver.

Twenty-five

The soirée was an elegant affair. All of the *ton* left in town were in attendance. It was a compliment to Lady Rathbone's hostessing abilities as much as a testimony of the interest to which Lord Rathbone's betrothal had given rise.

There were a number of individuals that Verity did not know, however. These personages turned out to be Lord Rathbone's relations. As Verity was introduced to the viscount's uncle, his aunts, and several cousins, she became progressively more aware of an oddness about the high degree of curiosity in their eyes. The manners of several of the younger female cousins could only be termed as spurious. But their example was obviously set by their mothers. The viscount's aunts shot more than one measuring glance in Verity's direction as they talked behind their hands.

A foppish young gentleman, whom Verity was told had lately come back to England from several years of living abroad in France, sauntered up to make her acquaintance. Mr. Harold Sandidge bowed elegantly over her hand and said all that was polite, but with such an indifferent air that Verity was positive that he was merely acting out of habit. Her suspicion was swiftly confirmed.

"I must make my father's apologies, Miss Worth. He is a

near-invalid or otherwise he would most definitely have graced this function with his presence," said Harold Sandidge languidly. He had not bothered to look at her as he had spoken, being occupied instead with surveying the company through a large, ornate quizzing glass.

"I regret that I shall not have the opportunity of making Mr. Sandidge's acquaintance," said Verity politely.

Harold Sandidge lowered the glass and swung round his body—his stiffened shirtpoints were so ridiculously high that it was virtually impossible for him to turn only his head. He glanced penetratingly at her. "Are you, indeed? How very praiseworthy of you, Miss Worth," he murmured.

Lord Rathbone came up then. His cousin almost immediately excused himself and sauntered off. The viscount looked after Harold Sandidge's elegant person with dispassionate contempt. "My cousin is a bit of a fop and a ne'er-do-well," he commented.

"I did think him not quite the thing," ventured Verity.

Lord Rathbone uttered a short bark of laughter. "Oh, I imagine that he is harmless enough. It is his father, Forde Sandidge, whom one must necessarily despise."

Verity looked up at him curiously. "Is your uncle so disagreeable, then?"

"Not more so than Bastion, I suppose," said Lord Rathbone, giving a nod in the direction of the one paternal uncle who was present.

Mr. Bastion Sandidge was a tall, stoop-shouldered gentleman. When Verity had met him, she had thought she had never seen a set of colder black eyes.

"I see," she said thoughtfully. She had observed all evening the mutual lack of cordiality between Lord Rathbone and his kinsmen. Though civil words had been exchanged, there had been no warmth in eyes nor expressions. With the exception of Bastion Sandidge's son, Philip, she did not think that any of Lord Rathbone's relations held him in the least degree of affection. "My lord, it seems to me that there is a singular lack of family feeling amongst your relations. The undercurrents of dislike are positively rife through this gathering."

Lord Rathbone looked down at her, a curious intentness in his stare. "Are they, Miss Worth?"

"One cannot help but notice it," said Verity quietly. "You will think me inquisitive, no doubt, but is there some animosity that lies between you and the others of your family?"

Lord Rathbone gave his peculiar twisted smile. "There is bad blood, certainly. But it was all a long time ago. It is nothing that need concern you, ma'am."

Verity was not at all certain of that since he had made such a point of guarding her against lengthy private conversation with any of the Sandidges. But she did not give voice to her thoughts. She was not on such terms with Lord Rathbone that she felt able to challenge his indifferent assertion.

Lord Rathbone's attention was claimed by a hail from Verity's brother. With a word, the viscount left her and went over to meet with Sir Charles.

Lady Rathbone swept up to Verity. "Are you enjoying yourself, my dear?"

Verity gave a polite smile. "It is a delightful soirée, ma'am."

Lady Rathbone gave vent to a throaty laugh. "What a poor liar you are, Verity. They are a bunch of quizzes and fools. You will understand now why I said that you would meet a number of personages that will not later come in your way. My son and I are quite divorced from mingling with either Forde's or Bastion's families. However, I did wish you to meet them this once."

"I suppose that I must thank you, my lady," said Verity. "Certainly it has been an interesting evening. If Lord Rathbone does not care for their company, I must make it an object to abide by his wishes."

"No, my son does not care for their company. Nor do I," said Lady Rathbone, somewhat harshly. Her keen gaze raked the gathering. "They none of them mean a single word of the civilities that they have mouthed this night. My son and I are not liked by this bunch. And because you are to wed my son, their dislike spills over onto you as well. You will not find it an onerous task to reject any encroachments, believe me."

Verity did not know what to say. She was grateful when her brother and Lord Rathbone joined her and Lady Rathbone. "Charles, I am glad to see you. I had hoped to enjoy another set with you. For an old soldier you do very well for yourself on the floor."

"I shall leave you to it, my dear," said Lady Rathbone, preparing to turn away.

"Pray do not abandon us so quickly, my lady. I should like you to hear the question I wish to put to my sister," said Sir Charles.

Lady Rathbone's brows rose. She glanced from Sir Charles to her son's closed face. Her gaze sharpened. "Of course, Sir Charles. You naturally command my full attention."

Verity cast a hasty glance up at the viscount's face. There was something in his expression that could not be defined. Turning to her brother with a prescience of trouble, she asked, "What is it, Charles?"

"I have just spoken to Lord Rathbone. He has agreed to a wedding date three weeks from today. Is that not correct, my lord?" said Sir Charles.

Lord Rathbone shrugged. "It is all one to me. As I told you, I shall agree if Miss Worth has no objections."

Sir Charles commandeered his sister's hand. "Verity, I think that I can persuade our mother to remain in London at least for that long. An early date will mean that she will not have to travel up again for a later wedding. You know how she detests leaving Crofthouse. It would mean, too, that she would not fret over wedding preparations during the holiday. You will not wish to put our mother through such anxiety, Verity."

"Of course I do not," said Verity, completely taken aback. "But it is so soon!"

She felt herself to be all at once in a stormy sea. Her brother's grip was compelling; she knew what he demanded of her. Her eyes sought and found Lord Rathbone's, but there was no help for her there. The viscount's gaze was shuttered.

Lady Rathbone wore a pleased smile. Her eyes glinted. "It is soon, of course. But I applaud Sir Charles's desire to make it as painless as possible for all concerned. I believe that your great-aunt would not otherwise be persuaded to attend, for the dear lady confided in me not two minutes ago that London is nothing like what she recalled and she was not going to set foot in town again for the remainder of her days."

Verity was diverted for an instant. "Yes, that sounds very like Great-aunt Mary," she agreed with a laugh.

"Then it is settled," said Lady Rathbone firmly. "We shall send a notice to the *Gazette* tomorrow, naturally. However, I should like to make the announcement tonight amongst all the family."

"Of course. What could be more appropriate or more satisfying?" murmured Lord Rathbone sardonically.

Verity looked quickly up at him, catching the hint of bitterness in his words but not understanding the reason for it. But he did not glance down at her. His attention was focused on Lady Rathbone as she signalled the butler to call for silence.

When all of the gathering was stilled and had turned inquiring faces toward her ladyship, Lady Rathbone said, "I wish to convey the gladdest of tidings to my friends and family. As you all are aware, my son is betrothed to Miss Worth. Tonight a wedding date has been set. I am happy to announce that I shall be able to address Verity as my daughter-in-law in truth three weeks from this very night!"

The company broke into surprised exclamations and laughter. Friends of both the viscount and his intended came forward to congratulate them. Verity was surrounded by her own family. A toast was called for and the suggestion was swiftly taken up.

Verity noticed that of all the Sandidges, only Lord Rathbone's cousin Philip offered uninhibited felicitations. Even as she noticed that, she chanced to catch sight of Lady Rathbone's face. Verity was startled by the raw emotion in the lady's expression.

Lady Rathbone was staring at her brother-in-law, Bastion Sandidge. There was triumph on her face. She slowly lifted her wineglass, toasting him, then deliberately she drained it.

Bastion Sandidge turned sharply on his heel and strode out of the ballroom. His leaving was the signal for a mass exodus of Sandidges.

With the end of the soirée, Verity returned to the Arnolds' completely exhausted. It had been a difficult evening, full of hidden emotions and contrasts. Verity herself had had to keep up a smiling front for her own family and her well-wishers, while her heart ached for what might have been. How different everything would have been if Lord Rathbone had actually cared for her.

Mr. Arnold departed at first light the morning following the soirée. Sir Charles Worth did not breakfast at the Arnolds' but went out to his club. Mrs. Arnold and Verity did not rise from their respective beds until nearly eleven o'clock. They met in the breakfast room, neither ascribing to the fashionable habit of taking morning chocolate and biscuits in bed.

Verity was heavy-eyed. Without appetite, she merely picked at her selection from the sideboard. After one comprehending glance, Mrs. Arnold poured a second cup of coffee for her. "Perhaps this will help, my dear. You do not look at all the thing this morning."

Verity covered an unexpected yawn with her hand. Apologizing, she said, "I am sorry, Betsy. I did not rest well."

"I do not wonder at it. We have been going the pace of late," said Mrs. Arnold.

Verity did not bother to reply. They both knew it was not a frenzy of social engagements and shopping that had worn Verity down. But there was little point in discussing what could not be changed.

The footman entered. As he handed a folded note to Verity, he said, "This was just brought for you, miss. A carriage is awaiting your convenience."

"A carriage? Verity, what is it about?" asked Mrs. Arnold.

Verity had read the note. She looked up, frowning. "The note is supposedly from my mother. I do not recognize the hand, however. It says that she requires me to come to her at once."

"How very odd!"

"Yes. I cannot imagine Mama sending for me through another's offices." Verity's expression altered suddenly. "Unless my great-aunt has been taken ill. Mama would not leave her in that instance, and she might very well direct a note to be written for her."

Verity rose from the table. "I must go at once. Mama would not be so very cryptic, nor would she send a carriage for me, if there was not an appalling crisis!"

"Of course you must go," said Mrs. Arnold, rising also. She walked with Verity out of the breakfast room, followed by the footman. "I shall make your excuses to any who might call and I will cancel those appointments that we had for today."

"Thank you, Betsy. I shall go up now to put on my bonnet," said Verity. "Will you have the driver informed, please?"

"Of course."

As Verity hurried up the stairs, Mrs. Arnold told the footman to notify Lady Worth's driver that it would be a few minutes before Miss Worth was ready.

"At once, ma'am. But I should perhaps mention that it is not Lady Worth's driver or carriage, but a hired vehicle," said the footman.

Mrs. Arnold raised her brows, entering into her servant's mild surprise. "How extraordinary. I expect that there is a logical explanation, however." The footman agreed, still disapproving of the circumstances, and went off to speak to the driver.

Shortly thereafter, Verity returned downstairs. She had put on her bonnet and an outer pelisse over her dress. Her slippers had been replaced by kid boots. A large muff hung from her arm. She was engaged in pulling on her second glove as she reached Mrs. Arnold. "I do not know how long I shall be, Betsy. I shall send word to you just as quick as I can."

Mrs. Arnold assured Verity that she need not concern herself with anything. She accompanied Verity out-of-doors and saw her into the carriage. "I shall see to everything on this end, my dear. Convey my regards to Lady Worth and my sincere hope that all will be well."

Verity waved, the carriage started away from the curb, and Mrs. Arnold returned shivering to the warmth of her town house. Mrs. Arnold's mind was already busy with the altered plans for the day.

Late that afternoon, Mrs. Arnold was surprised when Lady Worth was ushered into her drawing room. After greeting her ladyship affectionately, she said, "I hope that Mrs. Moffet is well?"

"Oh yes, she has never been better other than a twinge of the gout," said Lady Worth cheerfully. "I had hoped to catch you and Verity both in, Mrs. Arnold, for I wished to beg your company to the shops. I do so enjoy having someone with me when I go out."

Mrs. Arnold stared at her ladyship, disregarding most of this speech. "But is Verity not with you?"

Lady Worth looked her surprise. "No, why should she be?"

Mrs. Arnold's face drained of color. "Oh, my God."

Twenty-six

"I have been abducted." Verity said the words out loud, but still it seemed so unreal.

While in the carriage, preoccupied and anxious over what she had accepted as her mother's message, it had not immediately dawned on her that she had been riding for more minutes than the short trip should have taken. Glancing out of the window, she had been appalled to discover that the teeming streets of London were giving way to less-frequented byways.

She had rapped and raised her voice to catch the driver's attention, but to no avail. Then she had tried to open the doors, but they had been locked from the outside.

Verity had known panic and fear then, but there had been nothing she could do but watch the city environs disappear as the carriage carried her into the winter countryside.

Her destination had proved to be no great distance from London, but the estate was not one with which she was familiar and so she still had no inkling of the identity of her captor. The carriage had stopped, and then she had suffered the indignity of having a scratchy woolen cloak thrown over her head. Helpless, she had been carried up several flights of stairs before being dumped gracelessly in her present prison.

It seemed incredible. She had been abducted, but for what

purpose she had no notion. She knew, however, that she was very much afraid.

Shivering, Verity crossed her arms. Running her hands up and down her arms, she stepped to the cold window. It was a dizzying view. The barren ground was three stories below her vantage point. There would be no escape that way. If she was to leave the attic garret, it would only be at her abductor's pleasure.

The sound of a key grating in the lock spun her around. She stared at the door, fright pumping her heart to a fast cadence.

The door opened. A burly serving man in a livery unknown to her stood in the doorway. "The master's compliments, miss, and he requests that you join him in the drawing room."

The incongruity of the polite phrasing struck her. But it was illogically reassuring as well. It was something familiar in a most bizarre situation. Verity raised her chin. Stiffening her spine, she said coldly, "Thank you. I shall come at once."

Verity walked across the small, cramped room and through the door. In the narrow hall, she paused and looked an inquiry at the footman. The man bowed and guided her through twisting halls and down two levels to the first floor.

The footman led her across a parquet floor. Throwing open a door, he announced, "Miss Worth, sir." With a polite gesture, he invited Verity to pass through the doorway.

Verity entered into what proved to be a drawing room. She had a fleeting impression of a well-proportioned room furnished in an old-fashioned style, but her attention almost instantly focused on those who awaited her. With shock, she recognized all but one. Verity controlled her expression with difficulty.

Three of the gentlemen had risen in civil deference to her entrance. The last remained seated in his wheeled chair, a rug cast over his knees and a cane clasped in his withered hands.

"Miss Worth, we have been waiting for you. Pray come in and join us," said Bastion Sandidge. "It is cold. You will no doubt like a chair next to the fire. Philip, pray set a chair for our guest."

Once more Verity was struck by the outrageous contrast between her actual circumstances and the polite observances.

She had been brought to this house against her will and had remained under lock and key in an attic garret until this moment.

It was ridiculous to suppose that such civil addresses negated the undoubted criminality of her present company but, nevertheless, Verity felt somewhat reassured by the lack of overt brutality. In fact, the irony was so striking that it caused a glint of amusement to enter her eyes. She was therefore able to react with a collected air quite at variance with her former deep apprehension.

Verity inclined her head and walked over to take the chair that Philip had arranged for her. Quietly she thanked him, noticing that he avoided meeting her eyes. He bowed and moved away to stand in front of the mantel.

Verity turned her gaze on the entire company. "Gentlemen." Her tone expressed just the right shade of doubt for the aptness of the term.

Philip flushed. He turned away abruptly to claim a wineglass that was sitting on the mantel. With a twist of his wrist, he tossed down the contents.

His obvious discomfiture was ignored by the rest of the gentlemen. The elderly one in the wheeled chair stared at Verity from under bushy brows. It could be seen that at one time he had been a powerful man, but now the massive shoulders were sunken forward and the hand that rested on top of the cane showed both age and disease in its malformation. "You are very cool, miss," he remarked, almost disapprovingly.

"Perhaps a bout of screaming hysterics would be more to your taste, sir?" inquired Verity, raising her slim brows.

"No, by God!" exclaimed Philip. He looked her full in the face then. His mouth was taut. "Forgive me, Miss Worth. I had not meant to have a hand in this. You must believe that."

"Must I? Surely you will admit that circumstances argue against you," said Verity quietly. As she looked at him the dull flush once more surged upward over his sharply defined cheekbones.

"My son is uncomfortable in his unaccustomed role of villain, Miss Worth. His scruples are much nicer than mine," said Bastion Sandidge, smiling. "You must naturally have many questions, which of course we shall do our best to satisfy. You have made the acquaintance of my nephew, Harold, but I do not believe that you have previously met my brother, Forde Sandidge."

"No, that distinction was not mine. Under other circumstances perhaps the introduction would have been met with pleasure. You will, I know, understand my reservations upon this occasion, Mr. Sandidge," said Verity.

"Damned biting tongue you have, gel. Don't know that I care for it," said Forde Sandidge, scowling.

Bastion Sandidge laughed. "You have become too isolated, brother. Society has changed since your day. The ladies are more forthcoming than they were in our youth. Miss Worth has just delivered a civil setdown with what I might say is admirable aplomb given her awkward situation. She is obviously a young woman of considerable force of character."

"Somehow I am not astonished. Our dear thrice-damned viscount would scarcely choose someone who was not up to his weight," murmured Harold Sandidge, for the first time breaking his silence. He seated himself and thoughtfully regarded the cut of his boots.

"True enough. George has proven his mettle more than once," said Philip with almost a shade of defiance.

Bastion Sandidge's complacent smile thinned. He shot a withering stare at his son. Philip hunched a shoulder and turned his gaze to the fire in the grate. Bastion Sandidge returned his attention to Verity and his smile reappeared. "Now, Miss Worth. We have requested that you join us for a particular purpose. We wished you to have a fuller understanding of the situation and the history behind it. No doubt you have been regaled with tales. It is only proper that you should be made aware of our side of the story."

"My uncle is subtly offering justification for the attack against your person," said Harold indifferently. He did not glance at Verity, but continued to contemplate the highly polished toe of his boot.

"That will be enough, sirruh!" exclaimed Forde Sandidge wrathfully, rapping his cane on the floor. "You will keep a civil tongue in your head or you will see how sharply that neat independence I make you can be turned about."

Harold brushed an unseen fleck of dust from his sleeve.

"Forgive me, dear father. I forgot myself for a moment. As you were saying, uncle?"

"Perhaps I should apply first to Miss Worth. You undoubtedly have an opinion of our family. I should like to hear it, so that I may better explain matters," said Bastion Sandidge.

Verity looked at them. She wondered that the question could even be put forward. They had abducted her. Surely that could be said to be outside the realm of the conventional. "Bizarre is the word that comes to mind."

"Yes, it is as I thought," said Bastion, sighing. "Lady Rathbone has no doubt confided in you how deep runs her fear and hatred of us. We, who are her ladyship's closest kin, have always been treated like pariahs. But we do not altogether blame Lady Rathbone for her prejudice. She was infected by our brother's intolerance. Vincent viewed expressions of familial affection with unreasoning suspicion."

"What has this to do with me?" asked Verity.

"You are affianced to my cousin George," said Philip savagely. "That is reason enough!"

Verity glanced around at all of their faces, but could discover nothing in their expressions that was illuminating. A puzzled crease formed between her brows. "I do not understand. What has my becoming affianced to Lord Rathbone have to do with a long-standing feud between all of you and Lady Rathbone?"

"Either you are remarkably dense, Miss Worth, or you have been kept totally in the dark," murmured Harold.

"Miss Worth is neither," snapped Bastion. "She is merely fishing."

"Get on with it, Bastion," growled Forde., "This was your idiotic notion. I told you it was a waste of time. The gel is set to wed that bastard. To my mind, that settles the matter. She needs to be disposed of."

Verity felt something freeze within her. She stared at the old man hunched in the wheeled chair. He stared back with an implacability in his eyes that made her shudder. She turned her wide-eyed gaze to Bastion Sandidge. "Surely your brother speaks out of turn, sir."

Bastion Sandidge smiled slightly. He shrugged. "You must forgive my brother's impatience. Forde and I were confident of stepping into a wealthy inheritance with the demise of our eldest brother. Our expectations were quite unfairly cut up with the birth of the present viscount. Lord Rathbone's subsequent progress through life roused our hopes once again. He was always such a wild, reckless young fellow, you understand. But he has survived after all. Now he means to set up his nursery. Surely you can appreciate our dilemma. We don't know quite what to do with you."

Verity's mouth had gone dry. She was convinced that she was dealing with madmen. "I would prefer to be let go free, sir."

Bastion laughed gently. "My dear, that is not possible now that we have you in our hands. No, it is as my brother has stated. You must be disposed of in some fashion. I had thought perhaps to pawn you off on Philip or my nephew. What say you, Harold?"

Harold Sandidge lazily looked Verity up and down. "She is well enough, I suppose, but a bit on the tall side for my taste. I have no desire to take a wife, in any event. It would not suit me to change my way of living."

Bastion shrugged. "I should not like to foist a wife on you. And you, Philip? Do you also dislike the notion of taking Miss Worth to wife?"

Philip looked from his father to Verity. There was a very strange expression on his face.

Bastion showed his teeth. "No, my son, you need not give voice to your feelings. You lack the boldness to tame a reluctant bride." He swung his glance back around on Verity. "'Tis a pity that neither I nor my brother are free to offer ourselves, Miss Worth."

"On the contrary. I am most thankful for it," said Verity quietly. She looked at him curiously. "You seem to believe that I would have nothing at all to say in the matter."

"Believe me, you would not have the least say," said Bastion. "There are means that will bring even the most reluctant young lady to the altar."

Verity decided that she did not want to delve into that. Instead, she tried to pursue a course of logic. "I should like to point out that even if I were wed into your family, that would not answer. Lord Rathbone could simply get himself another bride. You cannot very well hope to dispose of all the women of England," she said.

"She's right," said Philip quickly. "You must see that."

Forde growled something deep in his throat. He rapped the cane on the floor. "Bastion."

"Pray do not be a nodcock, Philip," said Bastion wearily.

Under his contemptuous glance, his son flushed. Bastion returned his attention to Verity, once again smiling. "While it is quite true that we cannot precisely dissuade every lady from wedding our nephew, we have the means to prevent you from doing so. And to us, at the moment, that is of primary importance."

"But why should *I* be so important?" asked Verity, raising her hands in a slight gesture of bewilderment.

Bastion sighed. "Miss Worth, surely you must have realized by now. We have a vast acquaintance. We have had all the details of the scandal that arose out of the recent house party held by the Pettiforths. We know that Lord Rathbone made you the object of his gallantries. In light of the inordinately early date of the wedding, we have reasoned that Lord Rathbone seduced you and you have discovered that you are to be delivered of his heir."

"Can't let that happen," growled Forde.

Bastion spread his hands. "So there you have it, Miss Worth."

Verity's lips had parted with astonishment. Bemused, she shook her head. "My dear sirs, you operate under a gross misapprehension. I assure you that I was not seduced by Lord Rathbone. That may have been his ultimate intention, but it did not happen."

Forde guffawed, while Bastion merely regarded her with an expression of disappointment. The latter said pityingly, "Do you really think that we will believe that, Miss Worth?"

"Nevertheless, it is the truth."

"Bastion, I am done with waiting. You have enlightened the gel. Now let's do what needs to be done," said Forde.

"You were always so impetuous, brother," said Bastion.

"However, you are undoubtedly in the right. Miss Worth now perfectly understands our motives and the necessity of her removal. It only remains to devise a proper ending. Since neither of our respective sons is willing to sacrifice themselves, I suppose that we have no alternative but to sacrifice Miss Worth."

Harold Sandidge's head came up, his eyes narrowing on his uncle's face.

Bastion bowed slightly to the young woman who now stared at him, suddenly whitefaced. "Forgive me, Miss Worth. It is a pity, of course, but necessary."

"Enough, damn you!" Philip struck the mantel with his fist. He turned to face his kinsmen, his expression tight. "I won't hear another word! I fell in with this thing with the utmost reluctance, and then only at your word that Miss Worth was to be held only so long as to give George a disgust of her. You assured me that she would not be unduly harmed. Now you speak of murder! Well, I won't listen to any more of it. Do you understand me? You do what you must, but leave me out of the plot. It sickens me!"

Philip slammed out of the drawing room. In short order, his furious shout for his horse and whip could be heard ringing through the house.

Twenty-seven

The ensuing silence was broken. "Dear me! It appears that we have lost one of our number," said Harold quietly.

"He'll come back stone-drunk," predicted Forde. He stared at his brother from under lowered brows. "He has always lacked fortitude, Bastion."

Bastion stood, frowning. "Philip was always too much like his mother. I had once thought it possible to beat it out of him, but I failed."

"Will he betray us, I wonder?" asked Harold lightly.

Bastion stiffened. His cold black eyes raked his foppish nephew with dislike and contempt. "Philip fears me too much to set himself against me. He will be back, insensible and useless, but his loyalty to me still unquestioned. I may depend upon Philip's loyalty. It is ingrained in him. I suspect, however, that you will be loyal only as long as the purse remains open."

"I am such an avaristic soul," agreed Harold, sighing.

"Puppy!" growled Forde, "I will be glad when this business is done and I may send you back to France. You make me ill with your foppish ways and your die-away airs. Pah!"

"I cannot think why you did not strangle me in the cradle," said Harold amiably. His was a smiling expression, though it was noticeable that his drooping lids did not quite disguise the glittering dislike in his eyes.

Forde Bastion's withered hands worked on the head of his cane. "I wish I had. I wish that fall in the quarry had taken you. You could never hold a candle to your twin. I wish it had been you that had perished in that hole instead."

"But it was not. I am here and he is in hell. I am your only heir. I am the only son that you shall ever be able to call upon this side of perdition." Harold was no longer smiling. His eyes and face were as hard as his father's. "And you have called upon me, dear father."

"So he has. You are quite right, Harold. My brother should be gratetul for your expression of filial duty," said Bastion. His words did not seem to find favor with either combatant, for his nephew merely lowered his gaze to survey the toe of his boot while Forde hunched his shoulders.

Bastion shook his head. Lifting his hands, he smiled at Verity. "Forgive us, Miss Worth. For a moment, we quite forgot that you were present. All families have these little squabbles, but they are quickly overlooked in the press of more important matters." He paused, then said with deliberation, "The question of your fate, for instance."

"You must disregard my lack of enthusiasm for the proposed solution," said Verity with heavy irony. Her hands were clasped tightly in the folds of her skirt. Fear beat heavily in her veins. She knew that her life meant very little to these men, but it was of the greatest importance to her.

How strange it was that little less than a week ago she had felt that her existence had become in some respects intolerable. Now her one fervent desire was to exchange her present situation for her former state. Those things that had appeared to be so insurmountable now seemed peculiarly unimportant.

"What shall it be, then? Poison, garroting or shooting?" inquired Harold indifferently.

Forde scowled. "Fool! We would have the constables sniffing all over the countryside if her body turned up with signs of violence."

"Quite true, brother. We must be more subtle, more careful, than that. We must give it more thought," said Bastion.

Harold yawned and languidly rose to his feet. "Well, I shall leave it to you to decide. I don't intend to tease myself with it any more this evening. Do you not serve dinner in this house? We scarcely recommend ourselves as civilized beings to Miss Worth if we let her perish from hunger."

"Oh, surely one way is as good as the next," snapped Verity. The horror of it all had skewed in her mind. She scarcely realized what she said. It did not matter. Her fate was in the grip of madmen.

The three gentlemen stared at her, held by shocked astonishment.

Then Harold gave a shout of unaffected laughter. For that instant the attitude of studied indolence dropped away, as did the mask of indifference. His eyes danced. "That was very good. I could come to like you very well, Miss Worth."

"It's a pity that we shall not be given the opportunity to explore the possibility," said Verity, emboldened.

The shutter came down once more over Harold's countenance. He smiled slowly. "Yes," he agreed. "but at least I shall have the pleasure of your stimulating wit at dinner. Will you accept my escort, ma'am?"

"Since I have been granted the dubious honor of staying in this house, I shall accept," said Verity, putting her fingers on his extended elbow.

Harold walked with her to the door, remarking, "I doubt that we shall find much more than slivers of mutton or some meat pies on the sideboard. It is so tedious that the household was banished just at this time. I do dislike being inconvenienced."

A snarled insult was hurled after them. "Damned puppy!"

For Verity, it was a singularly macabre affair. She sat at the dining table with only two companions, Bastion Sandidge and his nephew, Harold, since Forde had opted to take dinner in solitary splendor in his rooms. Candlelight played over the silver settings and the expensive snowy linens; glimmerings of light touched fire from crystal wineglasses. By contrast, the offerings from the sideboard were much as Harold had predicted. A cold collation of meats, pies and cheeses; a weak barley soup; and vegetables indifferently cooked and ill-seasoned. There was only one servant in attendance—the burly footman who had let her out of the locked garret.

Verity refused nearly everything, her appetite nonexistent. She merely picked at the stringy beans and slivers of roast and mutton that Harold had insisted that she be served. The poor repast was accompanied by polite conversation between the Sandidges, punctuated several times by the younger man's oblique complaints of the fare.

"You do not eat, Miss Worth. I do not find it incomprehensible," said Harold, eyeing with distaste the remains of his own choices.

"You know that your mother and sisters and most of the staff were sent off," said Bastion, finally showing his growing irritation.

Harold sighed. His fingers played with the stem of his wineglass. "Yes, how inconvenient it has all been. I shall be glad to make an end of my stay here. My father's house has never produced warm feelings in me."

"You may leave the instant that everything has been arranged. Pray believe that I shall not throw any obstacle in your way," said Bastion, showing his teeth.

"You see what a close-knit affectionate family we are, Miss Worth," said Harold, mocking his uncle by raising his glass in salute. With the flick of an elegant wrist, he tossed back the wine.

"Yes, most definitely. I do believe that if left to yourselves, you would soon tear one another's throats out," said Verity quietly.

"How very astute of you, Miss Worth. It is only the shared antipathy for my cousin, Lord Rathbone, and his esteemed dame that has kept my father and my uncle from turning on one another long years past," said Harold. He had poured another glass of wine and now raised it to his lips.

"You are in your cups, Harold," said Bastion contemptuously.

"Perhaps I am. I am not usually so reflective. A pity that my father did not join us. His presence would undoubtedly have stymied any such tendency," said Harold.

Verity was thankful that the eldest Sandidge had chosen to retire to his rooms. Of them all, Forde Sandidge appeared to be the most inclined to do away with her with the least amount of time spared.

The thought of what was planned for her made her feel suddenly, overwhelmingly, claustrophobic. Verity started to rise from her chair. A heavy hand descended upon her shoulder, forcing her back into her chair. She looked up, her anger underlaid by fear. The burly footman stared back at her imperturbably.

Verity swung about to face Bastion Sandidge, her gray eyes resembling a sea storm. "Am I not to be allowed to retire into the drawing room while you *gentlemen* partake of your wine?" she asked witheringly.

"The man is perhaps overzealous in the interpretation of his duties. In this instance it is for the best. The house is virtually empty. I would not wish you to wander off and become lost, Miss Worth," said Bastion, smiling. "However, if you would prefer to retire to your room—"

"Thank you, but no," said Verity shortly. "I shall remain where I at least have the illusion of freedom."

A loud disturbance sounded outside the dining room. Quick, hard steps sounded on the parquet floor, then the door was thrust open. Philip stood swaying in the doorway. His eyes blinked, seeming to focus slowly. He let go of the door and walked into the room. "My family sitting at meat. I shall join you, if I may." He made a careful bow. "And you, Miss Worth."

"You're drunk, dear fellow," observed Harold.

Bastion's lips thinned, and his narrowed eyes glittered. With fury he snapped, "You're a fool, Philip!"

Philip had dropped into a chair beside Verity. He laughed. The aroma of spirits was strong. Slurring his words, he said, "So you have always told me, sir. But I am not such a fool as you think me. I have decided to take me a wife."

Under cover of the table his hand had found Verity's and squeezed her fingers. She stared at him, wide-eyed, wondering.

"I do believe that you have shocked Miss Worth, cousin," murmured Harold.

Philip's gaze swung around to meet Verity's. Though he wore a particularly loose grin, she was startled by the expression in his eyes. It was lucid, and one of warning. Her heart gave a great leap, yet still she did not dare to hope.

Philip leaned back in his chair. He passed a hand across his eyes. "Yes, I mean to take a wife."

Seated opposite, Harold chuckled softly. "Have you, indeed, cousin? But what has brought about this surprising turn?"

"Don't like the notion of murder." Philip hiccoughed and politely apologized before he continued. "But I do like Miss Worth. It came to me plain as day. I'll marry you, ma'am."

"Thank you, Mr. Sandidge. I believe that under the circumstances that I should like to accept your offer," said Verity.

"It is settled, then!" Philip stretched an arm across the table to reach for the bottle of brandy. "Let us drink a toast to it."

"I believe you have had enough." grated Bastion, removing the bottle beyond his son's fumbling grasp.

Philip shrugged, a sullen expression settling over his face. "Shouldn't have come back so soon. Shouldn't have come back at all."

"Ah, but then you could not have announced to us your intent to wed," said Harold, half-rising, and pushing another bottle across the table toward his cousin. "Drink up, my dear Philip. It is not every evening that a man makes such a momentous decision."

Philip grinned crookedly and laid hold of the bottle. Ignoring his father's explosive oath, he clumsily poured out a measure of wine, slopping a little onto the table linen as he did so. He held up the full wineglass. "To—to my bride!" He threw back his head and downed the brandy.

"There is no bride!" exclaimed Bastion Sandidge.

"Of course there is. There she sits," said Philip. He pointed a wavering finger at Verity. He lowered his head, staring at her as though he had difficulty bringing her into full focus. Then he smiled loosely again.

Bastion smashed a fist down on the table, causing some of the silver to jump. "Listen to me, you imbecile!"

"It is useless, dear uncle. He is not in a coherent state," interposed Harold. He had leaned back in his chair, an amused expression on his face. His long fingers played with the beribboned fob at his waist. "I have given some thought to the dilemna posed by Miss Worth. If you are adamantly opposed to Philip's surprising declaration, perhaps my own solution might be worthy of consideration."

At his nephew's soft words, Bastion abandoned his smouldering contemplation of his son. He narrowed his cold gaze onto Harold. "Well, what is it?"

"Deportation, dear uncle. The penal colonies are so distressingly short of good labor, one hears," said Harold.

Bastion stared at his nephew. "Deportation," he repeated slowly. His expression became increasingly thoughtful. "Many do not survive the harsh voyage. Those who do, never return. A trumped-up charge, a few pounds changing hands, and the thing is done. Very neat, indeed. It is a good thought, Harold. I might even say, one of brilliance."

Harold bent his head in ironic acknowledgement.

"I shall put it to Forde in the morning," said Bastion decisively. He rose from the table, tossing aside his napkin. "It is growing late. You there, put my son to bed. I shall myself escort Miss Worth upstairs."

The burly footman nodded. He bent to help the languishing Philip to his feet. Philip laughed and draped a heavy arm across the man's shoulders. "To bed, to bed, heigh-ho!" he chanted. His weight made the footman stagger as the two started out of the dining room.

Bastion mouthed his disgust. He held out a peremptory hand to Verity, who had also risen from the table. "Come, Miss Worth! I regret the necessity, but I must lock you in for the night."

"Pray do not put yourself to so much trouble, Mr. Sandidge. I can assure you that I do not walk in my sleep," retorted Verity, sweeping past him, her head held high.

Harold laughed quietly. He held open the door for her. "Ah, Miss Worth! I truly suspect that I shall miss you."

"The feeling is scarcely mutual, I assure you," said Verity.

She stepped into the wide hall, Bastion Sandidge coming immediately behind her. She saw that the footman was struggling to direct Philip's faltering steps up the stairs, while that young gentleman was bellowing a popular ballad. Verity felt a sinking of her spirits. Surely there could be no hope of rescue from that quarter, after all.

Verity felt a clutching hand close on her elbow. She whirled herself free, her eyes blazing at a startled Bastion Sandidge. "Do not dare to touch me!"

"Bravo, Miss Worth! Your fate is not your own and yet you meet it magnificently."

The ironic words had scarcely left Harold's mouth when the hall was shattered by a booming report.

Twenty-eight

Philip straightened and, with lightening-quick fists, dispatched the burly footman to unconsciousness. The servant slumped against the wall and slid down to sprawl awkwardly on the stairs.

Verity saw her brother seemingly materialize out of nowhere, smoking pistol in hand. She gave a glad cry. "Charles!"

He did not answer. Dropping the discharged pistol, he leaped forward, and with a savage twist, whipped Harold Sandidge's arm up behind his back. The dandy bit off a yelp of pain.

Bastion Sandidge uttered a sharp cry of rage. "No!" He spun round, his clawed hand snaking out.

"Verity!

An iron arm whipped about Verity's waist, yanking her out of Bastion's reach. She felt a hard male chest against her back, reassuringly warm and solid. A long-barreled pistol was leveled in a steady hand from beside her shoulder, pointing straight at the top button of Bastion Sandidge's tasteful waistcoat.

Hatred twisted the man's face. He took a hasty step toward Verity.

"Give me the excuse!" grated Lord Rathbone in a wrathful voice above Verity's head.

Bastion seemed to rock back on his heels. His eyes looked upon the viscount's savage visage and his expression altered to fear. His hands rose, palm outward, as though to ward off the threat.

Philip leaped down the stairs. Laughter spilled out of him and blazed in his eyes. "Well done, George! I knew that you would come!" He thrust out his hand.

The arm loosened from about Verity and slid away. She was suddenly conscious of a sharp sense of loss.

Lord Rathbone stepped forward to meet his cousin's hearty grasp. But the pistol in his other hand remained trained on Bastion Sandidge. "I am indebted to you, Philip. If it had not been for your quick action, I do not like to think what might have happened to Verity."

Lord Rathbone returned his arm to its former place. Its reassuring weight was welcome to Verity, and she relaxed into the tight embrace. For this moment, at least, she felt supremely cherished.

Bastion stared incredulously at his son. Malevolence flared in his eyes. Deliberately he turned his head, his profile flint-hard. "You are no longer a son of mine!"

"That is the greatest gift you could give me, sir! My freedom!" declared Philip, his lean face flushed with anger.

"You bastard! *You bastard!*"

As one, those in the hall looked up. They were startled and shocked by what they saw.

Upon hearing the commotion Forde Sandidge had somehow pulled himself along the floor from his bedroom. Somehow he had forced himself up onto his weakened legs. Braced against the stanchion at the top of the banister, he raised a pistol to his shoulder. Deadly intent burned fiercely in his craggy features.

Sir Charles whipped a second pistol free from his coat pocket.

The firearms bellowed. Acrid smoke burnt the air.

Forde Sandidge gave a choked cry, flinging up his arms. The pistol flew to one side as he toppled forward.

Verity watched, horrified, as Forde Sandidge's fall gathered momentum. He tumbled and rolled and crashed down the long stand of stairs.

At last he came to rest on the parquet floor. His head lay at a queer angle and his open, empty eyes glared impotently at the ceiling.

Verity hid her face against Lord Rathbone's shoulder.

Harold, who had been freed by Sir Charles in the excitement of the moment, walked forward to look down at his father. "The ball creased his skull. You are to be congratulated, sir. The wound will be attributed to the fall." His voice was detached. There was a singular smile on his face.

Harold raised his head. He looked slowly about the high-ceilinged hall without appearing to see any of the frozen company. His gaze lighted and focused on the footman. The servant had straightened, cradling his head. Harold's voice snapped out. All traces of the foppish gentleman were gone. "You! I am now the master of this cursed place. Take my father's body up to his bed. Then go for the justice of the peace."

The servant obediently got to his feet, shaking his rattled head. He staggered down the stairs and bent to take hold of the body. Grunting, he lifted it over his shoulders and proceeded to stump heavily up the stairs.

Harold turned then to look thoughtfully at a pasty-faced Bastion Sandidge. Harold's eyes glittered. The queer smile was still in place. "As for you, dear uncle, you have but a quarter hour. I forbid you to blacken my door for the extent of your lifetime. I shall make exception for my benighted aunt and my cousins, however."

In a wooden voice, Bastion Rathbone said, "I shall see to my belongings." He took a jerky step toward the stairs. He was stopped by Sir Charles's ringing voice.

"You, sir! If ever I discover that you have interfered again in my sister's life, I shall hunt you down and shoot you like the damnable cur you are."

Bastion Sandidge did not look around. He climbed the stairs, his shoulders hunched as though he was a broken man.

Lord Rathbone turned Verity toward him, his hands sliding up her arms to grasp her shoulders. In an urgent voice, he asked, "Are you quite all right?"

Verity nodded, a bubble of hope and happiness beginning to

grow inside her. She had never before seen that look in his lordship's eyes. She liked it; she liked it very much. "I am perfectly well. Oh, I am so glad that you and Charles came! You cannot conceive how glad I am!"

Sir Charles regarded his sister's face and read in her expression all of the trauma that she had undergone. He swung menacingly around on Harold Sandidge. "As for you, I shall cut out your liver if you dare—"

Harold threw up his hand. "Spare me, sir. I have not the least desire in the world to interfere with Miss Worth. I am completely indifferent to the lady."

"You would have let her die!" exclaimed Philip, glaring.

"That is a possibility, of course," agreed Harold without emotion. "However, I prefer to think that my suggestion of deportation would have delayed matters long enough that our hell-born cousin could ride to the rescue. As he has done. I congratulate you, my lord. Er . . . how did you manage to make your appearance so quickly?"

"It was my doing. I shot off a message from the inn. The boy met George enroute and brought him and Sir Charles straight to me," said Philip. "When I returned here, I left the front door open. All I had to do then was to pretend to be three sheets to the wind."

Harold looked at his cousin from under drooping lids. "Your enterprise astonishes me, Philip. I am all admiration, believe me. Since my uncle has cast you off, I suppose I am obligated to offer to support you."

Philip shook his head. "I mean to go into the army."

Harold shrugged. "As you will." He turned his head to regard the viscount and his lady, who seemed to have become rather absorbed in one another's faces. "It seems that you have us at a disasterous disadvantage, my lord. Under the circumstances, we could not withstand criminal prosecution. What will be your pleasure?"

"Quite frankly, the matter does not interest me. I shall leave the decision in Sir Charles's capable hands, whilst I seize the opportunity to speak privately with Miss Worth," said Lord Rathbone.

Without further ado, Lord Rathbone pulled Verity into the

drawing room and shut the door. He looked down at her silently.

Verity regarded his face, her heart pounding. "My lord, I—"

She was snatched into his lordship's arms and his mouth claimed hers.

Lord Rathbone kissed her with such ruthless abandon that she was made breathless. When his lips moved to her eyes, her neck, her hair, Verity's one coherent thought was that she was unbearably happy.

At last Lord Rathbone had satisfied his immediate hunger and he rested his cheek against her soft hair. His voice came harsh on her ear. "Do you know—can you possibly understand—the agony of suspense that I have suffered, knowing that you were in the hands of my enemies?"

"I did not know before that you had enemies," said Verity breathlessly. She clung to his lapel with one hand while her cheek nestled against his broad shoulder.

"My uncles have wished death upon me from the moment of my birth," said Lord Rathbone coolly.

"Yes, so I was given to understand," agreed Verity.

His head lifted and his hand came up to tilt her chin so that she met his eyes. "I never dreamed that you would be threatened, dearest Verity. I would have cut out my own heart rather than see you hurt. My dear girl, I know that I have been sunk below reproach in your eyes. But I must tell you! I never believed it possible to love a woman so deeply that her pain became mine. Verity, I want you for my wife in truth. I want to love you with everything in me. Can you accept me on those terms?"

Verity looked up into his grave face. The waiting, almost apprehensive, expression in his brilliant blue eyes smote her to the heart, excising all of the pain and disillusionment that had once haunted her. Tender laughter sprang into her own eyes. "My dear George, you quite succeeded with me, for I formed a passion for you weeks ago!"

A blazing light transformed Lord Rathbone's face. He caught her up in a kiss that threatened to crack her ribs—but Verity didn't care. She wrapped her arms about the viscount's neck and gave back passion for passion.

She had at last found the gentleman who was meant for her.

SIGNET REGENCY ROMANCE   (0451)

DILEMMAS OF THE HEART

☐ **THE SILENT SUITOR by Elisabeth Fairchild.** Miss Sarah Wilkes Lyndle was stunningly lovely. Nonetheless, she was startled to have two of the leading lords drawn to her on her very first visit to London. One was handsome, elegant, utterly charming Stewart Castleford, known in society as "Beauty," and the other was his cousin Lord Ashley Hawkes Castleford, nicknamed "Beast." Sarah found herself on the horns of a dilemma. (180704—$3.99)

☐ **AN INDEPENDENT WOMAN by Dawn Lindsey.** Gillian Thorncliff was ready to settle for a supremely sensible marriage to the Earl of Kintyre. This Scottish lord was attractive, attentive, intelligent, and kindly. Gillian's path to lasting if less than heavenly happiness lay open before her—when a tall, dark figure suddenly blocked her way. Rory Kilmartin was devastatingly handsome, marvelously mysterious, and irresistibly lawless ... (178742—$3.99)

☐ **THE AWAKENING HEART by Dorothy Mack.** The lovely Dinah Elcott finds herself in quite a predicament when she agrees to pose as a marriageable miss in public to the elegant Charles Talbot. In return, he will let Dinah puruse her artistic ambitions in private, but can she resist her own untested and shockingly susceptible heart? (178254—$3.99)

☐ **FALSE OF HEART by Elizabeth Hewitt.** A proud beauty follows passion's flaming path to love's shining truth. (171233—$4.50)

☐ **LORD ASHFORD'S WAGER by Marjorie Farrell.** Lady Joanna Barrand knows all there is to know about Lord Tony Ashford—his gambling habits, his wooing a beautiful older widow to rescue him from ruin, and worst of all, his guilt in a crime that made all his other sins seem innocent. What she doesn't know is how she has lost her heart to him? (180496—$3.99)

*Prices slightly higher in Canada

Buy them at your local bookstore or use this convenient coupon for ordering.

PENGUIN USA
P.O. Box 999 — Dept. #17109
Bergenfield, New Jersey 07621

Please send me the books I have checked above.
I am enclosing $_____ (please add $2.00 to cover postage and handling). Send check or money order (no cash or C.O.D.'s) or charge by Mastercard or VISA (with a $15.00 minimum). Prices and numbers are subject to change without notice.

Card #_____ Exp. Date _____
Signature_____
Name_____
Address_____
City _____ State _____ Zip Code _____

For faster service when ordering by credit card call **1-800-253-6476**

Allow a minimum of 4-6 weeks for delivery. This offer is subject to change without notice.

① SIGNET REGENCY ROMANCE (0451)

NOVELS OF LOVE AND DESIRE

☐ **DANGEROUS DIVERSIONS by Margaret Evans Porter.** Beautiful Rosalie de Barante knew the danger of being a dancer on the London stage. Thus when Gervase Marchant, Duke of Solway, showed interest in her, Rosalie had no illusions about his intentions. But when Gervase took her in his arms, she could feel her heart beating faster and hear the rhythm of ruin ... (180690—$3.99)

☐ **A REGENCY VALENTINE.** The joys and passions that surround St. Valentine's Day are captured in an extraordinary collection of all-new stories by five of the most highly acclaimed Regency authors: Mary Balogh, Katherine Kingsley, Emma Lange, Patricia Rice, and Joan Wolf. (168909—$4.50)

☐ **MISS DRAYTON'S DOWNFALL by Patricia Oliver.** Can the lovely Miss Cassandra Drayton continually refuse the marriage proposal of the licentious Earl of Mansfield as her defenses become weaker with his every passionate touch? (180194—$3.99)

☐ **FULL MOON MAGIC: Five Stories by Mary Balogh, Gayle Buck, Charlotte Louise Dolan, Anita Mills, and Patricia Rice.** In this wondrous collection are tales of enchanted love sprinkled with moonbeams, where ghosts roam castles, spirits travel through the realms of time, and the unlikeliest matchmakers bring lovers together.
(174577—$4.99)

☐ **TEMPTING HARRIET by Mary Balogh.** She had resisted scandalous seduction once before, six years ago. But now she was no longer that young and innocent girl. She was Lady Harriet Wingham, beautiful wealthy widow. The libertine who had almost taken her virtue then was the Duke of Tenby. He still wanted Harriet—not as a wife but as his mistress ... (179528—$3.99)

☐ **ELIZABETH'S GIFT by Donna Davison.** Elizabeth Wydner knew her own mind—and what she knew about her mind was remarkable. For Elizabeth had the power to read the thoughts of others, no matter how they masked them. She saw into the future as well, spotting lurking dangers and hidden snares. Elizabeth felt herself immune to falsehood and safe from surprise—until she met Nathan Lord Hawksley.
(180070—$3.99)

*Prices slightly higher in Canada

Buy them at your local bookstore or use this convenient coupon for ordering.

PENGUIN USA
P.O. Box 999 — Dept. #17109
Bergenfield, New Jersey 07621

Please send me the books I have checked above.
I am enclosing $_____ (please add $2.00 to cover postage and handling). Send check or money order (no cash or C.O.D.'s) or charge by Mastercard or VISA (with a $15.00 minimum). Prices and numbers are subject to change without notice.

Card #_____ Exp. Date _____
Signature_____
Name_____
Address_____
City _____ State _____ Zip Code _____

For faster service when ordering by credit card call **1-800-253-6476**

Allow a minimum of 4-6 weeks for delivery. This offer is subject to change without notice.

⓪ SIGNET REGENCY ROMANCE   (0451)

MAGICAL ROMANCES

☐ **GALATEA'S REVENGE by Elizabeth Jackson.** When the lovely Georgiana Oversham sets out to teach Sir Oliver Townsend a lesson, she finds that she is the one who needs instructing—in the ways of love. "A thoroughly entertaining read."—Mary Balogh   (177290—$3.99)

☐ **IN MY LADY'S CHAMBER by Laura Matthews.** Miss Theodosia Tremere finds herself in quite a predicament when her former fiance, Lord Steyen, reappears in her life, forcing her to risk seeing her dreams go up in smoke should the flames of love burn her again. "Laura Matthews has a magic touch. Her Regencies charm and enchant. Don't miss a single one!"—Catherine Coulter   (176502—$3.99)

☐ **MISS DOWER'S PARAGON by Gayle Buck.** Miss Evelyn Dower finds it hard to refuse Mr. Peter Hawkins's marriage proposal even though she knows he does not love her—or does he?   (173562—$3.99)

☐ **A PRECIOUS JEWEL by Mary Balogh.** Sir Gerald Stapleton wants Miss Priscilla Wentworth to be his most favored favorite—his mistress. Although they both believe that they know the ways of the world and that their fling could never turn into love, they know all too little about the ways of the heart.   (176197—$3.99)

☐ **LADY LEPRECHAUN by Melinda McRae.** When a lovely, young widow and a dashing duke are thrown together in a cross-country hunt for two schoolboy runaways, they are both faced with an unexpected pleasurable challenge. "One of the most exciting new voices in Regency fiction."—*Romantic Times*   (175247—$3.99)

Prices slightly higher in Canada.

Buy them at your local bookstore or use this convenient coupon for ordering.

PENGUIN USA
P.O. Box 999 – Dept. #17109
Bergenfield, New Jersey 07621

Please send me the books I have checked above.
I am enclosing $_____ (please add $2.00 to cover postage and handling). Send check or money order (no cash or C.O.D.'s) or charge by Mastercard or VISA (with a $15.00 minimum). Prices and numbers are subject to change without notice.

Card #_____ Exp. Date _____
Signature_____
Name_____
Address_____
City _____ State _____ Zip Code _____

For faster service when ordering by credit card call **1-800-253-6476**

Allow a minimum of 4-6 weeks for delivery. This offer is subject to change without notice.

ⓘ SIGNET REGENCY ROMANCE (0451)

SPECIAL REGENCIES TO CHERISH

- ☐ **A REGENCY CHRISTMAS: Five Stories by Mary Balogh, Gayle Buck, Edith Layton, Anita Mills, and Patricia Rice.** Warm your heart with the romance, generosities and cheer of the holiday seasons. (164849—$3.99)
- ☐ **A REGENCY CHRISTMAS II: Five Stories by Mary Balogh, Carla Kelly, Anita Mills, Mary Jo Putney, and Sheila Walsh.** This wonderful collection brings together five all-new stories of Christmas by some of the most beloved and highly acclaimed Regency authors.
(167910—$4.50)
- ☐ **A REGENCY CHRISTMAS III: Five Stories by Mary Balogh, Sandra Heath, Emma Lange, Edith Layton, and Mary Jo Putney.** Written especially for this new edition, these stories touch on all the great themes of Christmas. (170865—$4.50)
- ☐ **A REGENCY VALENTINE: Five Stories by Mary Balogh, Katherine Kingsley, Emma Lange, Patricia Rice, and Joan Wolf.** The joys and passions that surround St. Valentine's Day are captured in an extraordinary collection of all-new stories. (168909—$4.50)
- ☐ **A REGENCY VALENTINE II: Five Stories by Mary Balogh, Sandra Heath, Carla Kelly, Edith Layton, and Carol Proctor.** More delightful tales that capture the unique magic of the most passionate of holidays.
(171675—$4.50)
- ☐ **A REGENCY CHRISTMAS IV, with five new stories by Mary Balogh, Marjorie Farrell, Sandra Heath, Emma Lange, and Mary Jo Putney.** The holiday spirit comes alive in this wondrous new collection of enchanting Christmas stories. (173414—$4.99)
- ☐ **TOKENS OF LOVE Five Regency Love Stories by Mary Balogh, Sandra Heath, Carol Proctor, Sheila Walsh, and Margaret Westhaven.** Love and magic are in the air on St. Valentine's Day! (173422—$4.99)
- ☐ **A REGENCY SUMMER:** *Five Stories by Mary Balogh, Charlotte Louise Dolan, Sandra Heath, Melinda McRae, and Sheila Walsh.* Each tale celebrates the sweetness and excitement of a summer romance. (174011—$4.50)

Prices slightly higher in Canada.

Buy them at your local bookstore or use this convenient coupon for ordering.

PENGUIN USA
P.O. Box 999 – Dept. #17109
Bergenfield, New Jersey 07621

Please send me the books I have checked above.
I am enclosing $_____ (please add $2.00 to cover postage and handling). Send check or money order (no cash or C.O.D.'s) or charge by Mastercard or VISA (with a $15.00 minimum). Prices and numbers are subject to change without notice.

Card #_____ Exp. Date _____
Signature_____
Name_____
Address_____
City _____ State _____ Zip Code _____

For faster service when ordering by credit card call **1-800-253-6476**

Allow a minimum of 4-6 weeks for delivery. This offer is subject to change without notice.